Praise for *The 4 Disciplines of Execution*

"In place of the top-down, control-oriented management techniques of the industrial age, the 4 Disciplines offer a release-oriented, knowledge-worker-age approach to executing goals and strategies, an approach that engages people's hearts and minds toward a common goal unlike anything I've seen. Truly a profound work!"

—**Stephen R. Covey, #1** *New York Times* **bestselling author of** *The 7 Habits of Highly Effective People* **and** *The 3rd Alternative: Solving Life's Most Difficult Problems*

"Marriott was founded on the philosophy 'Take care of your employees and they'll take care of your customers.' Through the principles of *The 4 Disciplines of Execution*, we've been able to give our people a powerful tool for staying focused on what is most important to us: 'Our Guests' Experience.' I highly recommend this book for anyone who wants to create breakthrough results!"

—**David Grissen, President, The Americas, Marriott International, Inc.**

"The State of Georgia had unprecedented success as a result of implementing the principles outlined in *The 4 Disciplines of Execution.* We certified hundreds of leaders to take the disciplines to every department, achieving unprecedented results in customer service, quality improvement, and cost reduction. These execution principles are a must for any government agency that is seeking to be world class."

—**The Honorable Sonny Perdue, Governor of Georgia, 2003–2011**

"*The 4 Disciplines'* practical guidance on goal-setting and measurement resonates with groups at all levels in our organization. Many teams have applied this intuitive approach to build engagement and increase execution and accountability."

—**Dave Dillon, Chairman and Chief Executive Officer,**
The Kroger Co.

"We believe that *The 4 Disciplines of Execution* are the keys to growth and success. For years we have struggled with creating focus for our people. We have used priority sheets, standards of performance measures, and other methods. We have fallen in love with the concepts of 'whirlwind' and 'WIG'! When you read this book, you will never look at work or life the same!"

—**Danny Wegman, Chief Executive Officer, Wegmans Food**
Markets, Inc., #1 on *Fortune*'s 2005 list of the "100 Best
Companies to Work For"

"You don't have a strategy problem, you have an execution problem! *The 4 Disciplines of Execution* tells you everything you need to know to make your wildly important goals a reality. This simple, effective model is easy to understand, easy to apply, and delivers results. I've used it in my personal life, with my family, and in my organization. It works!"

—**Richard Stocking, President and Chief Operating Officer,**
Swift Transportation

"I've seen many great initiatives fail because of the inability to make the transition from strategy to execution. The authors here have developed a real-world, practical guide for navigating through the obstacles to success. While reading this book, I thought over and over again to myself, 'I wish I would have had this resource ten years ago.'"

—**Terry D. Scott, 10th Master Chief Petty Officer**
of the Navy, April 2002–July 2006, Retired

"Few things in business are harder than finding the handful of simple actions that every employee can take to help the company achieve its most important objectives. The 4 Disciplines provide a simple, common-sense way to help achieve real results."

—**Rob Markey, Partner, Bain & Company,**
and coauthor of *The Ultimate Question 2.0*

"*The 4 Disciplines of Execution* methodology and process, contained in this book, have been extremely helpful to our organization. It has allowed us to align and cascade our wildly important goals throughout our teams, which has resulted in an increase in employee engagement and improved client service and project delivery. As we continue to invest in our employees, this process remains critical to achieving our overall corporate goals."

—**Andrew Frawley, President, Epsilon**

"Genius and simplicity describe *The 4 Disciplines of Execution*. If you want to succeed with your strategic plan, utilizing this process and methodology will pay dividends. Focusing one's efforts on lead measures will result in success. And, the process of continual, quick accountability checkups encourages excellence."

—**Walter Levy, Co-President and Co-Chief Executive Officer,**
NCH Corporation

"'Wildly important goals,' 'lead measures,' 'compelling scoreboard,' 'cadence of accountability'—*The 4 Disciplines of Execution* delivers the essential battle cry every leader and organization requires, plus the guidelines on how to respond. The disciplines allow any leader the ability to move beyond the vision into the flawless execution of strategy. This book is a great gift to any leader in any organization."

—**Frances Hesselbein, President and Chief Executive**
Officer, The Frances Hesselbein Leadership Institute,
and founder of The Peter F. Drucker Foundation for
Nonprofit Management

"Well done! Disciplined leveraging of this work will profoundly help raise the standard of executional excellence in any and all organizations."

—**Douglas R. Conant, Chief Executive Officer, retired, Campbell Soup Company, and** *New York Times* **bestselling author**

"I've practiced and embraced the principles and process found in this book for many years and can attest this is a great framework to help organizations achieve their strategic goals."

—**Roger Morgan, President and Chief Executive Officer, Retail Products Group**

"The 4 Disciplines of Execution is a practical guide for organizational excellence. It provides a simple, actionable approach for success at all levels of any organization. The process creates maniacal focus and leads to uncommon results. Though the word 'proactive' is overused and underachieved in business, the 4DX process truly creates proactive momentum and sustainable results."

—**Matt Oldroyd, President and Chief Executive Officer, Partsmaster**

"Each person comes to this world packed with unlimited capacity. He can accomplish wonders. There is nothing in life more exhilarating than to achieve something important to him and to achieve it with excellence. In *The 4 Disciplines of Execution*, the authors have captured the principles and procedures that are key to human achievement."

—**Mohammed Yunus, Nobel Peace Prize Winner, 2006**

"Having worked in higher education administration for thirty-five years, with increasing management responsibility at both a private and public university, I have learned that the greatest obstacle any higher education leader faces is the challenge of execution, i.e., successfully and consistently achieving the institution's key strategic goals. Although *The 4 Disciplines of Execution* begins as it must with theory, the greatest contribution of this book to educational administrators is its powerful focus on the fundamentals of the *process* of execution.

For that reason, this book is *must* reading for every college and university administrator with responsibility for achieving strategic goals."
—Angelo Armenti, Jr., Ph.D., President,
California University of Pennsylvania

"Military leaders recognize that people are central and essential to achieving the organization's mission. The value of *The 4 Disciplines of Execution* centers on connecting everyone specifically, concretely, and visibly to the fulfillment of that mission. Every single person has a clear role to play, is measured on it, and can celebrate his or her contribution to its achievement. Whether delivering combat aircraft to the navy or dramatically improving an urban public education system, the focus on executing a few critical goals with excellence makes the difference between failure or success."
—Captain John W. Scanlan, USN Retired, Chief Financial
Officer, Cleveland Municipal School District

"The *4 Disciplines of Execution* is a leadership breakthrough enabling strategy into execution. Based on significant research, the book demystifies moving from 'knowing to doing.' With this approach everyone wins! Most important, employees are more engaged in their work. Employees clearly understand and experience how their efforts and results contribute to the execution of a company's strategy. Their work is meaningful. It contributes to a team, and they can be proud of what they have accomplished."
—Tom Halford, General Manager and Marketing, Whirlpool

"Having spent years working with organizations whose goal was to achieve greatness, I highly recommend reading *The 4 Disciplines of Execution*! It is truly a how-to manual for teams committed to achieving their wildest dreams and a must-read for leaders who have chosen to achieve greatness!"
—Ann Rhoades, President, People Ink, former Executive
Vice President, JetBlue, former Chief People Officer,
Southwest Airlines, and author of *Built on Values*

"*The 4 Disciplines of Execution* offers not only a clear description of the critical relationship of execution to viable strategy but also specific recommendations for increasing the likelihood of success. The approaches recommended will ensure focus, line-of-sight from tasks to goals, and the production of simple dashboards to give vital and timely feedback. As important as these, however, are the authors' granular examples, suggestions, and prescriptions."

—Joel Peterson, Chairman, JetBlue Airways; Robert L. Joss Consulting Professor of Management, Stanford Graduate School of Business; founding Partner, Peterson Partners

"*The 4 Disciplines of Execution* has a powerful way of inviting every frontline employee to commit to and then execute on the highest priority goals of their agency. As a leader in the public sector, I found myself revisiting these principles over and over again at a time when resources were dwindling, while the need for human services was rising."

—B. J. Walker, former Commissioner, Department of Human Services, State of Georgia

"My first experience with the 4 Disciplines of Execution was in a meeting with a group of front-line managers who were reporting their first six-month results. I saw a room full of winners. After applying these disciplines and this methodology throughout my entire organization, we saw improved employee engagement and teamwork during a time of downsizing, and we achieved our stretch business objectives."

—Alex M. Azar II, President, Lilly USA, LLC

"*The 4 Disciplines of Execution* is a principle-based system that simplifies the complexities of everyday execution and gets us consistent value increase over time. Thank you, FranklinCovey, for cracking the execution code!"

—Juan Bonifasi, Chief Executive Officer, Grupo Entero, Guatemala

"Keeping the eyes on execution is the single most important task for a leader. This book provides great guidance for leaders who want to stay focused on their most important goals. It is a practical guide to creating a cadence of accountability throughout their organizations. The book is as relevant in Europe as in the rest of the world, a great read, and a great method to achieve strong results over time."

—Sanna Rydberg, Head of Healthcare, sub-Region Europe North, AGA Gas AB, a member of the Linde Group

"The best way to prove the validity and effectiveness of any business concept or methodology is to apply it to real situations and observe the results obtained. At Bladex, we have had the opportunity to apply the principles proposed by *The 4 Disciplines of Execution* as a means to successfully achieve the strategic objectives of the organization. Our experience leads us to affirm that with consistency, once the degree of maturity in the application of these principles is attained, the desired objectives are gratifyingly achieved and justify the efforts required in the adoption process. The key lies in the discipline of the process."

—Miguel Moreno, Executive Vice President and Chief Operating Officer, Bladex, Foreign Trade Bank of Latin America, Inc.

"After approximately seven months working with the 4 Disciplines of Execution, we have seen the following improvements in my area; a cost savings from 5.9 percent to 26.1 percent and an improved bottom line from 3.7 percent to 43.3 percent. But most important, a quantum increase in employee engagement and trust. "

—Per Birkemose, Regional Manager, Euromaster Denmark

"The most important thing for us in using the 4 Disciplines of Execution was to have a real impact in the achievement of our goals, and that has been the case. The methodology has been an extraordinary tool to align the efforts of all our 7,168 collaborators toward the corporate goals, each knowing their role and the impact of this in our corporation. We also obtained additional benefits, such as an increased exchange of best practices, greater integration and teamwork, and even a tough but healthy competition between the different areas, generating enormous benefit for our organization."

—**Ricardo E. Fernández, Chief Operations Officer,**
Corporación BI, Guatemala

"All leaders must read *The 4 Disciplines of Execution* to help them consistently achieve breakthrough results. The 4D execution process is a true competitive advantage in present global markets and fast-paced business environments."

—**Giulio M. Zafferri, Associated Senior Management**
Consultant, Cegos Italia Spa

"The implementation of the methodology of the 4 Disciplines of Execution in our company has had a positive influence in the corporate culture to such extent that today each member of the organization understands the business priorities and knows the correct path to materialize them. Today, we have a better view with regard to what we expect from each team, and we have a common language that makes people feel more engaged, since their valuable individual contribution is better acknowledged. The methodology not only allows us to have an adequate follow-up on the fulfillment of the wildly important goals, but it has also influenced a more effective management of the way in which meetings are held, thus producing a better focus and prioritization. I really recommend the 4 Disciplines as an effective method to lead and set the course for the execution of strategy."

—**Luis Fernando Valladares Guillen, Chief Executive Officer,**
Tigo, Guatemala

"Beyond theories, the 4 Disciplines of Execution process is a truly useful guide on strategy execution. It has kept our organization focused on what really matters to achieve the objectives. This book is a great instrument for our business leaders to avoid the most common pitfalls in the execution of our strategy, based on our multiple business areas across the world."

—**Dr. Pietro Lori, President, Georg Fischer Piping Systems**

"The implementation of the 4 Disciplines of Execution at Progreso has been a great learning experience for everybody in the company. We have been able to work as a team—the board of directors and the top management—to establish what is wildly important for the company and at the same time define a cadence of accountability with the different business units, making sure everybody understands what is expected of them, but more important, being able to follow through week by week on the things that really help achieve results. The 4 Disciplines also helped us implement a leadership agenda based on the core values of the company, but with special emphasis on a culture of execution through performance-based management. For me, learning about the 4 Disciplines of Execution has changed the way I set goals in my life. Now, with every activity in which I get involved, I recommend or try to apply these concepts in goal setting and follow-through."

—José Miguel Torrebiarte, President, Grupo Progreso, Guatemala

"Over the last twenty years in charge of operations, I have made it a priority for associates and supervisors to execute our core operational routines. With the 4 Disciplines of Execution, we have been very effective in institutionalizing the adoption of these routines and have gained a common visibility around our wildly important goals. These three goals have been shared with every associate from the 212 Supercenter stores located across Mexico. This effort has increased satisfaction and teamwork, resulting in an improvement in the quality of the work life of our associates."

—Guadalupe Morales, Vice President of Operations, Supercenters, Mexico and Central America

"Working in a business environment characterized by a lot of changes and varied information, the 4 Disciplines of Execution have really given us a step change in organizational efficiency through prioritizing and setting up transparent goals and actions in close cooperation with the employees."

—Jens Erik Pedersen, Senior Vice President, Power Production, DONG Energy, Denmark

SIMON &
SCHUSTER

The 4 Disciplines of Execution

ACHIEVING YOUR WILDLY IMPORTANT GOALS

Chris McChesney

Sean Covey

Jim Huling

SIMON & SCHUSTER

London · New York · Sydney · Toronto · New Delhi

A CBS COMPANY

NOTE TO READERS

In some instances, people or companies portrayed in this book are
illustrative examples based on the authors' experiences, but they
are not intended to represent a particular person or organisation.

Video content available via QR code or at www.4dxbook.com. Message and
data rates may apply. Video content may not be available indefinitely.

First published in Great Britain by Simon & Schuster UK Ltd, 2012
This paperback edition first published by Simon & Schuster UK Ltd, 2015
A division of Simon & Schuster UK Ltd
A CBS COMPANY

Copyright © 2012 by FranklinCovey Co.

3 5 7 9 10 8 6 4

Simon & Schuster UK Ltd
1st Floor
222 Gray's Inn Road
London WC1X 8HB

www.simonandschuster.co.uk

Simon & Schuster Australia, Sydney
Simon & Schuster India, New Delhi

A CIP catalogue record for this book
is available from the British Library

ISBN: 978-1-47117-779-8
ebook ISBN: 978-0-85720-584-1

Designed by Julie Schroeder

Printed and bound by in by CPI Group (UK) Ltd, Croydon CR0 4YY

To Jim Stuart, our friend and colleague and the originator of this content, for your brilliance, insights, and your passion for great execution. May God bless you in your new endeavors.

1946 to 2006

Contents

CONTENTS

Foreword

> "*The 4 Disciplines of Execution* offers more than theories for making strategic organizational change. The authors explain not only the 'what' but also 'how' effective execution is achieved. They share numerous examples of companies that have done just that, not once, but over and over again. This is a book that every leader should read!"
> —**Clayton Christensen, Professor, Harvard Business School,**
> **and author of** *The Innovator's Dilemma*

Andy Grove, who helped found Intel and then led the enterprise for years as its CEO and chairman, has taught me some extraordinary things. One of them occurred in a meeting where he and several of his direct reports were plotting the launch of their Celeron microprocessor. I was there as a consultant. The theory of disruption had identified a threat to Intel. Two companies—AMD and Cyrix—had attacked the low end of the microprocessor market, selling much lower-cost chips to companies that were making entry-level computers. They had gained a significant market share and then had begun moving up-market. Intel needed to respond.

During a break in the meeting, Grove asked me, "How do I do this?"

I readily responded that he needed to set up a different, autonomous business unit that had a different overhead structure and its own sales force.

Andy said, in his typical gruff voice, "You are such a naïve academic. I asked you *how* to do it, and you told me *what* I should do." He swore and said, *"I know what I need to do. I just don't know how to do it."*

I felt like I was standing in front of a deity with no place to hide. Grove was right. I was indeed a naïve academic. I had just shown him that I didn't know the difference between *what* and *how.*

As I flew back to Boston I wondered whether I should change the focus of my research as an academic, trying to develop a theory of "how." I dismissed the idea, however, because I really couldn't conceive how I might develop a theory of "how."

My research has continued to focus, consequently, on the *what* of business—which we call strategy—and it has been quite productive. Most strategy researchers, consultants, and writers have given us static views of strategic issues—snapshots of technologies, companies and markets. The snapshots describe at a specific point in time the characteristics and practices of successful companies versus struggling ones; or of executives who perform better than others at the time of the snapshot. Explicitly or implicitly, they then assert that if you want to perform as well as the best-performing ones, you should follow what the best companies and the best executives do.

My colleagues and I have eschewed the profession of photography. Instead we have been making "movies" of strategy. These are not, however, typical movies that you might see at a theater, where you see fiction conceived in the minds of the producers and screenwriters. The unusual movies that we're making at Harvard are "theories." They describe what *causes* things to happen and *why*. These theories comprise the "plots" in these movies. In contrast to the movies in a theater that are filled with suspense and surprise, the plots of our movies are perfectly predictable. You can replace the actors in our movies—different people, companies and industries—and watch the movie again. You can choose the actions that these actors take in the movie. Because the plots in these movies are grounded in theories of causality, however, the results of these actions are perfectly predictable.

Boring, you ask? Probably, to those who seek entertainment. But managers, who must know whether their strategy—the *what* of their work—is the right one or the wrong one, need as much certainty as possible. Because the theory is the plot, you can rewind the movie and watch the past repeatedly, if you want, to understand what causes what and why to a certain point. Another feature of movies of this sort is that you can watch the future, too—before it actually occurs. You can change your plans, based upon different situations in which you might find yourself, and watch in the movie what will happen as a result.

Without boasting, I think it is fair to say that our research on strategy, innovation, and growth has helped managers who have taken the time to read and understand the theories, or movies, of strategy to become and sustain success more frequently than was historically the case.

What remains is the "how" of managing a company during times of change. This "how" has been studied minimally, until this book.

The reason why good research on "how" has taken so long to emerge is that it requires a different scale of research. Causal theories of strategy—the "what"—typically come from a deep study of one company, as was the case with my disk-drive study. The "how" of strategic change, in contrast, arises incessantly in every company. Developing a theory of "how" means that you can't study this phenomenon once in one company. You can't take snapshots of "how." Rather, you need to study it in deep detail over and over again, over years, in many companies. The scale of this endeavor is why I and other academics have ignored the "how" of strategic change. We simply could not do it. It requires the perspective, insight, and the scale of a company like FranklinCovey to do it.

This is the reason why I am so excited about the book. It isn't a book filled with anecdotes about companies that succeeded once. Rather, the book truly contains a theory of causality of "how" effective execution is achieved. The authors have given us not snapshots of execution but movies—movies that we can rewind and study over and over, into which you, as a leader can insert your company and your people as actors. And you can watch your future before it emerges. This book is derived from deep study of many companies over time as they deployed new ways of doing "how," store by store, hotel by hotel, division by division.

I hope you will enjoy this book as much as I have.

—Clayton Christensen,
Harvard Business School

Strategy and Execution

There are two principal things a leader can influence when it comes to producing results: your *strategy* (or plan) and your ability to *execute* that strategy.

Stop for a moment and ask yourself this question:

Which of these do leaders struggle with more? Is it creating a strategy, or executing the strategy?

Every time we pose this question to leaders anywhere in the world, their answer is immediate: "Execution!"

Now, ask yourself a second question:

If you have an MBA or have taken business classes, what did you study more—execution or strategy?

When we ask leaders this question, the response, once again, is immediate: "Strategy!" It's perhaps not surprising that the area with which leaders struggle most is also the one in which they have the least education.

After working with thousands of leaders and teams in every kind of industry, and in schools and government agencies worldwide, this is what we have learned: once you've decided what to do, your biggest challenge is in getting people to execute it at the level of excellence you need.

Why is execution so difficult? After all, if the strategy is clear, and you as the leader are driving it, won't the team naturally engage to achieve it? The answer is "no," and it's likely that your own experience has proven this more than once.

The book you are reading represents the most actionable and impactful insights from all that we've learned. In it, you will discover a set of disciplines that have been embraced by thousands of leaders and hundreds of thousands of front-line workers, enabling them to produce extraordinary results.

A Letter

When I saw a three-hour meeting on my calendar that day, I was skeptical. As a new VP of Eli Lilly and Company's U.S. affiliate, I was swamped. But since one of my leaders was running the meeting, I decided to attend.

It was a decision I will always be glad I made, because within the first few minutes of the meeting I realized I was seeing something special. I watched a team reporting on the remarkable results they had achieved by piloting a new set of practices known as the 4 Disciplines of Execution. These were individuals who had not only achieved their goals, but who walked and talked like *winners*. Their chests were out and their heads held high. As a leader, I wanted those results, but more important, I wanted that *mindset* throughout my entire organization.

We launched the 4 Disciplines throughout our managed healthcare business, aiming at two critical goals: to dramatically increase customer access to our medicines while simultaneously improving bottom-line profitability. During this same period, there was a larger initiative throughout Lilly to reorganize for more effective operations. We could not have chosen a more difficult context for creating engagement. In the end, we exceeded both of our goals by a significant margin, but these results were not really our greatest outcome.

Our greatest outcome was strengthening our culture by raising the engagement of our teams. During a time of high demand coupled with a reorganization that brought significant change, our employee engagement scores actually *went up.*

I often look back on the decision to attend that initial meeting, and more important, on the journey we've made to create not only great business results but also a high-performing culture. It was a pivotal decision for me—one that changed the way I lead forever.

Alex Azar
President, Lilly USA, LLC

The Real Problem with Execution

B. J. Walker was facing the greatest challenge of her career. When she was the newly appointed Commissioner of the Department of Human Services for the U.S. State of Georgia in 2004, she could see that her twenty thousand employees were completely demoralized. The department had burned through six commissioners in five years and was under constant media scrutiny, due to the number of deaths and accidents involving children in the state's care. For months, her employees had operated under constant fear of making a mistake, which only made their poor productivity worse and led to some of the largest backlogs in the country. B. J. Walker needed a way to bring focus and direction to her team and she knew that the clock was ticking.

Less than eighteen months later, B. J. and her team had reduced repeat cases of child maltreatment by a stunning 60 percent.

· · ·

One of the hotels near Marriott International's headquarters, the Bethesda Marriott, wanted to improve performance measures, an effort magnified by being so close to the company's leadership. General Manager Brian Hilger, his team and the hotel's owners worked together on a $20 million renovation that included remodeled rooms, an impressive lobby and a new restaurant—improvements critical to higher guest scores. And the results were amazing—the hotel looked fantastic. *But the guest scores were still not at desired levels . . . yet.*

Android - Barcode Scanner
iPhone - Red Laser

LINK: http://www.4dxbook.com/qr/CaseStudies

Scan the image above to see case study videos of Eli Lilly, the State of Georgia, and Marriott.

The second part of the equation would involve how associates interacted with guests and executed at the hotel—a strategy dependent on new behaviors.

After one year Brian and his team proudly celebrated earning the highest Guest Satisfaction Scores in the thirty-year history of the hotel. As Brian said, "I used to dread the arrival of our new Guest Satisfaction Scores every Friday. Now, I'm excited to get up on Friday mornings."

• • •

These stories from Eli Lilly, the State of Georgia, and Marriott sound very different from each other, but they aren't. For each of these leaders, the challenge was essentially the same. So was the solution.

Their common challenge? Executing a strategy that required a significant change in human behavior—the behavior of many, or even all, of the people in the team or organization.

Their common solution? Deeply implanting The 4 Disciplines of Execution (4DX).

All leaders struggle with this challenge even if they don't realize it. If you're leading people, right now you are probably trying to get them to do something different. Whether you lead a small work team or a whole company, a family or a factory, no significant result is achievable unless people change their behavior. Yet, to be successful, you will need more than just their compliance; you will need their commitment. As every leader knows, getting the commitment of hearts and minds, the kind of commitment that will endure in the midst of the daily grind, is not easy.

We completed more than fifteen hundred implementations of the 4 Disciplines before we were ready to write this book. Why? Because we wanted to test and refine the 4 Disciplines against hundreds of real-world challenges like the ones faced by Alex Azar, B. J. Walker, and Brian Hilger.

When you execute a strategy that requires a lasting change in the behavior of other people, you are facing one of the greatest leadership challenges you will ever meet. With the 4 Disciplines of Execution, you are not experimenting with an interesting theory; you are implementing a set of proven practices that meet that challenge successfully every time.

THE REAL CHALLENGE

Whether you call it a strategy, a goal, or simply an improvement effort, any initiative you as a leader drive in order to significantly move your team or organization forward will fall into one of two categories: The first requires mainly a stroke of the pen; the second requires behavioral change.

Stroke-of-the-pen strategies are those that you execute just by ordering or authorizing them to be done. Simply put, if you have the money and the authority, you can make them happen. It might be a major capital investment, a change in the compensation system, a realignment of roles and responsibilities, adding staff, or a new advertising campaign. While executing these strategies may require planning, consensus, guts, brains, and money, you know that in the end it is going to happen.

Behavioral-change strategies are very different from stroke-of-the-pen strategies. You can't just order them to happen, because executing them requires getting people—often a lot of people—to do something different. And if you've ever tried to get other people to change their ways, you know how tough it is. Changing yourself is hard enough.

For example, you may have to get all of your store employees to greet every customer that enters the store within thirty seconds, or get your entire sales force to begin using the new CRM system, or get your product development team to collaborate with the marketing team. If you're Alex Azar or B. J. Walker, you may be changing routines that have been entrenched for decades. This stuff is hard!

STROKE OF THE PEN Strategy	BEHAVIOR CHANGE Strategy
Capital Investment	Improved Customer Experience
Expansion of Staff	Higher Quality
Process Change	Faster Responsiveness
Strategic Acquisition	Operational Consistency
Media Buy	Consultative Sales Approach
Change in Product Mix	Reduced Cost Overruns

Examples of strategic moves that require people to change their behavior contrasted with those that can be executed by "the stroke of a pen."

It's also not uncommon to find many stroke-of-the-pen strategies that, once approved, evolve into those that require significant behavioral change.

Our colleague Jim Stuart summarized this challenge as follows: "To achieve a goal you have never achieved before, you must start doing things you have never done before." It could be a new sales approach, an effort to improve patient satisfaction, better project management discipline, or adherence to a new manufacturing process. If it requires people to do something different, you are driving a behavioral-change strategy and it's not going to be easy.

Have you ever found yourself on the way to work muttering something like, "For the love of heaven, can't we just do this one thing?"

If so, then you remember how it felt when the inability to get people to change was the one thing standing between you and the results you wanted. And you're not alone.

In a key study on organizational change, the global management-consulting firm Bain & Company reports these findings: "About 65 percent of initiatives required significant behavioral change on the part of front-line employees—something that managers often fail to consider or plan for in advance."[1]

Despite the significance of this problem, leaders seldom recognize it. You don't hear leaders saying, "I wish I were better at driving strategies that require people to do things differently." What you are more likely to hear is a leader saying, "I wish I didn't have Tom, Paul, and Sue to deal with!"

It's natural for a leader to assume the people are the problem. After all, they are the ones not doing what we need to have done. But you would be wrong. *The people are not the problem!*

W. Edwards Deming, the father of the quality movement, taught that any time the majority of the people behave a particular way the majority of the time, the people are not the problem. The problem is inherent in the system.[2] As a leader, you own responsibility for the system. Although a particular person can be a big problem, if you find yourself blaming the people, you should look again.

When we began to study this challenge several years ago, we first wanted to understand the root causes of weak execution. We commissioned an international survey of working people and examined hundreds of businesses and government agencies. During the early stages of our research we found problems everywhere we looked.

One prime suspect behind execution breakdown was clarity of the objective: People simply didn't understand the goal they were supposed to execute. In fact, in our initial surveys we learned that only one employee in seven could name even one of their organization's most important goals. That's right—15 percent could not name even one of the top three goals their leaders had identified. The other 85 percent named what they *thought* was the goal, but it often didn't remotely resemble what their leaders had said. The further from the top of the organization, the lower the clarity. And that was just the beginning of the problems we uncovered.

Lack of commitment to the goal was another problem. Even those people who knew the goal lacked commitment to achieving it. Only 51 percent could say that they were passionate about the team's goal, leaving almost half the team simply going through the motions.

Accountability was also an issue. A staggering 81 percent of the people surveyed said they were not held accountable for regular progress on the organization's goals. And the goals were not translated into specific actions—87 percent had no clear idea what they should be doing to achieve the goal. No wonder execution is so inconsistent.

In short, people weren't sure what the goal was, weren't committed to it, didn't know what to do about it specifically, and weren't being held accountable for it.

These were only the most obvious explanations as to why execution breaks down. On a more subtle level, there were problems with lack of trust, misaligned compensation systems, poor development processes and poor decision making.

Our first instinct was to say "Fix everything! Fix it all, and then you'll be able to execute your strategy." It was like advising them to boil the ocean.

As we dug in further, we began to put our finger on a far more fundamental cause of execution breakdown. Certainly all of the problems we just cited—the lack of clarity, commitment, collaboration, and accountability—exacerbate the difficulty of strategy execution. But, in reality, they initially distracted us from seeing the deeper problem. You may have heard the expression, "Fish discover water last." That expression sums up our discovery very well. Like a fish discovering the water it's been swimming in the whole time, we finally realized that the fundamental problem with execution had always been right in front of us. We hadn't seen it because it was everywhere, hiding in plain sight.

THE WHIRLWIND

The real enemy of execution is your day job! We call it the *whirlwind*. It's the massive amount of energy that's necessary just to keep your operation going on a day-to-day basis; and, ironically, it's also the thing that makes it so hard to execute anything new. The whirlwind robs from you the focus required to move your team forward.

Leaders seldom differentiate between the whirlwind and strategic goals because both are necessary to the survival of the organization. However, they are clearly different, and more important, they compete relentlessly for time, resources, energy, and attention. We don't have to tell you which will usually win this fight.

The whirlwind is urgent and it acts on you and everyone working for you every minute of every day. The goals you've set for moving forward are important, but when urgency and importance clash, urgency will win every time. Once you become aware of this struggle, you will see it playing out everywhere, in any team that is trying to execute anything new.

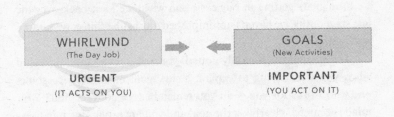

Important goals that require you to do new and different things often conflict with the "whirlwind" of the day job, made up of urgencies that consume your time and energy.

Consider your own experience. Can you remember an important initiative that launched well and then died? How did the end come? Was it with a loud crash and a tremendous explosion? Or did it go down quietly over time, suffocated by the whirlwind? We've asked thousands of leaders this question and we always get the same answer: "Slow suffocation!" It's like finding that faded tee-shirt in the bottom of your drawer and saying, "Oh yeah, Operation Summit. I wonder whatever happened to that." It died, and you didn't even have a funeral.

Executing in spite of the whirlwind means overcoming not only its powerful distraction, but also the inertia of "the way it's always been done." We're not saying that the whirlwind is bad. It isn't. It keeps your organization alive and you can't ignore it. If you ignore the urgent, it can kill you today. It's also true, however, that if you ignore the important, it can kill you tomorrow. In other words, if you and your team operate solely from within the whirlwind, you won't progress—all your energy is spent just trying to stay upright in the wind. The challenge is executing your most important goals in the midst of the urgent!

Different leaders experience the whirlwind in different ways. A senior executive with one of the world's largest home-improvement retailers describes it this way: "We don't have dragons swooping down and knocking us off our priorities. What we have are gnats. Every day we have gnats getting in our eyes, and when we look back over the last six months, we haven't accomplished any of the things we said we were going to."

You've almost certainly found yourself facing the whirlwind when you were trying to explain a new goal or strategy to someone who works for you. Can you remember the conversation? Your mind is centered clearly on the goal and you are explaining it in easy-to-understand terms. But, while you're talking, the person you are talking to is backing slowly out of the room, all the while nodding and reassuring you, but trying to get back to what they would call *the real work,* another name for the whirlwind.

Is that employee fully engaged in achieving that goal? Not a chance. Is he trying to sabotage your goal or undercut your authority? No. He's just trying to survive in his whirlwind.

To illustrate, one of our colleagues shares this story:

"I was chair of the community council for my local high school, and we as a council developed a serious goal of improving test scores. My job was to orient the teachers to the new goal, so I made an appointment with key teachers to explain what we were doing and get things started.

"At first I was baffled—they didn't seem to be listening to me. Slowly, I learned why: On one teacher's little desk was a stack that looked like a thousand papers. It was just one day's collection of essays she would have to evaluate and grade. Plus, she had a parent conference to go to and the next day's lessons to plan. She looked kind of helpless while I jabbered on and on, but she wasn't really listening. There wasn't room in her brain for this, and I didn't blame her!"

Let's summarize what we've said so far. First, if you are going to create significant results you will eventually have to execute a behavioral-change strategy. Stroke-of-the-pen moves will only take you so far. Second, when you undertake a behavioral-change strategy you will be battling the whirlwind—and it is a very worthy adversary, undefeated in many organizations.

The 4 Disciplines of Execution aren't designed for managing your whirlwind. The 4 Disciplines are rules for executing your most critical strategy *in the midst of* your whirlwind.

THE 4 DISCIPLINES OF EXECUTION

Tim Harford, author of *The Undercover Economist,* said, "You show me a successful complex system, and I will show you a system that has evolved through trial and error."[3] In the case of the 4 Disciplines of Execution he is absolutely right. It benefited from well-researched ideas, but it *evolved* through trial and error.

In our initial research with Harris Interactive we surveyed nearly thirteen thousand people internationally across seventeen different industry groups and completed internal assessments with five hundred different companies. Over the years, we've added to this foundation by surveying almost three-hundred thousand leaders and team members. This research has been valuable as a foundation for the principles and in guiding our early conclusions, but the real insights did not come from research. They came from working with people like you in over fifteen hundred implementations. This effort is what enabled us to develop principles and methods that we know will work regardless of the industry or the nation in which they are implemented.

There is good news and bad news here. The good news is that

there are rules—rules for executing in the face of the whirlwind. The bad news? The bad news is that there are rules—the kinds of rules that have immediate consequences if you violate them.

Although the disciplines may seem simple at first glance, they are not simplistic. They will profoundly change the way you approach your goals. Once you adopt them, you will never lead in the same way again, whether you are a project coordinator, lead a small sales team, or run a Fortune 500 company. We believe they represent a major breakthrough in how to move teams and organizations forward.

Here's a quick overview of the 4 Disciplines.

Discipline 1: Focus on the Wildly Important

Basically, the more you try to do, the less you actually accomplish. This is a stark, inescapable principle that we all live with. Somewhere along the way, most leaders forget this. Why? Because smart, ambitious leaders don't want to do less, they want to do more, even when they know better. Isn't it really difficult for you to say *no* to a good idea, much less a great one? And yet, there will always be more good ideas than you and your teams have the capacity to execute. That's why your first challenge is focusing on the wildly important.

Focus is a natural principle. The sun's scattered rays are too weak to start a fire, but once you focus them with a magnifying glass they will bring paper to flame in seconds. The same is true of human beings—once their collective energy is focused on a challenge, there is little they can't accomplish.

Discipline 1: Focus on the wildly important requires you to go against your basic wiring as a leader and focus on *less* so that your team can achieve *more*. When you implement Discipline 1 you start by selecting one (or, at the most, two) extremely important goals, instead of trying to significantly improve everything all at once. We call this a *wildly important goal* (WIG) to make it clear to the team that this is the goal that matters most. Failure to achieve it will make every other accomplishment seem secondary, or possibly even inconsequential.

Take champion cyclist Lance Armstrong. At one point in his career, he completely dedicated himself to winning the Tour de France.

His WIG was to win the big one—again and again. Achieving that goal meant that even when he competed in other races, they were always in service to his WIG of winning the Tour, no matter how important or prestigious they may have been. It also meant constant specialized training and going over every centimeter of the route and planning precisely how to execute every stage of the Tour. The result of this powerful focus? Lance Armstrong won seven Tours de France—more than anyone in history.[4]

If you're currently trying to execute five, ten, or even twenty important goals, the truth is that your team can't focus. This lack of focus magnifies the intensity of the whirlwind, dilutes your efforts, and makes success almost impossible. This is especially problematic when there are too many goals at the highest levels of the organization, all of which eventually cascade into dozens and ultimately hundreds of goals as they work their way down throughout the organization, creating a web of complexity.

However, when you narrow the focus of your team to one or two wildly important goals, the team can easily distinguish between what is truly top priority and what is the whirlwind. They move from a loosely defined and difficult-to-communicate collection of objectives to a small, focused set of achievable targets. Discipline 1 is the discipline of focus. Without it, you will never get the results you want. It's also only the beginning.

Discipline 2: Act on the Lead Measures

This is the discipline of leverage. It's based on the simple principle that all actions are not created equal. Some actions have more impact than others when reaching for a goal. And it is those that you want to identify and act on if you want to reach your goal.

Whatever strategy you're pursuing, your progress and your success will be based on two kinds of measures: lag and lead.

Lag measures are the tracking measurements of the wildly important goal, and they are usually the ones you spend most of your time praying over. Revenue, profit, market share, and customer satisfaction are all lag measures, meaning that when you receive them, the performance that drove them is already in the past. That's why you're praying—by the time you get a lag measure, you can't fix it. It's history.

Lead measures are quite different in that they are the measures of the most high-impact things your team must do to reach the goal. In essence, they measure the new behaviors that will drive success on the lag measures, whether those behaviors are as simple as offering a sample to every customer in the bakery or as complex as adhering to standards in jet-engine design.

A good lead measure has two basic characteristics: It's *predictive* of achieving the goal and it can be *influenced* by the team members. To understand these two characteristics, consider the simple goal of losing weight. While the lag measure is pounds lost, two lead measures might be a specific limit on calories per day and a specific number of hours of exercise per week. These lead measures are predictive because by performing to them, you can predict what the scale (the lag measure) will tell you next week. They are influenceable because both of these new behaviors are within your control.

Acting on the lead measures is one of the little-known secrets of execution. Most leaders, even some of the most experienced, are so focused on lag measures that the discipline to focus on the lead measures feels counterintuitive.

Don't misunderstand. Lag measures are ultimately the most important things you are trying to accomplish. But lead measures, true to their name, are what will get you to the lag measures. Once you've identified your lead measures, they become the key leverage points for achieving your goal.

Discipline 3: Keep a Compelling Scoreboard

People play differently when they're keeping score. If you doubt this, watch any group of teenagers playing basketball and see how the game changes the minute scorekeeping begins. However, the truth of this statement is more clearly revealed by a change in emphasis: People play differently when *they* are keeping score. It's not about you keeping score for them.

Discipline 3 is the discipline of engagement. In principle, the highest level of performance always comes from people who are emotionally engaged and the highest level of engagement comes from knowing the score—that is, if people know whether they are winning or losing. It's that simple. Bowling through a curtain might be fun in the beginning; but if you can't see the pins fall it will soon become boring, even if you really love bowling.

If you've narrowed your focus in Discipline 1 (your WIG with a lag measure) and determined the critical lead measures that will keep you on course toward that goal in Discipline 2, you have the elements of a winnable game. The next step is to capture that game on a simple but compelling scoreboard.

The kind of scoreboard that will drive the highest levels of engagement with your team will be one that is designed solely for (and often by) the players. This players' scoreboard is quite different from the complex coach's scoreboard that leaders love to create. It must be simple, so simple that members of the team can determine instantly if they are winning or losing. Why does this matter? If the scoreboard isn't clear, the game you want people to play will be abandoned in the whirlwind of other activities. And if your team doesn't know whether or not they are winning the game, they are probably on their way to losing.

Discipline 4: Create a Cadence of Accountability

Discipline 4 is where execution really happens. The first three disciplines set up the game, but until you apply Discipline 4, your team isn't *in* the game. It is based on the principle of accountability: that unless we consistently hold each other accountable, the goal naturally disintegrates in the whirlwind.

The cadence of accountability is a rhythm of regular and frequent meetings of any team that owns a wildly important goal. These meetings happen at least weekly and ideally last no more than twenty to thirty minutes. In that brief time, team members hold each other accountable for producing results, despite the whirlwind.

Why is the *cadence* of accountability so important?

Consider the experience of someone with whom we've worked. He and his teen-age daughter made an agreement that she would be allowed the use of the family car if she washed it every Saturday morning. He would meet with her each Saturday to make sure the car was clean.

They met on Saturday for several weeks and everything went well, but then he had to go out of town for two Saturdays in a row. When he returned, he found that the car had not been cleaned. He asked his daughter why she hadn't taken care of her job.

"Oh," she replied. "Are we still doing that?"

It took only two weeks for the accountability system to break down. If this was the case in a one-on-one situation, think how much more it applies to a work team or a whole organization. The magic is in the cadence. Team members must be able to hold each other accountable regularly and rhythmically. Each week, one by one, team members answer a simple question: "What are the one or two most important things I can do in the next week (outside the whirlwind) that will have the biggest impact on the scoreboard?" Then members report on whether they met the previous week's commitments, how well they are moving the lead and lag measures on the scoreboard, and their commitments for the coming week, all in only a few minutes.

The secret to Discipline 4, in addition to the repeated cadence, is that team members create their own commitments. It's common to find teams where the members expect, even want, simply to be told what to do. However, because they make their own commitments, their ownership of them increases. Team members will always be more committed to their own ideas than they will to orders from above. Even more important, making commitments to their team members, rather than solely to the boss, shifts the emphasis from professional to personal. Simply put, the commitments go beyond their job performance to become promises to the team.

Because the team commits to a new set of objectives each week, this discipline creates a just-in-time weekly execution plan that adapts to challenges and opportunities that can never be foreseen in an annual strategic plan. In this way, the plan is adapting as fast as the business is changing. The result? The team can direct enormous energy to the wildly important goal without getting blocked by the shifting whirlwind of change all around them.

When your team begins to see the lag measure of a big goal moving as a direct result of their efforts, they will know they are winning. And we have found nothing that drives the morale and engagement of a team more than winning.

A remarkable example is a world-class luxury hotel chain that set a WIG with a lag measure of 97 percent guest retention. "If you stay here once, we

SCAN
WITH
YOUR
SMART
PHONE

Android - Barcode Scanner
iPhone - Red Laser

LINK: http://www.4dxbook.com/qr/17Overview

Scan the image above to watch a video overview of 4DX.

want you back!" was their mantra. And they executed that goal with excellence.

They chose to achieve their goal through lead measures of individualized personal service.

So, what did they do differently?

Every staff member had a role in achieving that goal. Housekeepers, for example, carefully recorded on computers the individual preferences of each guest so they could provide the same services each time the customer came back. One guest asked the maid to leave his partially smoked cigar in the ashtray because he would be returning to the room. When he returned, there was a new cigar of the same brand in the ashtray. He thought that was nice, but what he never expected was to find a new cigar of that brand waiting for him in his room in another hotel in the chain months later! He says, "Now, I have to go back just to see if the cigar will be there. They own me!"

In addition to their whirlwind, the housekeepers had quite a few new things to do: note guest preferences, enter and retrieve guest preferences from a computer, and fulfill guest preferences. Clearly, the housekeepers would not have done all those new things if they hadn't known without question:

- That the goal of customer retention was top priority
- That a few new activities were vital to achieving that goal
- That they would track those activities carefully
- That they would account for their commitments daily

In other words:

- They knew the goal (Discipline 1)
- They knew what to do to achieve the goal (Discipline 2)
- They knew the score at all times (Discipline 3)
- They held themselves accountable regularly and frequently for the results (Discipline 4)

These are the characteristics of organizations that practice the 4 Disciplines of Execution.

People want to win. They want to make a contribution that matters. However, too many organizations lack this kind of discipline—the conscious, consistent regimen needed to execute key goals with excellence. The financial impact of a failure to execute can be huge, but it is only one of the impacts. Another is the human cost to people who want to give their best and be part of a winning team. By contrast, nothing is more motivating than belonging to a team of people who know the goal and are determined to get there.

The 4 Disciplines work because they are based on principles, not practices. Practices are situational, subjective, and always evolving. Principles are timeless and self-evident, and they apply everywhere. They are natural laws, like gravity. Whether you understand them or even agree with them doesn't matter—they still apply.

One of the best-selling business books of all time is *The 7 Habits of Highly Effective People* written by Stephen R. Covey. In his book, Stephen identified some of the core principles that govern human behavior and effectiveness, such as responsibility, vision, integrity, understanding, collaboration, and renewal.

Just as there are principles that govern human behavior, there are principles that govern how teams get things done, or how they execute. We believe the principles of execution have always been focus, leverage, engagement, and accountability. Are there other principles at play when it comes to execution? Yes. But is there something special about these four and their sequencing? Absolutely. We didn't invent them and we freely acknowledge that understanding them has never been the problem. The challenge for leaders has been finding a way to implement them, especially when the whirlwind is raging.

HOW THIS BOOK IS ORGANIZED

The 4 Disciplines of Execution is organized into three parts to provide you with a progressively deeper understanding of the disciplines and their application to any team.

Section 1, "The 4 Disciplines of Execution," presents a thorough understanding of the 4 Disciplines. This section also explains why these apparently simple concepts are actually so difficult to practice and why they are the key to successfully meeting any leader's greatest challenge.

Section 2, "Installing 4DX with Your Team," is designed like a field guide. It gives very detailed step-by-step instructions for implementing the disciplines within your team. A separate chapter is devoted to each discipline. The final chapter of this section introduces you to an online system for managing the 4 Disciplines with your team.

Section 3, "Installing 4DX in Your Organization," provides you with some rules of the road that have evolved from the hundreds of implementations we've guided over the past decade. You will gain insights from the leaders of top companies who are successfully using 4DX to drive strategy and create breakthrough results in their organizations. This section also answers, from our direct experience, many of the questions that arise in executing strategies in a wide range of industries.

Throughout all three of these sections you will find links to FranklinCovey's execution website where you can watch video case studies of many of the examples cited in this book.

At the end of the book we've included a chapter of Frequently Asked Questions and a short chapter which shows how the 4 Disciplines can help you accomplish personal or family-oriented goals.

This book is a little different from most other business books you've read. Most business books share a lot of very helpful ideas and theories but are shallow on application. In this book we are heavy on application and will tell you exactly what you can do to implement these disciplines—the specifics, the tips, the watch outs, the must do's. We'll share everything we know. Section 1 will teach you The 4 disciplines of Execution. Sections 2 and 3 will show you how to apply them, in vivid detail. We hope you'll find this approach refreshing.

. . .

Before you begin . . .

We've learned that there are three things to watch out for when you begin studying the 4 Disciplines more deeply:

4DX says easy, does hard. First, the disciplines will sound deceptively simple, but they take sustained work to implement. As one of our clients put it, "Says easy, does hard." Don't be misled by this simplicity: The 4 Disciplines are powerful in part because they are easy to understand. But successful implementation takes significant effort over an extended period. It requires sustained commitment. If the goal you're seeking isn't one you just have to achieve, you might not make the sustained commitment necessary. The payoff, however, is that you will not only achieve this goal but also build the organizational muscle and capability to achieve the next goal and the next.

4DX is counterintuitive. Second, each of the 4 Disciplines are paradigm shifting and might even fly in the face of your intuition. While it might seem instinctive to you to have a lot of goals, the more you have the fewer you will achieve with excellence. If you want to achieve a certain goal, don't focus on the goal itself but on the lead measures that drive the goal. As you implement each discipline, at least initially, you'll be doing things that, at first glance, might not seem to make sense and that run counter to your instincts. Let us emphasize, though, that the 4 Disciplines are the result of serious, intense experimentation and hypothesis testing over many years; everything you learn here has been thoroughly vetted. The good news is that once you gain some experience with the 4 Disciplines, what seemed awkward in the beginning will become more comfortable and more effective.

4DX is an operating system. Third, the 4 Disciplines are a matched set, not a menu of choices. While every one of the disciplines has value, their real power is in how they work together in sequence. Each discipline sets the stage for the next discipline; leave one out and you'll have a far less effective result. Think of the 4 Disciplines as the operating system of a computer—once it's installed, you can use it to run almost any strategy you choose, but you need the whole system for it to work. As we move through the next chapters, the reasons for this will become clear.

Section 1

The 4 Disciplines
of Execution

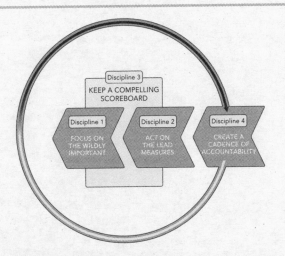

The 4 Disciplines of Execution are all about producing great results. The disciplines point from right to left because great teams execute from right to left—they hold themselves consistently accountable for performance on lead measures, which in turn drives achievement of wildly important goals.

The compelling scoreboard, Discipline 3, is central because it displays the success measures on the goals for all to see.

The cadence of accountability, Discipline 4, surrounds the other disciplines because it holds everything together. The circling arrow symbolizes the practice of regular, frequent accountability for the success measures on the scoreboard.

Discipline 1:
Focus on the Wildly Important

The first discipline is to *focus* your finest effort on the one or two goals that will make all the difference, instead of giving mediocre effort to dozens of goals.

Execution starts with focus. Without it, the other three disciplines won't be able to help you.

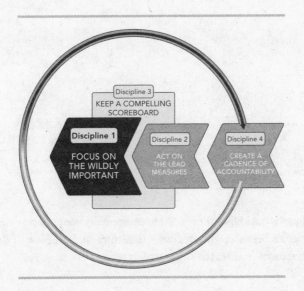

Why do almost all leaders struggle to narrow their focus? It's not because they don't think focus is needed. Every week, we work with dozens of leadership teams across the world and, almost without exception, they acknowledge that they need greater focus. Despite this desire, they continue to find themselves with too many competing priorities, pulling their teams in too many different directions. One of the first things we want you to know is that you are not alone. The inability of leaders to focus is a problem of epidemic proportions.

We also want you to know that when we talk about narrowing your focus in Discipline 1, we are not talking about narrowing the size and complexity of your whirlwind, although, over time, attention to WIGs might have that effect. Your whirlwind includes all of the urgent activities that are necessary to sustain your business day to day. Focusing on the wildly important means narrowing the number of goals you are attempting to accomplish beyond the day-to-day demands of your whirlwind.

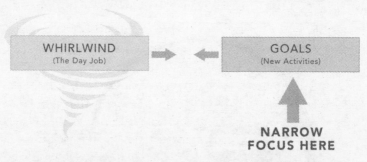

Practicing Discipline 1 means narrowing your focus to a few highly important goals so you can manageably achieve them in the midst of the whirlwind of the day job.

Simply put, Discipline 1 is about applying more energy against fewer goals because, when it comes to setting goals, the law of diminishing returns is as real as the law of gravity.

NUMBER OF GOALS (In addition to the Whirlwind)	2-3	4-10	11-20
	⬇	⬇	⬇
GOALS ACHIEVED WITH EXCELLENCE	2-3	1-2	0

Your chances of achieving 2 or 3 goals with excellence are high, but the more goals you try to juggle at once, the less likely you will be to reach them.

If a team focuses on two or even three goals beyond the demands of their whirlwind, they can often accomplish them. However, if they set four to ten goals, our experience has been that they will achieve only one or two. They'll be going backward! If they go after eleven to twenty goals in addition to the whirlwind, they'll lose all focus. Confronted with so many goals the team members will stop listening let alone executing.

Why is this so?

The fundamental principle at work in Discipline 1 is that human beings are genetically hardwired to do one thing at a time *with excellence*. You're probably thinking—proudly—that you're great at multitasking and can get a lot of things done at the same time. But to the wildly important goal you want to devote your best effort. Steve Jobs of Apple had a big company to run, and he could have proudly brought many more products to market than he did; but he chose to focus on a handful of "wildly important" products. His focus was legendary. And so were his results. Science tells us the human brain can give full focus to only a single object at any given moment. You can't even give your best effort to driving a car while talking on a mobile phone and eating a burger, let alone juggle multiple important business goals at once.

MIT neuroscientist Earl Miller says, "Trying to concentrate on two tasks causes an overload of the brain's processing capacity. . . . Particularly when people try to perform similar tasks at the same time, such as writing an email and talking on the phone, they compete to use the same part of the brain. Trying to carry too much, the brain simply slows down."[5] If this is true of simple tasks like processing emails and phone calls, think of the impact of losing focus on the goals that could transform your business.

The prefrontal cortex, the brain's gateway, just can't handle the daily flood that comes at us, because it is designed to deal with teaspoons rather than tidal waves of information.

In our culture of multitasking, according to Professor Clifford Nass of Stanford University, "The neural circuits devoted to scanning, skimming, and multitasking are expanding and strengthening, while those used for reading and thinking deeply, with sustained concentration, are weakening or eroding."

What's the consequence? "Habitual multitaskers may be sacrificing performance on the primary task. They are suckers for irrelevancy." (Another term for the *primary task* is the WIG.)

"Improving our ability to multitask actually hampers our ability to think deeply and creatively. . . the more you multitask . . . the less deliberative you become; the less you're able to think and reason out a problem," says Jordan Grafman of the National Institute of Neurological Disorders and Stroke in the USA.[6]

Of course, you don't have to overload the brain. You can leverage the brain's capacity to concentrate superbly on one *wildly important goal* at a time, while still being aware of the other priorities. There's no better illustration of this principle than an airport control tower.

Right now more than a hundred airplanes might be approaching, taking off, or taxiing around, and all of them are very important, especially if you happen to be on one of them! But for the air traffic controller, only one airplane is *wildly important* right now—the one that's landing at this moment.

The controller is aware of all the other planes on the radar. She's keeping track of them, but right now all her talent and expertise is solely focused on one flight. If she doesn't get that flight on the ground safely and with total excellence, then nothing else she might achieve is really going to matter much. She lands *one airplane at a time.*

WIGs are like that. They are the goals you must achieve with total excellence beyond the circling priorities of your day to day. To succeed, you must be willing to make the hard choices that separate what is wildly important from all the many other merely important goals on your radar. Then, you must approach that WIG with focus and diligence until it is delivered as promised, with excellence.

That doesn't mean you abandon all your other important goals. They're still on your radar, but they don't require your finest diligence and effort *right now.* (Still, some of those goals might never be worthy of your finest diligence and effort—some of them never should have taken off in the first place!)

People who try to push many goals at once usually wind up doing a mediocre job on all of them. You can ignore the principle of focus, but it won't ignore you. Or you can leverage this principle to achieve your top goals, one at a time, again and again.

CONVENTIONAL THINKING	4DX PRINCIPLE
All of our goals are Priority 1. We can successfully multitask and succeed at five, ten, or fifteen important goals. All we need to do is work harder and longer. . .	Many of our goals are important, but only one or two are wildly important. We call them WIGs. They are the goals we must achieve. Our finest effort can only be given to one or two wildly important goals at a time.

THE LEADER'S CHALLENGE

So, here's the big question: Why is there so much pressure toward expanding, rather than narrowing, the goals? If you understand the need to focus, why is it so difficult to actually do it?

You might say that, as a leader, it's because you can always see more than a dozen existing things that need improvement and another dozen new opportunities you'd like to be chasing on any given day. On top of that, there are other people (and other peoples' agendas) that can be adding to your goals, especially if they are from higher up in the organization.

However, more often than any of these external forces, there's one real culprit that creates most of the problem: you. In the words of the old cartoon, *Pogo,* "We have met the enemy and he is us."

Although the tendencies that drive you to the higher side of the scale are well-intentioned, in a very real sense, you are often your own worst enemy. Being aware of these tendencies is a good place to start. Let's examine a few of them candidly.

One reason you may drive your team to take on too much is that, as a leader, you tend to be ambitious and creative. You are exactly the kind of individual organizations like to promote. The problem is that creative, ambitious people always want to do more, not less. If this describes you, you're almost hardwired to violate the first discipline of execution.

Another reason you might lead your team to go after too many goals is to hedge your bets. In other words, if your team pursues everything, then it seems likely that something might work. It also ensures that, if you fail, no one can question the level of effort your team gave. Even though you know that more is not better, it *looks* better, especially to the person above you. So, you may resist the increased accountability for results that would come with fewer goals and instead rely on the sheer volume of effort to drive your success.

However, the greatest challenge you face in narrowing your goals is simply that it requires you to say no to a lot of good ideas. 4DX may even mean saying no to some *great* ideas, at least for now. Nothing is more counterintuitive for a leader than saying no to a good idea, and nothing is a bigger destroyer of focus than always saying yes.

What makes it even harder is that these good ideas aren't presented all at once, wrapped in a nice little bundle so that choosing among them would be simple. Instead, they filter in one at a time. Alone, each idea seems to make so much sense that it's almost impossible for you to say no, so you fall into a trap of your own making.

We believe all leaders facing this challenge should have this quote prominently displayed in their offices:

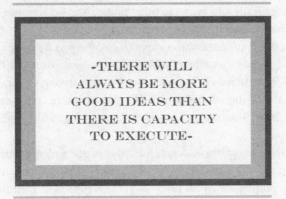

-THERE WILL
ALWAYS BE MORE
GOOD IDEAS THAN
THERE IS CAPACITY
TO EXECUTE-

We can't overemphasize the importance of focusing on only one or two WIGs at once. It's counterintuitive, but it must happen.

Before Apple was named company of the decade in the United States by multiple sources,[7] then COO Tim Cook (now CEO) said this to the company's shareholders:

"We are the most focused company that I know of or have read of or have any knowledge of. We say no to good ideas every day. We say no to great ideas in order to keep the amount of things we focus on very small in number so that we can put enormous energy behind the ones we do choose. The table each of you is sitting at today, you could probably put every product on it that Apple makes, yet Apple's revenue last year was $40 billion."[8]

Apple's determination to say no to good ideas has had devastating consequences for their competitors. We once worked with a manufacturer that competed directly with Apple's iPhone. When we met with the leader responsible for creating a new interface to compete with the iPhone (How would you like that assignment?), he was more than a little discouraged. "It's really not fair," he said, shaking his head. "Between our domestic and international operations we make over forty different phones. They only make one."

We couldn't have said it better ourselves.

As Stephen R. Covey says, "You have to decide what your highest priorities are and have the courage—pleasantly, smilingly, unapologetically—to say no to other things. And the way you do that is by having a bigger 'yes' burning inside."

Once you understand the importance of saying no to good ideas in order to keep your team's focus narrow, you can avoid the first of two focus traps. However, the second trap, trying to turn everything in the whirlwind into a WIG, is even more common. Once caught in it, you try to turn everything in the whirlwind into a goal.

Within the whirlwind are all of your existing measurements for running the organization today, illustrated below as dials. It's perfectly appropriate for your team to spend 80 percent of their time and energy sustaining or incrementally improving the whirlwind. Keeping the ship afloat should be job one, but if they are spending 100 percent of their energy trying to significantly improve all of those dials at once, you will have lost your focus.

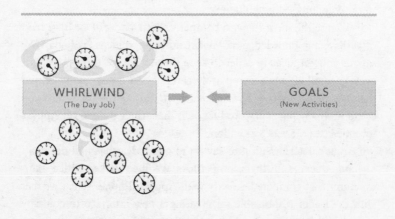

In the organizational whirlwind, people track countless numbers—finances, customer satisfaction scores, product life cycles, and so forth. A new, wildly important goal can get lost in this storm.

Applying even pressure to all these dials is like trying to make holes in a piece of paper by applying even pressure with all your fingers. You can't press on any one dial with enough force to drive a change in human behavior. Many of the dials require dozens of changes in human behavior in order to move them. Focusing on one WIG is like punching one finger through the paper—all your strength goes into making that hole.

Unless you can achieve your goal with a stroke of the pen, success is going to require your team to change their behavior; and they simply cannot change that many behaviors at once, no matter how badly you want them to. Trying to significantly improve every measure in the whirlwind will consume all of your time and leave you with very little to show for it.

So, beyond avoiding these two focus traps—refusing to say no to all the good ideas and trying to make everything in the whirlwind a goal—what should you do? Narrow your focus to one or two wildly important goals and consistently invest the team's time and energy into them. In other words, if you want high-focus, high-performance team members, they must have something wildly important to focus *on*.

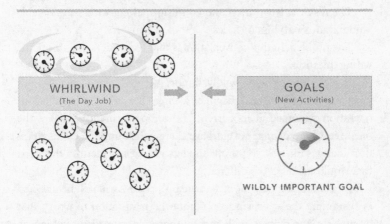

While you don't lose track of the numbers in the whirlwind, Discipline 1 requires intense focus on one number—the measure of success on the "wildly important goal."

IDENTIFYING YOUR WILDLY IMPORTANT GOALS

A wildly important goal (WIG) is a goal that can make all the difference. Because it's your strategic tipping point, you're going to commit to apply a disproportionate amount of energy to it—the 20 percent that is not used up in the whirlwind. But how do you decide which of many possible goals should be your WIG?

Sometimes, the choice of a WIG is obvious, but at other times it can be confusing. If you try to select your WIG by asking yourself what's most important, you may find your mind running in circles. Why? Because the urgent priorities in your whirlwind are always competing to be the most important and a very good argument can usually be made for choosing any one of them.

To illustrate this problem, imagine the leadership team in a manufacturing plant having this conversation: "I'm telling you, quality is the most important thing and it should be our WIG!" says one person. "Well don't forget, it's our production that pays the bills around here," says another. "I'm sorry, but I disagree with both of you," says a third. "Safety has to be the most important. Have you ever had one of your people seriously hurt in an accident? If you had, you'd agree."

The result is frustration and confusion, along with an inevitable (and paradoxical) loss of focus.

The problem in this conversation is that the leaders are asking the wrong question.

In determining your wildly important goal, don't ask "What's most important?" Instead, begin by asking "If every other area of our operation remained at its current level of performance, what is the one area where change would have the greatest impact?" This question changes the way you think and lets you clearly identify the focus that would make all the difference.

Remember, 80 percent of your team's energy will still be directed at sustaining the whirlwind, so ignore the temptation to worry that by making one or two goals most important, your team will ignore everything else. And once you stop worrying about everything else going backward, you can start moving forward on your WIG. In the words of Discipline 1, you can focus on the wildly important.

Your wildly important goal will come from one of two categories: either from within the whirlwind or from outside it.

Within the whirlwind, it could be something so badly broken that it must be fixed, or it could be a key element of your value proposition that isn't being delivered. Poor project completion time, out-of-control costs, or unsatisfactory customer service are all good examples. However, it could also be an area in which your team is already performing well and where leveraging this strength could result in significant impact. For example, increasing patient satisfaction in a hospital from the 85th percentile to the 95th percentile could increase your revenue dramatically.

Outside the whirlwind, the choices tend to be about repositioning yourself strategically. Launching a new product or service, either to counter a competitive threat or seize a huge opportunity, could be a WIG that would make all the difference. Remember that this type of WIG will require an even greater change in behavior, since it will be completely new to your team.

Whether your WIG comes from within the whirlwind or outside it, your real aim is not only to achieve it, but also to then make the new level of performance a natural part of your team's operation. In essence, once a WIG is achieved, it goes back into the whirlwind. Every time this happens, the whirlwind changes. It isn't as chaotic, chronic problems are resolved, and new performance levels are sustained; in essence, it's a much higher performing whirlwind. Ultimately, this is what enables your team to pursue the next WIG from a stronger foundation.

Sometimes, choosing your WIG is about more than selecting the aspect of your business where the greatest results are desired; it's about a WIG so fundamental to the heart of your mission that achieving it defines your existence as an organization.

We got to work with the new president of a large thrift-store chain just as he was asking himself these questions. His predecessor had put the company on a firm financial and operational footing, updating marketing and advertising, the look and feel of the stores, and the accounting procedures. When we got into the WIG discussion, some of his reports thought this emphasis needed to continue. Others wanted more emphasis on hiring more disabled workers. Still others argued that their top WIG should be growth. The range of choices was baffling.

To help the team find common ground, the new leader asked everyone to ponder the mission of the organization: "To promote self-reliance among the disabled and displaced." With the company in a solid financial and operational position, could it be that the area where they now wanted the greatest results might be more directly related to their mission?

Gradually, a WIG emerged from this experience; one they had not even considered before: "Help disabled workers find jobs outside our organization that can sustain them." While they couldn't hire every disabled person in their region, they had the operational capacity to train thousands in the retail business and find better jobs for them, so that they could escape from dependency. The organization's new measure of success? "Increasing the number of disabled people placed in sustainable jobs."

This WIG transformed the organization. They helped thousands become self-reliant and find a new sense of self-worth, while sustaining the day-to-day financial and operational results that made their mission possible.

FOCUSING THE ORGANIZATION

Up to this point, we've talked a lot about narrowing the focus as it relates to you and your team. This in itself is a huge challenge. Narrowing the focus for an entire organization or even a large portion of an organization, however, is a much bigger challenge. Although we'll cover this in more detail on page 235, we want you to gain a high-level understanding of the rules for applying Discipline 1 organizationally before we move into Discipline 2.

Rule #1: No team focuses on more than two WIGs at the same time. This rule acts like a governor on an engine. When you are deeply into the 4 Disciplines of Execution there may be dozens or even hundreds of WIGs across the entire organization, but the key is not to overload any single leader, team, or individual performer. Remember, they are all dealing with the incessant demands of the whirlwind. Keep this rule in mind as you consider the remaining three rules. If you violate this one, you will have lost your focus as an organization.

Rule #2: The battles you choose must win the war. Whether it's a military conflict, or the war on hunger, cancer, or poverty, there's a relationship between battles and wars. The only reason you fight a battle is to win the war. The sole purpose of WIGs at lower levels in the organization is to help achieve the WIGs at higher levels. It isn't enough that the lower-level WIGs support or align with the higher WIGs. The lower-level WIGs must *ensure* the success of the higher WIGs.

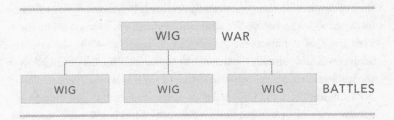

For example, a provider of Internet financial services we worked with knew they had to increase revenues from $160 million to $200 million by fiscal year end in order to fulfill the expectations of their investors. A new outside-sales team committed to provide $8 million of new revenue and the major-account division committed to the other $32 million.

What about the other major division—the technology team? What role did they play in this revenue WIG? Did they have any role at all? At first, they felt left out of the WIG.

After some careful research, they determined that the most impactful lower-level WIG they could set for themselves would be to improve their record for continuous, uninterrupted service. This was a major criterion new customers would use to choose a provider—perhaps the most important criterion. As it turned out, this group had to fight the key battle in achieving the WIG, which in turn cleared the path for the other divisions as well.

Once the top-level WIG is chosen, the next question is critical. Instead of asking, "What are all the things we could do to win this war?"—a common mistake that results in a long to-do list—ask, "What are the fewest number of battles necessary to win this war?" The answer to that question determines which and how many lower-level WIGs will be needed to achieve the top-level WIG. As you begin to choose the battles to win the war, you have begun to both clarify and simplify your strategy. This process will be covered in detail on page 94.

Rule #3: Senior leaders can veto, but not dictate. The highest levels of execution are never reached when the strategy is devised solely by the top leaders of the organization and simply handed down to the leaders and teams below. Without involvement, you cannot create the high levels of commitment that execution requires. While the senior leaders will undoubtedly determine the top-level WIG, they must allow the leaders at each level below to define the WIGs *for their teams*. This not only leverages the knowledge of these leaders, but also creates a greater sense of ownership and involvement. Simply put, they become more engaged in a goal that they choose themselves and that supports a worthy organizational goal. Senior leaders then exercise their right to veto if the battles chosen are not going to win the war.

Implementing Discipline 1 enables an organization to quickly turn a broad strategy into clearly defined WIGs at every level. It is not solely a top-down process, but neither is it exclusively bottom-up. Through this process, the senior leader's choice of the overall WIG brings clarity (top down), and allowing the leaders and teams below to choose their WIGs (bottom up) brings engagement. In the process, the entire organization mobilizes around the focus that matters most and takes ownership for driving the result.

Rule #4: All WIGs must have a finish line in the form of from *X to Y by when.* Every WIG at every level must contain a clearly measurable result, as well as the date by which that result must be achieved. For example, a revenue-focused WIG might be: "Increase percent of annual revenue from new products from 15 percent to 21 percent by December 31st." This *from X to Y by when* format recognizes where you are today, where you want to go, and the deadline for reaching that goal. As deceptively simple as this formula may seem, many leaders often struggle to translate their strategic concepts into a single *from X to Y by when* finish line. But once they've done it, both they and the teams they lead have gained tremendous clarity.

Typically, however, goals lack this kind of clarity. We constantly see goals like these that no one can achieve because there's no finish line; no way of telling whether you completed the goal or not and where you stand at any given point:

- From a major global retail company: "Improve inventory processing."
- From a British publisher: "Develop and strengthen new and existing client relationships."
- From an Australian tourist authority: "Influence effective tourism workforce development in Queensland."
- From a European investment firm: "Successfully convert our portfolio to a life-cycle strategy."
- From a multinational agribusiness company: "Identify, recruit, and retain the best employees."

These goals lack the measurement that can tell the team when they've won the game. "Improve inventory processing?" How much? "Strengthen new client relationships?" How do we measure "stronger"? "Successfully convert a portfolio to a life-cycle strategy?" How will we know if we've done that?

Effective lag measures look like this:

- "Improve inventory processing by increasing per-year inventory turns from eight to ten by December 31."
- "Raise our client-relationship score from forty to seventy on the loyalty scale within two years."
- "Move 40 percent of our customers from fixed categories to life-cycle categories of investments within five years."
- "Launch the new CRM solution at an 85 percent quality beta rating by the end of our fiscal year."

If a goal is wildly important, surely you should be able to tell if you've achieved it or not. The formula *from X to Y by when* makes that possible.

In setting a finish line, we often hear the question, "Over what period of time should the achievement of a WIG be spread?" Our answer is, "It depends." Since teams and organizations often think and measure themselves in terms of a calendar or a fiscal year, a one-year time frame makes a good starting point for a WIG. That said, remember that a WIG is not a strategy. A WIG is a tactical goal with a limited time frame. We've seen some WIGs that take two years and some that take six months. The length of a project-based WIG, such as "Complete the new website within budget by July 1," will usually correspond with the time frame of the project itself. Use your own judgment. Just remember that a WIG should be within a time frame that balances the need to create a compelling vision with the need to create an achievable goal.

SHOOTING FOR THE MOON

In 1958, the fledgling National Aeronautics and Space Administration (NASA) had many very important goals like this one: "The expansion of human knowledge of phenomena in the atmosphere and space." It sounded like many of the goals you hear in business today: "Become world class . . ." or "Lead the industry . . ." Although the leaders at NASA had ways to measure various aspects of this goal, they lacked the clarity of a defined finish line. They also lacked the results that the Soviet Union was producing.

But in 1961, President John F. Kennedy shook NASA to its foundations when he made the pronouncement "land a man on the moon and return him safely to the earth before this decade is out." Suddenly, NASA had a formidable new challenge, the war it would fight for the next ten years, and it was stated in exactly the way WIGs should be stated: "X" is earthbound, "Y" is to the moon and back, and "when" is by December 31, 1969.

Just a glance at this table[9] shows the difference between conventional organizational goals and a true WIG.

NASA'S GOALS IN 1958	NASA'S GOALS AS OF 1961
1. The expansion of human knowledge of phenomena in the atmosphere and space;	*"I believe that this nation should commit itself to achieving the goal, before this decade is out, of landing a man on the moon and returning him safely to the earth."* –John F. Kennedy
2. The improvement of the usefulness, performance, speed, safety, and efficiency of aeronautical and space vehicles;	
3. The development and operation of vehicles capable of carrying instruments, equipment, supplies, and living organisms through space;	
4. The establishment of long-range studies of the potential benefits to be gained from, the opportunities for, and the problems involved in the utilization of aeronautical and space activities for peaceful and scientific purposes;	
5. The preservation of the role of the United States as a leader in aeronautical and space science and technology and in the application thereof to the conduct of peaceful activities within and outside the atmosphere;	
6. The making available to agencies directly concerned with national defense of discoveries that have military value or significance, and the furnishing by such agencies, to the civilian agency established to direct and control nonmilitary aeronautical and space activities, of information as to discoveries which have value or significance to that agency;	
7. Cooperation by the United States with other nations and groups of nations in work done pursuant to this Act and in the peaceful application of the results thereof;	
8. The most effective utilization of the scientific and engineering resources of the United States, with close cooperation among all interested agencies of the United States in order to avoid unnecessary duplication of effort, facilities and equipment.	

Consider the 1958 goals:

- Are they clear and measurable?
- How many are there?
- Is there a finish line for any of them?

So, what kind of results were these objectives driving for NASA? Russia went into space first with satellites and cosmonauts while the United States was still blowing up rockets on launchpads.

Contrast the 1958 goals with the 1961 goal: one clear, measurable WIG.

Now, with its reputation at stake on the world stage, NASA had to determine the few key battles that would win that war.

In the end, three critical battles were chosen: navigation, propulsion, and life support. Navigation posed the formidable challenge of moving a spacecraft through space at eighteen miles per second to a precise location on the moon, which was also moving rapidly in its elliptical orbit around Earth. Propulsion was no less of a challenge because a rocket heavy enough to carry a lunar module had never yet achieved a velocity sufficient to break free of Earth's gravitational pull. Life support was the most critical of all because it required developing a capsule and landing module that would keep astronauts alive, both for the journey to and from the moon and while they explored the moon's surface.

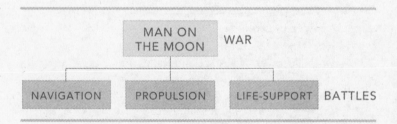

President Kennedy's speech also included another key aspect of Discipline 1—saying no to good ideas—when he acknowledged that were many other worthy objectives that the country would not pursue in order to achieve this goal. But, as he asked, "Why, some say, the moon? Why choose this as our goal? . . . That goal will serve to organize and measure the best of our energies and skills, because that challenge is one that we are willing to accept, one we are unwilling to postpone, and one which we intend to win."[10] In this way, he narrowed the focus of NASA to a finish line whose achievement became one of the most important ventures in human history.

What do you think happened to accountability within NASA when the challenge of putting a man on the moon was publicly announced? It went through the roof. This is particularly clear when you remember that the spacecraft they would use had only a tiny fraction of the computing power of the smartphone in your pocket. Even worse, the engineers and scientists still had no operational technology for winning the three necessary battles. Looking back, you might say human beings had no business being on the moon in 1969.

Now, consider a different question: When accountability soared, what happened to morale and engagement? It, too, went through the roof. Most leaders find this surprising. We tend to think that when accountability is at its highest, the pressure makes morale go down. The reality is the opposite: Narrowing your focus increases both accountability and the engagement of your team.

When a team moves from having a dozen we-really-hope goals to one or two no-matter-what goals, the effect on morale is dramatic. It's as though a switch exists in every team member's head called "Game on!" If you can throw that switch, you have laid the foundation for extraordinary execution. When President Kennedy said to the moon and back by the end of the decade, he threw that switch.

Can you remember what it's like to be part of a team when the game-on switch is activated? It's a remarkable experience. Even though you still have to deal with the whirlwind and its myriad demands, you also have a finish line, something clear and important at which you can win. Even more meaningful, it's something whereby every member of the team can see that their contribution makes a difference. Everyone wants to feel that they are winning and that they are contributing to something meaningful. And, when times are tough, they want it even more.

When we started on this journey years ago, we did not intend to focus on defining or even refining strategy. However, we quickly learned that the line separating strategy and execution is blurry. Applying this first discipline will sharpen your strategy more than you think it will. But what it will really do is make your strategy executable.

Think of it this way: Above your head is a thought bubble, and inside that bubble are all the various aspects of your strategy, including opportunities you wish you were pursuing, new ideas and concepts, problems you know you need to fix, and a lot of "whats" and "hows" to get it all done. Your bubble is complicated and chaotic. It's also completely different from the bubbles above every other leader.

This is why Discipline 1 requires you to translate your strategy from concepts to targets, from a vague strategic intent to a set of specific finish lines. The four rules for implementing Discipline 1, outlined above, give an entire organization a framework for doing this successfully. (For more examples and process steps, see sections 2 and 3.)

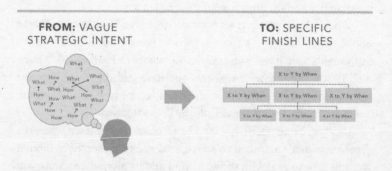

FROM: VAGUE STRATEGIC INTENT

TO: SPECIFIC FINISH LINES

Too many organizational goals are hazy and imprecise, leaving people wondering "what" they are supposed to do and "how" they are supposed to do it. Discipline 1 provides clear, unmistakable finish lines so people know exactly what success looks like.

Finally, remember that the four rules of focus are unforgiving. At some point, you will want to cheat on them, even just a little. We know. We often want to do the same inside our organization. However, what we've learned is that the rules governing focus are like the rules governing gravity: They aren't concerned with what you think or with the details of your particular situation. They simply yield predictable consequences.

When you think about it, the principle of focusing on the vital few goals is common sense; it's just not common practice. In one of Aesop's fables, a young boy put his hand into a pot full of hazelnuts. He grasped as many as he could possibly hold, but when he tried to pull out his hand, he found the neck of the pot was too narrow. Unwilling to lose his catch, and yet unable to withdraw his hand, he burst into tears and bitterly lamented his disappointment.

Like the boy, you might find it hard to let go of a lot of good goals until you start serving a greater goal. As Steve Jobs often said, "I'm as proud of what we don't do as I am of what we do." [11] Discipline 1 is about defining that greater goal, and it *is* a discipline. In Section 2 of this book, we'll give you more guidance about the exact process of defining an organizational WIG.

Discipline 2:
Act on the Lead Measures

The second discipline is to apply disproportionate energy to the activities that drive your lead measures. This provides the leverage for achieving the lag measures.

Discipline 2 is the discipline of leverage. Lead measures are the "measures" of the activities most connected to achieving the goal.

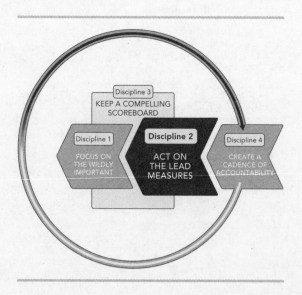

Discipline 1 takes the wildly important goal for an organization and breaks it down into a set of specific, measurable targets until every team has a wildly important goal that it can own. Discipline 2 then defines the leveraged actions that will enable the team to achieve that goal. The illustration below shows the relationship between lag measures and lead measures at the team level.

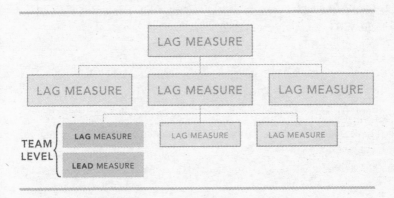

While a lag measure tells you if you've achieved the goal, a lead measure tells you if you are *likely* to achieve the goal. While a lag measure is hard to do anything about, a lead measure is virtually within your control.

For example, while you can't control how often your car breaks down on the road (a lag measure) you can certainly control how often your car receives routine maintenance (a lead measure). And, the more you act on the lead measure, the more likely you are to avoid that roadside breakdown.

Once you have defined your wildly important goal it would seem natural, even intuitive, to then create a detailed plan listing all of the specific tasks and sub tasks required for achieving the goal in the coming months. But with Discipline 2, that's not what you are going to do.

Long-term plans created by most organizations are often too rigid. They lack the ability to adapt to the constantly changing needs and environment of the business. Not surprisingly, they also end up on your shelf collecting dust after only a few months.

With Discipline 2, you do something quite different from that.

Discipline 2 requires you to define the daily or weekly measures, the achievement of which will lead to the goal. Then, each day or week, your team identifies the most important actions that will drive those lead measures. In this way, your team is creating a just-in-time plan that enables them to quickly adapt, while remaining focused on the WIG.

CONVENTIONAL THINKING	4DX PRINCIPLE
Keep your eye on the **lag** measures: the quarterly results, the sales numbers, pounds lost. Stress out. Bite your nails while you wait.	Focus on moving the **lead** measures. These are the high-leverage actions you take to get the lag measures to move.

LAG VERSUS LEAD MEASURES

Let's drill down into the distinction between lag and lead measures. A lag measure is the measurement of a result you are trying to achieve. We call them *lag* measures because by the time you get the data the result has already happened; they are always lagging. The formula *from X to Y by when* in a WIG gives us a lag measure, but WIGs are not the only lag measures in your world. The whirlwind is full of lag measures such as revenue, accounts payable, inventory numbers, hospitalization rates, asset utilization, and so forth.

Lead measures are different; they foretell the result. They have two primary characteristics. First, a lead measure is *predictive,* meaning that if the lead measure changes, you can predict that the lag measure also will change. Second, a lead measure is *influenceable;* it can be directly influenced by the team. That is, the team can make a lead measure happen without a significant dependence on another team.

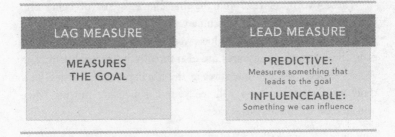

In Discipline 2, you create lead measures, the movement of which will become the driving force for achieving the WIG. In the months ahead, your team will invest consistent energy toward moving these lead measures and, as we have seen with hundreds of teams, this investment will be the key to their success.

We strongly believe that understanding lead measures will be one of the most important insights you take from this book.

Let's explore the two characteristics of a good lead measure further by first assuming you have a WIG to "Increase corn production from 200 tons to 300 tons by September 1." The *X to Y* of corn tonnage is your lag measure. You know that rainfall is an important factor in corn production, so rainfall can be predictive of the corn harvest. But is it a good lead measure? No, because you can't influence the weather to produce the right amount of rain. Rainfall is predictive, but it isn't influenceable. Rainfall fails the test because both characteristics are equally important. Other measures, such as soil quality or fertilization rates, however, easily meet the test.

Now take another illustration with which many people are intimately familiar: a WIG of achieving weight loss. Obviously, the lag measure will be your weight as reflected by the bathroom scale. If you format this WIG correctly, you might define it as "Decrease total body weight from 190 pounds to 175 pounds by May 30" (*from X to Y by when*). This is a good start, but what are the lead measures that will be predictive of achieving the goal and, equally important, that you can influence? You would likely choose both diet and exercise, and, of course, you'd be right.

These two measures fulfill the first characteristic of being predictive: Reducing calories consumed and increasing calories burned strongly indicates that you'll lose weight. Just as important, however, these two lead measures are also directly influenceable by you. Achieve these two lead measures at the level specified, outside your daily whirlwind, and you will see your lag measure moving when you step on the bathroom scale.

LEAD MEASURES CAN BE COUNTERINTUITIVE

There's a problem with lead measures. Where do leaders normally fixate, on lead measures or on lag measures? That's right. As a leader, you've likely spent your entire career focusing on lag measures even though you can't directly affect them. And you're not alone. Think about your last meeting with the other leaders in your organization. What were you discussing, analyzing, planning, and agonizing about? Lag measures and, usually, your inability to move them.

For example, it's easy for schoolteachers to measure the reading levels of students with a standardized test. Often, they obsess over these lag measures. However, it's harder to come up with lead measures that *predict* how students will do on the test. The school might hire tutors or reserve more time for uninterrupted reading. In any case, the school is likely to do better if it tracks data on time spent reading or in tutoring (lead measures) rather than hope and pray that the reading scores (lag measures) will rise of their own accord.

We see this syndrome every day all over the world and in every area of life. The sales leader fixates on total sales, the service leader fixates on customer satisfaction, parents fixate on their children's grades, and dieters fixate on the scale. And, in virtually every case, fixating solely on the lag measures fails to drive results.

There are two reasons almost all leaders do this. First, lag measures are the measures of success; they are the results you have to achieve. Second, data on lag measures is almost always much easier to obtain and more visible than data on lead measures. It's easy to step on a scale and know exactly how much you weigh, but how easy is it to find out how many calories you've eaten today or how many you've burned? That data is often hard to get, and it can take real discipline to *keep* getting it.

Here's a warning: Right about now you might be tempted to oversimplify what we're saying.

If you're thinking something like "So, all you're saying is that if you want to lose weight, you should diet and exercise? What's revolutionary about that?" then you've missed the point of Discipline 2.

There's a huge difference between merely *understanding* the importance of diet and exercise and *measuring* how many calories you've eaten and how many you've burned. Everyone knows you should diet and exercise, but the people who actually measure how many calories they've eaten and how many they've burned each day are the ones actually *losing* weight!

In the end, it's the *data* on lead measures that makes the difference, that enables you to close the gap between what you know your team should do and what they are actually doing. Without lead measures, you are left to try to manage to the lag measures, an approach that seldom produces significant results.

W. Edwards Deming, the management and quality guru, said it best when he told executives that managing a company by looking at financial data (lag measures) is the equivalent of "driving a car by looking in the rearview mirror."[12]

Lead measures also eliminate the element of surprise that a sole focus on lag measures can bring. Imagine this scenario: You and your team have been working hard on a goal to improve customer satisfaction. It's your most important measure and the one on which your bonus is based, and the new customer satisfaction scores have just arrived in your inbox. As one of our clients expressed it, you are about to have one of two reactions: "Oh, cool!" or "Oh, no!" But either way, there is nothing you can do to change the results: They are in the past.

49

That same client also pointed out, "If luck is playing a significant role in your career, then you're fixating on lag measures."

We couldn't agree more.

Now, imagine instead that you are tracking the two most predictive lead measures of customer satisfaction, and for the past three weeks your team has performed well above the standard on those measures. Do you think your experience will change when the new customer satisfaction results arrive? Absolutely. It will be like stepping on the scale knowing that you have met your diet and exercise measures every day. You already know that the lag measure will change.

DEFINING LEAD MEASURES

"Increase annual water production from 175 million liters to 185 million liters by December 31." That was the WIG for the water-bottling plant of a large beverage company when we began working with the senior executive in charge of the supply chain to implement 4DX. The plant had been struggling to meet its targeted water production levels for several years and the leaders were anxious to identify the lead measures that would drive water production to new levels.

We began by asking them to discuss what they thought a good lead measure for increasing annual water production would be.

"Monthly water production," they quickly answered.

Sorry, we said, that won't work.

They seemed confused. "Why not?" asked the plant manager. "If we hit our monthly water production targets, then we'll hit our annual production, right?"

"You're absolutely right that monthly water production is predictive of annual water production," we replied, "but monthly production isn't any more influenceable by your teams than annual production. All you're doing is identifying a different lag measure that you can get more frequently than annual production. It is still a lag."

This dialogue is very common when teams first determine lead measures, and unfortunately, the leaders at the water plant still weren't quite getting it.

To help, we asked them what their lead measure would be for monthly water production.

"Daily water production!" they responded.

We knew that we weren't getting through. The discussion grew more animated until the production manager finally demanded everyone's attention.

"I've got it," he said with real excitement. "I know what our lead measures should be!" He walked to the front of the room and began to explain. "We're constantly running shifts without full crews and we have way too much machine downtime. Those are the two main things that keep us from producing more water."

Now, we were getting somewhere.

Everyone in the room agreed with his diagnosis. They still didn't have usable lead measures—they needed to translate full crews and preventive maintenance into actual measures—but they had captured the idea. Quickly, they identified their first lead measure: Increase percentage of shifts with full crews from 80 percent to 95 percent. The second lead measure was even easier: Increase percentage of compliance to preventive maintenance schedules from 72 percent to 100 percent.

Their strategic bet was that if the plant ensured full crews and a reduction in machine downtime, it would achieve a significant increase in water production. Over the next few months, the teams put a disproportionate amount of effort into those two lead measures, above their day-to-day whirlwind. Not only did their water production increase, it grew at a rate far greater than expected.

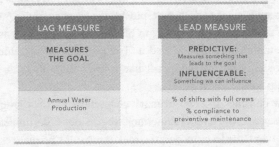

This is a good illustration of the process for defining lead measures, but it also helps to make an important point. Our consultant on the project lauded the plant's results, but then asked an important question: "Why weren't you already doing those two things?"

His point was that their lead measures didn't come from Franklin-Covey. The leaders at the plant already knew the importance of running shifts with full crews and compliance to preventive-maintenance standards, but despite knowing it, they weren't doing it. Why?

As with most teams, their problem was not that they didn't *know*, it was a matter of focus—they didn't *do*. There were dozens of things that needed improvement and focus, not just crew staffing and preventive maintenance; and by trying to improve everything, they remained trapped in their whirlwind. They spent every day spreading their energy across so many urgent priorities and trying to move all the dials at once that in the end, nothing moved. As in the illustration we offered earlier, it was like trying to make holes in a piece of paper by applying even pressure on all your fingers.

Obviously, this problem is not unique to the leaders in this plant. If we followed you around for a few days we would likely observe two predominant activities. One, you would spend most of your time battling your whirlwind, and two, a lot of your remaining time would be spent worrying over your lag measures. The problem with these two activities is that they consume enormous energy and produce little, if any, leverage beyond sustaining your whirlwind. And it's leverage that you need most.

The key principle behind lead measures is simply this: leverage. Think of it this way: achieving your wildly important goal is like trying to move a giant rock; but despite all the energy your team exerts, it doesn't move. It's not a question of effort; if it were, you and your team would already have moved it. The problem is that effort alone isn't enough. Lead measures act like a lever, making it possible to move that rock.

Now consider the two primary characteristics of a lever. First, unlike the rock, the lever is something we *can* move: It's influenceable. Second, when the lever moves, the rock moves: It's predictive.

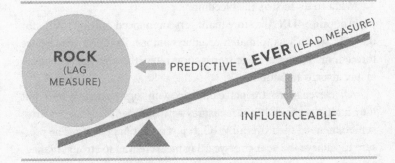

How do you choose the right levers?

To achieve a goal you've never achieved before, you must do things you've never done before. Look around you. Who else has achieved this goal or something like it? What did they do differently? Analyze carefully any barriers you foresee and decide together how to overcome them. Use your imagination. What haven't you thought of that might make all the difference?

Then select the activities you believe will have the greatest impact on achieving the WIG: the 80/20 activities. What 20 percent of what you do has as much or more leverage on the WIG than 80 percent of what you do? In the words of consultant and entrepreneur Richard Koch, in business, "The mass of activity will always be pointless, poorly conceived, badly directed, wastefully executed, and largely beside the point. A small portion of activity will always be terrifically effective. . . . it is probably not what you think it is; it is opaque and buried within a basket of less effective activity." [13]

Finding the right lever among many possibilities is perhaps the toughest and most intriguing challenge for leaders trying to execute a WIG.

A distinguished high-end department store at the prestigious Phipps Plaza Mall near Atlanta was under heavy pressure from new competitors—discounters as well as two major national chain stores that had recently moved into the area. Revenues were down 8 percent from the previous year.

What to do to stop the bleeding?

Adopting 4DX, the store managers announced only one WIG for the year, which was to match revenue numbers from the year before through increasing average transaction rates (the amount purchased in any given transaction).

All eleven departments came up with supporting WIGS but they hadn't yet found lead measures with sufficient leverage to drive achievement of their overall WIG. It just wasn't happening. The pressure to achieve the year-over-year lag measure was so strong, managers were screaming at everyone, "Sell more! Sell more!" All of their energy was poured into raising transaction averages (a lag measure) with no specific idea of what to do differently.

We worked late one night with the manager of the shoe department, which seemed to be doing better than the other departments. We drilled down, looking for the right levers: "Tell us about your people. How do they sell?"

Then he told us about his best salesperson, a woman who sold three times more shoes than the average. We asked, "What does she do differently?"

The manager knew immediately what she did differently. She would get lost in the customer's world, notice what they were wearing, ask about their families, and understand their needs. Then she would bring out six pairs of shoes instead of one pair to show the customer. She would say, "Oh, it's spring, how about this open-toed pair? I noticed your Gucci bag will go really well with those sandals. You like those red shoes? How about these?"

Also, instead of asking customers if they wanted to set up a charge account and getting a refusal, she would simply ring up the sale and say: "And you're getting 10 percent off that purchase by setting up a charge account with us today. All you need to do is sign here."

The lights went on for us. "How many of your people do these things? How many pairs of shoes do your people show in a day?"

"I have no idea. How would our systems monitor that?"

"Well, they can't, but that doesn't mean it can't be measured."

So they set an experimental standard in the shoe department:

Each associate would do three things consistently: (1) Show at least four pairs of shoes to every customer, (2) Write thank-you notes, and (3) Invite every customer to set up a charge account.

"So, how can I tell if they're doing these things?" the manager asked.

"You won't. Your people will track themselves."

Behind the cashier's desk they set up a simple spreadsheet with three columns. Each time a salesperson did these three things with a customer, he or she would check off a column.

"How do I know it's accurate?" the manager asked. "What if they lie?"

We bet he could trust them. Besides, a fraud would surface eventually. Transaction averages were tracked for every employee. When the lead measures started moving the lag measure, they would be able to see the correlation.

The result? The sales team became maniacally focused on the three lead measures, and these levers worked. It was exciting when the lag measure started to move up—it turned out there was a direct correlation between the leads and the achievement of the lag measure. They installed these measures across all the departments in the store and, by year-end, they had not only achieved their WIG of matching the previous year's revenues, they surpassed it by 2 percent. That was a ten-point improvement in three months.

For the store managers, the doorway of understanding opened.

None of the lead measures were news to them. Suggestive selling is just "Retail 101," but they didn't know if their team members were actually doing it. We knew they could measure that behavior. We have learned that the lead measures are usually already there in the business, but no one is tracking them. Management was swimming in data, but not focusing on the data that would really make a *difference.* The key is to isolate and consistently track the right levers.

Finally, instead of hounding the staff to "do better," managers could manage to the data. They could see if Jane was showing one hundred or three hundred pairs of shoes per day. They could track the number of charge accounts each salesperson set up. They became teachers, watching people, demonstrating how to do suggestive selling and sharing best practices. Their energy went up, and their results followed.

They will never manage the same way again. Of course, at times it may take some intense effort to identify the lead measures with the most leverage.

An intriguing example comes from the amazing turnaround of the Oakland Athletics, in the 1990s one of the poorest teams in Major League Baseball. The team played in a dilapidated stadium, attendance was low, and signing great players seemed more and more out of reach.

No way could they bid successfully for players against wealthy teams like the New York Yankees, who could dip into a budget five times that of Oakland.

Caught between financial pressure from the owners and the fans' outcry for better, more expensive baseball players, General Manager Sandy Alderson's WIG was to save the team, and to achieve that he had to fill the stadium. But how?

He knew that people come to watch baseball for many reasons: Some want to see star players, some enjoy the atmosphere of the ballpark, and some just want a night out. But people always come to see a winning team. It's winning that matters most.

So, he began to ask himself what really produces wins in baseball. No one had asked this question seriously before. Most people assumed that great players were essential to a winning team. If you had stars, you'd win. But, Alderson thought, suppose there were more to it?

He and his assistant manager Billy Beane brought together the best thinkers they could find on the subject: What produces wins? The answer, of course, is the highest number of runs, but what exactly contributes to runs? What are the lead measures that create a run?

That's how statisticians and computer scientists got into the picture. Their hard research began to serve up factors that had always been there but that no one had ever noticed before. They discovered that the mighty sluggers who hit home runs were often not all that productive. The most productive players were the ones who could just get on base. If they could get to one base and then another and then another, they could score runs much more reliably than the power hitters everyone valued so much, and who commanded astronomical salaries. As in the old fable, the tortoises turned out to provide much more leverage than the hares.

After Alderson left, Billy Beane became the new manager. He did the unthinkable, going on a binge of recruiting nobodies. The players he hired were some of the most awkward and unvalued prospects, and he paid relatively little for them. Oakland became a laughing-stock. What was Beane thinking?

Then, a sort of magic developed on the field. Unaccountably, Oakland started winning games again. The poorest team in the league—at least financially—won the division title. The next year they did it again. Soon they were locked in battle with the mighty, wealthy, Yankees for the pennant. Although they didn't quite make it, Oakland astonished everyone in baseball by regularly beating teams much more gifted in terms of money and talent. Stirred by victory, the fans returned, and little Oakland with its dingy stadium consistently finished near the top of the standings year after year.

For a decade, the Oakland A's maintained the fifth best record in Major League Baseball while ranking twenty-fourth of the thirty major-league teams in player salaries. Instead of falling to the bottom where they belonged, they rarely stood lower than first or second in their division.

What Billy Beane did was to track the on-base record of players across the league and then recruit from those who were very good at getting on base. These players were usually not flashy, not the big-name athletes, and didn't pull down big money. But they were de-pendable workhorses who could be relied on to get on base. Getting on base was the best predictor of producing runs. And, in baseball, runs are the name of the game.

The Oakland management team reframed the game by acting on the lead measures that produce wins. Through hard research, sifting through endless statistics to get at the key factors that produced runs, they discovered high-leverage lead measures no one had noticed before.[14] This exciting turnaround story was eventually chronicled in a popular film, *Moneyball*.

In section 2, we'll give you more guidance on how to arrive at effective lead measures, drawn from the lessons our clients have learned.

Over the years, we've seen thousands of leaders learn that an important key to execution is putting disproportionate energy against the leverage points by focusing on moving lead measures. If you have a big rock to move, you're going to need a lever that is highly predictive and controllable. The bigger the rock, the more leverage you will need.

TRACKING LEAD MEASURE DATA

Younger Brothers Construction is a residential construction company in Arizona that had a big problem: a rising rate of accidents and injuries. Not only did each incident mean that a member of their crew was hurt, it also meant a delay in the completion of a tightly scheduled construction project, increased insurance rates, and potentially, the loss of their safety rating. Reducing safety incidents had become the company's most important focus, so it wasn't difficult for them to arrive at their wildly important goal: to reduce safety incidents from 7 percent to 1 percent by December 31.

Once the WIG was established, they had to determine the lead measures that were both predictive of fewer accidents and influenceable by the team.

The first idea they considered was to conduct more intensive safety training. It was highly influenceable, as they could simply make everyone go to more training. The leaders ultimately rejected that idea, however, since their people had already undergone significant amounts of training that had allowed them to achieve their current levels of safety. They decided that additional hours of training wouldn't be sufficiently predictive of achieving their new goal.

The leaders at Younger Brothers then looked more carefully at the primary causes of accidents plaguing the company and developed a different idea for their lead measure: Compliance to safety standards. They decided to measure compliance via six safety standards: wearing hard hats, gloves, boots, and eyewear, as well as using scaffolds and roof braces to keep workers from sliding off the roof. They were certain that enforcing these six standards at high levels of compliance would be both predictive and influenceable in reducing accidents.

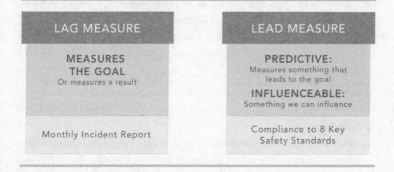

LAG MEASURE	LEAD MEASURE
MEASURES THE GOAL Or measures a result	**PREDICTIVE:** Measures something that leads to the goal **INFLUENCEABLE:** Something we can influence
Monthly Incident Report	Compliance to 8 Key Safety Standards

Within one year of focusing on the lead measure of compliance to safety standards Younger Brothers Construction achieved the best safety record in the thirty-year history of the company. But it wasn't easy.

One of the most challenging aspects of their lead measure was simply getting the data. The lag measure data of accidents and injuries came automatically from the company's system each week. The lead measure, compliance to safety standards, had to be physically observed.

This meant that construction supervisors had to move among the various crews to check whether the people were wearing their hard hats, gloves, and safety glasses and that scaffolds and roof braces were firmly in place. Moreover, they had to do this despite a never-ending stream of distractions: subcontractor issues, late shipments, customer concerns, and weather delays. In the middle of that whirlwind, checking for safety compliance might not seem "wildly important" to a construction foreman. However, because reducing safety incidents was the wildly important goal, and because safety compliance was the primary leverage point for achieving it, they made it happen week after week.

The lesson in this story is that lead measure data is almost always more difficult to acquire than lag measure data, but you must pay the price to track your lead measures. We often see teams struggle with this, zeroing in on a high-leverage lead measure only to say, "Wow, getting that data is going to take real work! We're too busy to do that." If you're serious about your WIG, then you must create a way to track your lead measures. Without data, you can't drive performance on the lead measures; without lead measures, you don't have leverage.

And when the WIG is truly wildly important, you've got to have that leverage.

The WIG for every airline flight is a safe landing. Flying today is actually remarkably safe, but that wasn't always true. In the 1930s many serious airplane crashes were caused by pilot error. In 1935, Major Pete Hill, a very experienced test pilot with the US Army, crashed one of the biggest airplanes ever built because he forgot to make sure the tail elevators were unlocked before taking off.

As a result, pilots got together and adopted a clear set of lead measures called a preflight checklist.[15] After that, there were far fewer crashes due to pilot error. Today, the preflight checklist is the greatest predictor of arriving safely.

The preflight checklist is a perfect example of what we mean by a high-leverage activity. Going through the checklist takes a few minutes but can have enormous impact. One hundred percent compliance with the checklist is also an excellent example of a lead measure: It is predictive of a safe landing and influenceable by the pilots.

Once you and your team begin to develop lead measures in Discipline 2, you'll gain an even greater appreciation for the work you did in narrowing your focus in Discipline 1. Driving the lead measures for a single WIG is a challenging enough objective in the midst of your whirlwind. Leaders who insist on more than two WIGs in Discipline 1 (despite our advice) always change their minds once they begin to understand lead measures in Discipline 2.

LEAD MEASURES AND ENGAGEMENT

Once a team is clear about its lead measures, their view of the goal changes.

Let's take a look at what happened when Beth Wood, a grocery store manager, set out to achieve a very challenging goal of increasing year-over-year sales.

Beth called in Bob, her bakery manager, to get his support in improving their sagging year-over-year sales numbers.

Bob is a good-natured manager and, on a typical day, he would likely have said, "Sure, Beth, I'd be glad to help," even if he didn't have a clue what he could do to drive more sales. On this day, however, Bob had reached his limit and wasn't in the mood to just go along.

"You want improved sales?" he said sarcastically "Knock yourself out, Beth."

Startled by Bob's response, Beth came back quickly "Look, Bob, I can't do this alone. You're closer to the customers than I am and you're closer to your employees than I am."

Now, Bob was really frustrated. "What exactly would you like me to do? It's not like I can hit people over the head and drag them into the store. I run the bakery. If you want a bagel, I'm your guy."

If you didn't know Beth and Bob well, you might think that Bob has a chronically bad attitude, or doesn't respect Beth, or worse, is just lazy.

But none of these things are true.

Bob actually likes Beth and would also like to help the store improve sales. But two things are holding him back: one, he doesn't know how, and two, he doesn't think he can. At this moment, what's really going through Bob's mind is "We're a thirty-year old store that just had a Walmart Supercenter move in down the street. We're also on the wrong side of the intersection and all the traffic has to make a left to get in here, if they can even see our sign. And Beth wants me to improve store sales?"

Bob continues, "If I knew how to improve sales don't you think I'd already be doing it? I'm not holding out on you!"

When you see Bob's perspective, you can better understand his response to this frustrating situation. Bob is representative of so many people. They can see the rock all too well. The problem is that they just don't see the lever.

Now, let's replay this same scenario, but this time with Beth using a lead measure to drive her goal. She calls her managers together and poses this question: "Above sustaining our day-to-day operation, what is the one thing your teams could do to improve year-over-year sales the most?" In effect, she is asking them what influenceable outcome or behavior is the most predictive of moving the lag measure of sales, but she's limiting it to a very narrow focus.

They begin to discuss a lot of possibilities, such as raising customer service, improving store conditions, or giving away more free samples. After a lot of back and forth, they finally come to the agreement that the single biggest thing they can do to improve sales in *their* store is to reduce the number of out-of-stock items.

This lead measure of reducing out-of-stocks is highly predictive of better store sales—this is well known in the retail world. Equally important, out-of-stocks is a highly influenceable lead measure. Now, Bob sees what he can do in the bakery to drive sales. Reducing out-of-stocks is something he and his team can really influence. They can perform extra shelf reviews to check for items that are sold out, they can organize their back room so that fast moving products are easier to restock, or they can change the frequency and volume of reordering. In other words, it's a game he and his team can win, and now *he's engaged*.

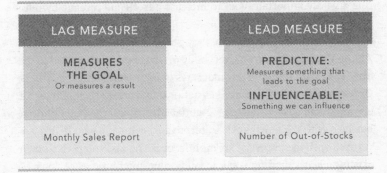

When a team defines its lead measures they are making a strategic bet. In a sense, they are saying, "We're betting that by driving these lead measures we are going to achieve our wildly important goal." They believe that the lever is going to move the rock, and because of that belief, they engage.

Disciplines 3 and 4 are designed to help the team put energy into moving the lead measures. However, the real impact and beauty of good lead measures in Discipline 2 is that they truly connect your team to the achievement of the WIG. And, ultimately, it's the front line of an organization that creates the bottom-line result you're after.

Coming up with the right lead measures is really about helping everyone see themselves as strategic business partners and engaging them in dialogue about what can be done better or differently in order to achieve the WIGs.

A good example is the advertising department of the *Savannah Morning News,* a venerable newspaper in the American South. When we met with them, their WIG was to close a serious revenue gap. They had fallen into the trap of trying to focus on everything at once, including pushing new products, daily inserts specials, and other add-ons, in an attempt to incrementally move the revenue number. Their focus was spread across so many initiatives that they had taken their eye off of their main product. So, they began with Discipline 1, setting a wildly important goal to increase advertising revenue by refocusing on their core product.

Everything changed when they started practicing Discipline 2: Act on the lead measures. Everybody on the team was involved in the dialogue. After thinking through ways to increase advertising dollars, they agreed together on three key actions: to increase their number of contacts with new customers, potential advertisers who had not done business with the newspaper; to reactivate customers who hadn't advertised with the paper for six months or more; and to upsell to their existing clients, finding ways to add value to the message—maybe adding color to an ad, giving it better placement, or increasing the size of an ad.

In practice, the plan broke down into simple lead measures: in the weekly WIG sessions people committed to hit a certain number of new-customer contacts, reactivation calls, and upsell offers. The next week they reported the results. Individual salespeople were not only managing their own business more effectively, but also regularly communicating to each other best practices, refinements to approaches, and ways of overcoming barriers.

The advertising director said, "I've been in this business for twenty years, and I've spent my entire career basically praying over lag measures and putting out fires." For the first time, she felt able to help her people achieve their goals in tangible ways. The newspaper closed their revenue gap and shot past their goals for the year. Acting consistently on the right lead measures made it all possible. Based on her success, Morris Communications, the parent company of the *Savannah Morning News,* went on to implement 4DX with their forty other newspapers.

We'll talk more about selecting the right lead measures in section 2.

Discipline 3:
Keep a Compelling Scoreboard

The third discipline is to make sure everyone knows the score at all times, so that they can tell whether or not they are winning.

This is the discipline of engagement.

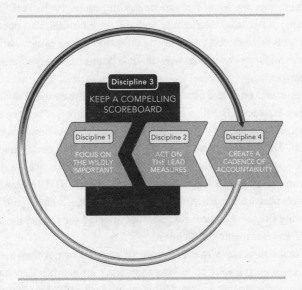

Remember, people play differently when they are keeping score.

The difference in performance between a team that simply understands their lead and lag measures *as a concept,* and a team that actually knows their score, is remarkable. If the lead and lag measures are not captured on a visual scoreboard and updated regularly, they will disappear into the distraction of the whirlwind. Simply put, people disengage when they don't know the score. When they can see at a glance whether or not they are winning they become profoundly engaged.

In Discipline 3, the strategic bet for your team, their lead and lag measures, are translated into a visible, compelling scoreboard.

Several years ago, we were working with a group of leaders at Northrop Grumman to apply 4DX to the design and building of Coast Guard cutters. Our project began only a few months after Hurricane Katrina had significantly damaged their facility, and as we were introducing Discipline 3, they offered an example that perfectly illustrated the importance of having a compelling scoreboard.

On the previous Friday night, the local high-school team had played an important football game. As expected, the stands were full and there was the usual excitement leading up to the kickoff. But as the game progressed, something was missing. No one was cheering. In fact, no one seemed to be paying attention to the game at all. The only sound from the stands was the dull hum of conversation. What was happening?

The scoreboard had blown down during the hurricane and had not yet been repaired. The fans couldn't see any numbers. "No one could tell you what the score was, what down it was, or even how much time was left. There was a game going on, but it was like no one even knew."

This story really caught our attention. Have you ever wanted to shout in frustration to your team "Don't you get it? There's a game going on here and it really matters!" If you have, it's likely your team is missing the same critical element that affected the fans at the game: a clear and compelling scoreboard.

Great teams know at every moment whether or not they are winning. They *must* know, otherwise, they don't know what they have to do to win the game. A compelling scoreboard tells the team where they are and where they should be, information essential to team problem solving and decision making.

That's why a great team can't function without a scoreboard that *compels* action. Without it, energy dissipates, intensity lags, and the team goes back to business as usual.

We need to be very clear here. Visually displaying data is not new to you or your team. In fact, you may be thinking that you already have a scoreboard, or even lots of scoreboards, all captured in complex spreadsheets inside your computer. And the data just keeps coming in. Most of this data is in the form of lag measures accompanied by historical trends, forward projections, and detailed financial analysis. The data is important and it serves a purpose for you as the leader; your spreadsheets are what we would call a coach's scoreboard.

But what we're after in Discipline 3 is something quite different. In implementing Discipline 3, you and your team need to build a players' scoreboard, one that's designed solely to engage the players on your team to win.

CONVENTIONAL THINKING	4DX PRINCIPLE
Scoreboards are for leaders. They are coach's scoreboards that consist of complex spreadsheets with thousands of numbers. The big picture is in there somewhere, but few (if anyone) can easily see it.	*The scoreboard is for the whole team.* To drive execution you need a players' scoreboard that has a few simple graphs on it indicating: Here's where we need to be and here's where we are right now. In five seconds or less, anyone can determine whether we are winning or losing?

To understand the impact of this kind of scoreboard, imagine that you are at a park where a group of teenagers is playing basketball. You're not close enough to hear them, but you can see them. Can you tell, just by watching, if they are keeping score? You can, and the indicators are obvious.

First, you'll see a level of intensity in their play that you wouldn't see if they weren't keeping score. You'll also see teamwork, better shot selection, aggressive defense, and celebration each time they make a basket. These are the behaviors of a fully engaged team, and they only play at this level when the game matters—in other words, when it matters enough that they are keeping score.

If your scoreboard includes complicated data that only you, the leader, understand, it represents a leader's game. But for maximum engagement and performance you need a players' scoreboard that makes it the team's game. Jim Stuart (one of the originators of 4DX) said it best: "The fundamental purpose of a players' scoreboard is to motivate the players to win."

We began this chapter with a critically important statement: people play differently when they are keeping score. Now, we need to shift the emphasis to be even clearer: People play differently when *they* are keeping score. This creates a very different feeling than when you keep score for them. When team members themselves are keeping score, they truly understand the connection between their performance and reaching their goal, and this changes the level at which they play.

When everyone on the team can see the score, the level of play rises, not only because they can see what's working and what adjustments are needed, but also because they now want to *win*.

You see here the contrast between a coach's scoreboard and a player's scoreboard.

TOTAL REVENUE							GROSS MARGIN							EBITDA						
2/12	Bud	Var	2/8	Var	2007	Var	2/12	Bud	Var	2/8	Var	2007	Var	2/12	Bud	Var	2/8	Var	2007	Var
0	0	0	0	0	0	0	0	0	0	143	(143)	0	0	0	0	0	143	(143)	0	0
(1)	53	(54)	182	(183)	1	(2)	(0)	35	(35)	0	(0)	1	(2)	(96)	(49)	(37)	(84)	(2)	(114)	28
0	0	0	0	0	0	0	0	0	0	0	0	0	0	(61)	(65)	4	(73)	12	(11)	(51)
1,008	1,080	(71)	1,150	(142)	1,146	(137)	699	754	(55)	812	(113)	892	(193)	384	384	1	439	(54)	530	(146)
		-6.6%		-12.3%		-12.0%	69.3%	69.9%	-7.3%	70.6%	-13.9%	77.9%	-21.6%	38.1%	35.5%	0.2%	38.1%	-12.4%	46.3%	-27.5%
699	843	(144)	700	(1)	963	(264)	486	594	(108)	498	(12)	730	(245)	242	297	(56)	218	24	392	(151)
		-17.1%		-0.2%		-27.4%	69.5%	70.4%	-18.2%	71.1%	-2.4%	75.8%	-33.5%	34.6%	35.3%	-18.8%	31.1%	10.8%	40.7%	-38.5%
592	682	(90)	524	68	613	(21)	422	483	(60)	361	62	459	(36)	260	276	(16)	187	73	270	(10)
		-13.1%		13.0%		-3.4%	71.3%	70.8%	-12.5%	68.9%	17.1%	74.8%	-7.9%	43.9%	40.5%	-5.7%	35.8%	38.9%	44.0%	-3.5%
879	937	(58)	840	39	828	51	607	695	(88)	582	25	539	68	354	370	(16)	292	62	235	119

A coach's scoreboard is complex and data rich, but it requires careful study to figure out if the team is winning.

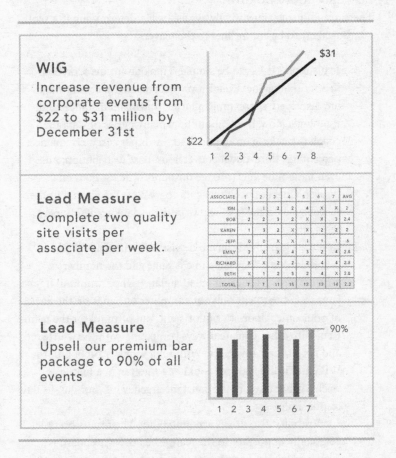

WIG
Increase revenue from corporate events from $22 to $31 million by December 31st

Lead Measure
Complete two quality site visits per associate per week.

Lead Measure
Upsell our premium bar package to 90% of all events

In this players' scoreboard, the goal (represented by the black line) is to increase revenue. The gray line is actual performance. At any moment, team members can see if they are winning.

The players' scoreboard is essential to motivating the players to win.

CHARACTERISTICS OF A COMPELLING PLAYERS' SCOREBOARD

There are four questions we always ask when determining if a scoreboard is likely to be compelling to the players:

1. Is it simple? It has to be simple. Think about the scoreboard in a football game. Usually, only six distinct pieces of data are displayed: score, time, quarter, down and distance, and time-outs. Now, think about how many pieces of data the coach is tracking on the sideline: yards per carry, completion percentage, third-down conversions, pass distribution, and even hang time and yardage for punts. The list goes on forever. Coaches need this data to manage the game, but the scoreboard on the field shows only the data needed to play the game.

2. Can I see it easily? It has to be visible to the team. The scoreboard at a football game is huge and the numbers gigantic so everyone can tell at a glance who's winning. If your scoreboard sits on your computer or hangs on the back of your office door, it's out of sight, out of mind for the team. Remember that you are always competing with the whirlwind and it's a tough adversary. Without a visible scoreboard, the WIG and lead measures could be forgotten in a matter of weeks, if not days, in the constant urgency of your day-to-day responsibilities.

   Visibility also drives accountability. The results become personally important to the team when the scoreboard is displayed where it can be seen by everyone. We've observed this again and again. We've seen a union shift at a giant juice-bottling plant in Michigan choose to skip their lunch break in order to increase the number of full truckloads they delivered so they could move the scoreboard. Why? So they can move past other shifts on the scoreboard. In another instance, we observed the night shift come to work at midnight and saw that the first thing they looked at was the scoreboard to see how their team was doing compared to the day shift. If your team is geographically dispersed, the scoreboard should be visible on your desktop computer or mobile phone (more on electronic scoreboards on page 194).

3. Does it show lead *and* lag measures? It should show both the lead and lag measures. This really helps a scoreboard come to life. The lead measure is what the team can affect. The lag measure is the result they want. The team needs to see both or they will quickly lose interest. When they can see both the lead and lag, they can watch the bet play out. They can see what they are doing (the lead), and what they are getting (the lag). Once the team sees that the lag measure is moving because of the efforts they have made on the leads, it has a dramatic effect on engagement because they know they are having a direct impact on the results.

4. Can I tell at a glance if I'm winning? It has to tell you immediately if you are winning or losing. If the team can't quickly determine if they are winning or losing by looking at the scoreboard then it's not a game, it's just data. Check your next report, graph, scorecard, or scoreboard before you dismiss this as obvious. Glance at the spreadsheets that show the weekly financial data. Can you *instantly* tell if you are winning or losing? Could other people tell? We call it the *five-second rule*. If you can't tell within five seconds whether you're winning or losing you haven't passed this test.

This simple illustration comes from one of our clients, an events management company responsible for booking trade shows for outdoor retailers. The WIG was to book a certain number of exhibitors by a certain date.

In the scoreboard on the left you can see the status of the team's progress to date, but you have no idea if they are winning or losing. Winning or losing requires you to know two things: where you are now and where you *should* be now.

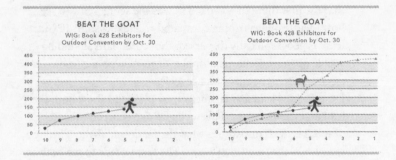

The difference in the scoreboard on the right is the addition of where the team should be, illustrated by the goat. Because so many of their customers were mountain climbers, they used a mountain goat to represent the performance needed each week to achieve their goal. Now you can easily see that they are losing, and several other important aspects of the team's performance are also immediately apparent: You know how long they have been losing (two weeks). You know that achieving the goal is getting harder, not easier. You know that the performance of the team is starting to level off, instead of climbing. And you know that the team is closer to the end of the race than the beginning.

As basic as this may seem, when we ask leaders in our programs to report this sort of data on the spot they will often say, "I think I can get most of that, but I'll need a few minutes to pull it together." Keep in mind that these are capable leaders. Their problem is not the absence of data; their problem is too much of it and little sense of what data is most important.

Imagine if not only you, but every member of your team understood the team's performance this clearly. Would it change the way they engaged in the game? After implementing 4DX in thousands of teams, we can assure you that it will.

Like Disciplines 1 and 2, Discipline 3 is not intuitive for most leaders. You don't naturally create a player's scoreboard. Your instinct will be to create a coach's scoreboard: a complex scoreboard with lots of data, analysis, and projections designed for the coaches, not the players. And you're not alone. We seldom find even a single scoreboard in most organizations that meets the four criteria listed here.

Android - Barcode Scanner
iPhone - Red Laser

LINK: http://www.4dxbook.com/qr/Scoreboards

Scan the image above to see full-color examples of "Players' Scoreboards."

In the end, it isn't actually the scoreboard that's compelling. Although teams enjoy creating their own scoreboards, what ultimately drives engagement is the game the scoreboard represents. You'll never hear a sports fan saying, "Did you see that game last night? What an amazing scoreboard!" The scoreboard was absolutely necessary, but it was the game that interested them.

One of the most demoralizing aspects of life in the whirlwind is that you don't feel you can win. If your team is operating exclusively in the whirlwind, they're giving everything they have just to sustain their day to day operation and survive. They're not playing *to win*; they're playing *not to lose*. And the result is a big difference in performance.

But with 4DX, not only do you create a game for your team, you create a *winnable* game. And the secret to that game being winnable is the relationship between the lead and lag measures that plays out on the scoreboard every day.

In essence, you and your team make a bet that you can move the lead measures and that those lead measures will move the lag measure. When it starts to work, even people who have shown little interest become very engaged as the entire team starts to see that they are winning, often for the first time. Keep in mind that their engagement is not because the *organization* is winning, or even that *you* as their leader are winning: it's because *they* are winning.

Some years ago, we were invited to help a low-performing plant run by a global manufacturing company to come up to the quality standards of the rest of the company. The plant was old, struggling with outdated technology, and in a remote location. For us, it required all-day flights and a long drive to the end of a forest road in Canada to reach the plant.

In 25 years, this plant had never hit its targeted production number. Additionally, they had massive quality issues in their work product, particularly with the night shifts that employed the least experienced workers. The quality score was in the low seventies, while the rest of the company was in the high eighties.

It wasn't until the scoreboards went up that things changed radically. They had been playing in the dark, and the new scoreboards "turned on the lights." Data is like light—the best growth agent known. When winners are given data that shows that they are losing, they figure out a way to win. With the lights on, they can see what they need to do to improve.

A shift would come in at midnight, compare their scoreboard with those of the shifts who had been working all day, and get energized to go beyond whatever the previous shift had done. This was a hockey-playing culture: For entertainment in this remote locale, there were two hockey rinks and not much else. The workers knew they'd be playing hockey and drinking with the guys from the other shift on the weekends, and they wanted to be the shift with bragging rights about higher scores.

As 4DX leveraged the natural urge to compete, the quality score soared from 74 to 94, from worst in the fleet to best and far above the industry standard. And within a year, this plant that had never hit its production number exceeded it by 4,000 metric tons, adding at least $5 million to the bottom line.

The players' scoreboard is a powerful device for changing human behavior anywhere, even deep in the woods.

In section 2, we'll give you guidance on exactly how to create and maintain a compelling scoreboard.

THE 4 DISCIPLINES AND TEAM ENGAGEMENT

We'd like to be able to say that we understood the connection between the implementation of 4DX and team engagement all along, but we didn't. We learned it through experience. As we began to implement 4DX with teams around the world, we saw significant increases in morale and engagement, even though their WIGs weren't about morale and engagement. That outcome might not come as a surprise to you, based on how we've described 4DX so far, but at the time, it did to us.

FranklinCovey had built a worldwide reputation for helping to increase the personal effectiveness of individuals and teams, and with it, their morale and engagement. 4DX was designed to occupy the other end of the FranklinCovey offering continuum, with an exclusive focus on business results. However, in our early implementations, the increase in engagement that we observed as teams began to feel they were winning was not a subtle thing. It was palpable. In fact, we would have to have been blind to miss it.

Our implementations usually involved several days of intensive work with leaders and teams, and these teams included their share of naysayers and resisters. To our surprise, we would return two months later and find that these initial resisters, along with everyone else on the team, were excited to show us what they were accomplishing.

Many believe that engagement drives results, and so do we. However, we know now, and have witnessed consistently over the years, that results drive engagement. This is particularly true when the team can see the direct impact their actions have on the results. In our experience, nothing affects morale and engagement more powerfully than when a person feels he or she is winning. In many cases, winning is a more powerful driver of engagement than money, benefits packages, working conditions, whether you have a best friend at work, or even whether you like your boss, all of which are typical measures of engagement. People will work for money and they will quit over money, but many teams are filled with people who are both well paid and miserable in their jobs.

In 1968, author Frederick Herzberg published an article in the *Harvard Business Review* aptly titled: "One More Time: How Do You Motivate Employees?" In it, he emphasizes the powerful connection between results and engagement: "People are most satisfied with their jobs (and therefore most motivated) when those jobs give them the opportunity to experience achievement."

Forty-three years later in another *Harvard Business Review* article, "The Power of Small Wins," authors Teresa Amabile and Steven Kramer emphasize the importance of achievement to team members: "The power of progress is fundamental to human nature, but few managers understand it or know how to leverage progress to boost motivation." [16]

We have learned that scoreboards can be a powerful way to engage employees. A motivating players' scoreboard not only drives results but uses the visible power of progress to instill the mindset of *winning*.

If you still have doubts about the impact of winning on team engagement, think of a time in your own career when you were the most excited and engaged in what you were doing, a time when you couldn't wait to get out of bed in the morning, when you were consumed with what you were doing professionally. Now ask yourself this question, "At that time, did I feel like I was winning?" If you are like the vast majority of people, your answer will be "yes."

4DX enables you to set up a winnable game. Discipline 1 narrows your focus to a wildly important goal and establishes a clear finish line. Discipline 2 creates lead measures that give your team leverage to achieve the goal. This is what makes it a game: The team is making a bet on their lead measures. But, without Discipline 3, without a compelling players' scoreboard, not only would the game be lost in the whirlwind, no one would care.

A winning team doesn't need artificial morale boosting. All the psyching up and rah-rah exercises companies do to raise morale aren't nearly as effective in engaging people as the satisfaction that comes from executing with excellence a goal that really matters.

Disciplines 1, 2, and 3 are powerful drivers of execution, and yet, they are really only the beginning of the story. The first three disciplines set up the game, but your team may still not be *in* the game, as you are about to learn.

Discipline 4:
Create a Cadence of Accountability

The fourth discipline is to create a cadence of accountability, a frequently recurring cycle of accounting for past performance and planning to move the score forward.

Discipline 4 is where execution actually happens. As we've said, Disciplines 1, 2, and 3 set up the game; but until you apply Discipline 4, your team isn't *in* the game.

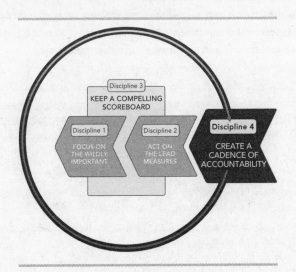

This is the discipline that brings the team members all together, and that is why it encompasses the other disciplines.

Many leaders define *execution* simply as the ability to set a goal and achieve it. After years of teaching these principles, we can tell you that this definition is insufficient. But, as discussed above, what's difficult—and rare—is the ability to achieve a critical goal while living *in the midst of a raging whirlwind.* And it is even more difficult when achieving the goal requires changing the behaviors of a lot of people.

Great teams operate with a high level of accountability. Without it, team members go off in all directions with each doing what he/she thinks is most important. Under this approach, the whirlwind soon takes over.

Disciplines 1, 2, and 3 bring focus, clarity, and engagement, which are powerful and necessary elements for your success. But with Discipline 4, you and your team ensure that the goal is achieved, no matter what is happening around you.

In most organizations, accountability means the annual performance review, hardly an engaging experience whether you are giving or receiving the review. It can also mean being called on the carpet for something you failed to accomplish.

On the other hand, in a 4DX organization, *accountability* means making personal commitments to the entire team to move the scores forward and then following through in a disciplined way.

CONVENTIONAL THINKING	4DX PRINCIPLE
Accountability on our team is always top down. We meet with the boss periodically and he lets us know how we're doing and what we should focus on next.	Accountability on our team is shared. We make commitments and then we're accountable to our boss, but more important, to each other, for following through.

THE WIG SESSION

In Discipline 4, your team meets at least weekly in a WIG session. This meeting, which lasts no longer than twenty to thirty minutes, has a set agenda and goes quickly, establishing your weekly rhythm of accountability for driving progress toward the WIG.

This discipline literally makes the difference between successful and failed execution.

In May 1996, noted author Jon Krakauer tried climbing Mt. Everest with a group of paying climbers. As they encountered obstacles such as blizzards, 62 mph winds, and high-altitude sickness, the group began to fall apart. Some of the more headstrong climbers decided to try for the summit themselves and struck out on their own. Team discipline was abandoned. They all had the same goal, but the loss of discipline and sense of accountability for each other in an extremely unforgiving environment turned out to be lethal. The result: eight people died.[17]

Five years later, another group set out to climb Mt. Everest; their goal was to help a blind climber, Erik Weihenmayer, reach the summit. The team carefully planned the route, just as Krakauer's group had done. A big difference, however, was that at the end of each day Weihenmayer's group huddled together in what they called the "tent meeting" to talk over what they had accomplished and what they had learned, which would help them to plan and make adjustments for the next day. Faster climbers on the team "cleared the path," fixed ropes, and then worked their way back to meet Erik along the trail. Erik said, "Our team stuck together and took care of each other, which gave me just enough courage to finish."

At one critical point, it took thirteen hours for their blind leader to cross the aluminum extension ladders that spanned the bottomless crevasses of the extremely dangerous Khumbu Icefall. The team knew that on summit day they would have to get across in two hours. In nightly tent meetings (a form of WIG Session), they shared lessons learned and committed to the next day's strategy. It took days and days of practice and night after night of tent meetings.

The result? On summit day, they actually passed sighted teams as they worked to get the entire team to the other side of the icefall in record time.

This cadence of accountability was the key to successful execution of the goal. On May 25, 2001, Erik Weihenmayer became the first blind person to stand on the summit of Mt. Everest. His team's other remarkable first: The greatest number of people from one team to reach the top of Everest in a single day, eighteen in all. In the end, Erik and almost everyone on his team reached the highest peak on the planet and returned safely.[18]

The focus of the WIG session is simple: to hold each other accountable for taking the actions that will move the lead measures, resulting in the achievement of the WIG despite the whirlwind. Easy to say, but hard to do. To ensure that this focus is achieved every week, two rules of WIG sessions must absolutely be followed.

First, the WIG session should be held on the same day and at the same time every week (sometimes even more often—daily, for instance—but *never* less often than weekly). This consistency is critical. Without it, your team will never be able to establish a sustained rhythm of performance. Missing even a single week causes you to lose valuable momentum, and this loss of momentum impacts your results. This means that the WIG session is sacred—it takes place every week, even if the leader can't attend and has to delegate the role of leading it.

It is truly amazing what you can accomplish by the simple discipline of meeting around a goal on a weekly basis over an extended period of time. There is nothing quite like it. Frankly, we're dumbfounded that this discipline isn't practiced more frequently. We have asked hundreds of thousands of employees in various industries around the globe to respond to the statement: "I meet at least monthly with my manager to discuss my progress on goals." To our surprise, only 34 percent can respond positively to this statement, even when the review is only once each month, let alone weekly—the best practice of high-performing teams. It's no wonder that high accountability is absent in so many organizations.

What is so special about holding a WIG session each week, you may ask? We have found that for most organizational units, the week embodies a perfect slice of "life." It is a short enough period of time to keep people focused and remain highly relevant, but long enough to allow for commitments made in these meetings to actually get done. In many operating environments, weeks represent a natural rhythm of organizational life. We think in weeks. We talk in weeks. They have beginnings and ends. They are a staple of the human condition and make for a perfect cadence of accountability.

Second, the whirlwind is never allowed into a WIG session. No matter how urgent an issue may seem, discussion in the WIG session is limited solely to actions and results that move the scoreboard. If you need to discuss other things, hold a staff meeting *after* the WIG session, but keep the WIG session separate. This high level of focus makes the WIG session not only fast, but extremely effective at producing the results you want. It also reaffirms the importance of the WIG to every team member. It sends a clear message that, as it relates to achieving the WIG, no success in the whirlwind can compensate for a failure to keep the commitments made in last week's WIG session. Many of our client organizations do exactly this: They hold a WIG session for twenty to thirty minutes and then hold a staff meeting right after, during which they can discuss whirlwind issues.

Keeping your WIG sessions to twenty to thirty minutes is a standard to strive for. When you first start holding WIG sessions they may take more time. But, ultimately, as you increasingly focus your time and attention on moving the scoreboard and nothing more, your sessions will become increasingly effective and efficient. We also recognize that depending upon the particular function or nature of your team, they may take a bit more time. But even then, any team in any function can learn to conduct fast, efficient sessions centered on the wildly important goal in place of protracted meetings covering everything under the sun. Often, to keep your WIG sessions fast and focused, you may need to schedule other meetings to resolve issues that grow out of the WIG session. For example, you might say, "Bill, you bring up an important problem that has to be resolved this week. Why don't we set up another meeting this Thursday to do a deep dive on this problem to see if we can solve it," and then continue with your WIG session.

WIG sessions might vary in content, but the agenda is always the same. Here's the three-part agenda for a WIG session along with the kind of language you should be hearing in the session:

1. **Account: Report on commitments.**
   - *"I committed to make a personal call to three customers who gave us lower scores. I did, and here's what I learned . . ."*
   - *"I committed to book at least three prospects for a site visit and ended up getting four!"*
   - *"I met with our VP, but wasn't able to get the approval we wanted. Here's why . . ."*

2. **Review the scoreboard: Learn from successes and failures.**
   - *"Our lag measure is green, but we've got a challenge with one of our lead measures that just fell to yellow. Here's what happened . . ."*
   - *"We're trending upward on our lead measures, but our lag measure isn't moving yet. We've agreed as a team to double our efforts this week to get the score moving."*
   - *"Although we're tracking toward achieving our WIG, we implemented a great suggestion from a customer this week that improved our lead measure score even further!"*

3. **Plan: Clear the path and make new commitments.**
   - *"I can clear your path on that problem. I know someone who . . ."*
   - *"I'll make sure the inventory issue impacting our lead measure is resolved by next week, no matter what I have to do."*
   - *"I'll meet with Bob on our numbers and come back next week with at least three ideas for helping us improve."*

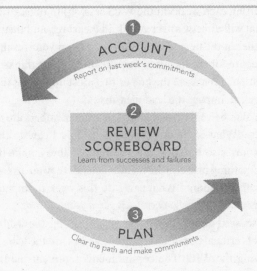

A WIG Session is a short, intense team meeting devoted to these three—and only these three—activities. The purpose of the WIG Session is to account for prior commitments and make commitments to move the WIG scoreboard.

Android - Barcode Scanner
iPhone - Red Laser

LINK: http://www.4dxbook.com/qr/WIGSession

Scan the image above to see a short video about WIG Sessions from different organizations.

STAYING FOCUSED IN SPITE OF THE WHIRLWIND

In a WIG session, you and every member of your team are accountable for moving the metrics on the scoreboard. You accomplish this by committing each week (in the WIG session) to one or two specific actions that will directly affect your lead measures, and then reporting to each other in the next week's WIG session on your results.

To prepare for the meeting, every team member thinks about the same question: "What are the one or two most important things I can do this week to impact the lead measures?"

We need to be very careful here. The team members are not asking themselves, "What is the most important thing I can do this week?" That question is so broad that it will almost always take their focus back to something in their whirlwind. Instead, they are asking a much more specific question: "What can I do this week to impact the lead measures?"

As discussed above, this focus on impacting the lead measures each week is critical because the lead measures are the team's leverage for achieving the WIG. The commitments represent the things that must happen, beyond the day to day, to move the lead measures. This is why so much emphasis is placed in Discipline 2 on ensuring that the lead measures are influenceable: so that the team can actually move them through their performance each week. Simply put, the keeping of weekly commitments drives the lead measures, and the lead measures drive achievement of the WIG.

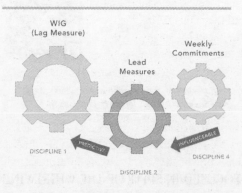

By keeping their weekly commitments, team members influence the lead measure, which in turn is predictive of success on the lag measure of the WIG.

Let's take the example of Susan, a nurse manager whose lead measure is to reduce the time it takes to administer pain medication to patients. Susan can see from her scoreboard that two of her teams, seventh floor day shift and eighth floor intensive care, are lagging behind the others. She knows that the seventh floor team has a new supervisor who is still learning the pain-management procedures. She also knows that the eighth floor team is understaffed. So Susan's commitments to move the lead measures for this week might be to review the pain-management procedures with the seventh floor team and to fill the open position on the eighth floor team.

Now, let's take the example of Tom, a member of a sales team whose lead measure is to get out two new proposals each week. Tom knows that his list of prospects is running low, so for this week his commitment might be to acquire names and contact information for ten additional prospects, ensuring he has enough to successfully move two of them to the proposal stage.

In these two examples, both leaders and team members make weekly commitments (more on this on page 179). The nature of the commitments might change every week because the business, along with the performance of the team, is always changing; only the process is constant.

Realize that these weekly commitments are often not urgent or necessarily even new. They often are things the team should be doing naturally, but the reality is that these are the actions the whirlwind devours first. Without the steady rhythm of accountability of Discipline 4, there will always be things the team members know they should do, but never actually do with real consistency.

CREATING A CADENCE

MICARE, which produces the coal that fuels many of Mexico's power plants, is one of the largest private enterprises in Mexico. 4DX permeates everything at MICARE.

Monday morning WIG sessions take place in every department of this vast company. The meetings are connected by videophone to remote locations so that everyone will be on the same page at the same time. Every manager's results are visible on the screen for all to see.

Each group (production, delivery, human resources, finance, operations, and so forth) has scoreboards that are posted around the company and kept constantly updated. Everyone in the company—engineers, miners, even maintenance workers—can recite their team WIGs to you. When touring MICARE, we were reminded of this observation by Jack Welch, the legendary leader of GE:

"Goals cannot sound noble but vague. Targets cannot be so blurry they can't be hit. Your direction has to be so vivid that if you randomly woke one of your employees in the middle of the night and asked him, 'Where are we going?' he could still answer in a half-asleep stupor." [19]

That is the level of strategic clarity and commitment evident throughout MICARE.

What has the 4DX operating system meant to the achievement of MICARE's WIGs? Over a seven-year period:

- Lost-time accidents dropped from nearly seven hundred per year to fewer than sixty.
- Water consumed in processing coal—a major environmental concern—dropped by two-thirds.
- Annual rehabilitation of mined-out properties rose from six hectares to more than two hundred.
- Suspended particulates in the air around the mines dropped from three hundred forty-six units per cubic meter to eighty-four.
- Metric tons of coal produced per worker grew from six thousand to ten thousand per year.

In summary, and according to MICARE's CEO, 4DX has produced dramatic hard business results for MICARE and enabled major improvements to safety and the environment as well.

MICARE credits concentrated attention to the cadence of accountability as the major factor in MICARE's success. The regular

WIG session, as simple in concept as it is, keeps bringing the whole organization's focus back to what matters most.

Remember that the WIG session should move at a fast pace. If each person simply addresses the three cadence items described earlier, it doesn't require a lot of talking. As one of our largest clients is fond of saying, "The more they talk, the less they did."

The WIG session also gives the team the chance to process what they've learned about what does and doesn't work. If the lead measures aren't moving the lag, the team brings creative thinking to the table, suggesting new hypotheses to try. If people are running into obstacles keeping their commitments, team members can commit to clear the path for each other. What might be tough for a frontline worker to achieve might take just a stroke of the pen for the team leader. In fact, as the leader you should often ask each team member "What can I do this week to clear the path for you?"

It's also important to note that, unless you are a frontline person, you will likely be in two WIG sessions every week: one led by your boss and one that you lead with your team (more on this on page 171).

For now, let's apply Discipline 4 to the example of Younger Brothers Construction that we discussed earlier. Remember that the WIG for Younger Brothers was to reduce safety incidents from fifty-seven to twelve by December 31, and their lead measure was compliance to the six safety standards they believed would eliminate the vast majority of accidents.

Imagine that you are a project manager at Younger Brothers responsible for a number of crews. In the WIG session with your boss, you would do three things:

1. **Report on last week's commitments**: "Last week I committed to order new braces for the scaffolding so that conditions for all my crews were up to code (one of the six safety standards) and I completed that."
2. **Review the scoreboard**: "My lag measure for safety incidents is currently averaging five per month, slightly above where we

should be for this quarter. My lead measure for compliance to safety standards is green at 91 percent, but crews nine, eleven, and thirteen are hurting the score because they aren't consistently wearing their safety glasses."

3. **Make commitments for the coming week**: "This week I will meet with the supervisors of crews nine, eleven, and thirteen, review their safety records, and ensure that they have enough safety glasses for everyone."

Each commitment must meet two standards: First, the commitment must represent a specific deliverable. For example, a commitment to "focus on" or "work on" crews nine, eleven, and thirteen is too vague. Because this type of commitment doesn't make you accountable for a specific result, it usually gets lost in the whirlwind. Second, the commitment must influence the lead measure. If the commitment doesn't directly target the lead measure, it won't advance the team toward achieving the WIG.

As you begin to understand the WIG session, you'll also see more clearly the importance of the two characteristics of lead measures we discussed in Discipline 2. If the lead measures are influenceable, they can be moved by the weekly commitments. If they are predictive, then moving them will lead to achievement of the WIG.

The WIG session is like an ongoing science experiment. Team members bring their best thinking as to how to influence the scoreboard. They commit to try new ideas, test hypotheses, and bring back the results.

For example, at the Minnesota Cystic Fibrosis Center at the University of Minnesota Medical Center, Fairview, staff doctors hold a weekly meeting to review lung function among their vulnerable patients, most of them infants and small children. Cystic fibrosis gradually reduces the victim's ability to breathe, so the WIG for this world-class treatment center is 100 percent lung function for all their patients. They are not satisfied with 80 percent of normal, or even 90 percent, as a lag measure.

In these weekly meetings, the doctors review what they've observed that week about improving lung function and they make commitments to follow up. For example, because body weight might be a lead measure in lung health, doctors carefully monitor it and give some infants supplemental feedings. They conduct experiments with mist tents and massage vests and other ways to clear lungs. Then they report back to the team on the outcomes.

Each week they learn more and share their learning.

Few people hold themselves as rigorously accountable for a WIG as the Fairview team does, and the results show the value of their cadence of accountability: They haven't lost a patient to cystic fibrosis in many years.[20]

While the leader of the WIG session is responsible for ensuring the quality of commitments, it's critical that the commitments come from the participants. We cannot emphasize this strongly enough. If you simply tell your team what to do, they will learn little. But when they are able to consistently tell *you* what's needed to achieve the WIG, they will have learned a lot about execution, and so will you.

Having team members generate their own commitments may seem counterintuitive, especially when you can see so clearly what should be done and when your team may even expect or want you to just tell them what to do. However, what you ultimately want is for each member of your team to take personal ownership of the commitments they make. As a leader, you may still coach people who are struggling to make high-impact commitments, but you want to ensure that, in the end, the ideas are theirs, not yours.

THE BLACK AND THE GRAY

Finally, the WIG session saves your wildly important goals from being engulfed by the whirlwind. Below is the calendar for a typical week. The black blocks represent your WIG session commitments and the gray blocks represent your whirlwind. This simple visual is ideal for showing what the balance of time and energy invested in execution looks like.

When we introduce Discipline 4 in our process, some leaders mistakenly picture a week that's mostly black, meaning that the commitments are the predominant focus for the week. This seldom represents reality. The vast majority of your energy will still be spent managing your day-to-day priorities, as it should be. But the critical value of the 4 Disciplines is ensuring that the black—your investment over and above your day to day—stays consistently focused on your WIG.

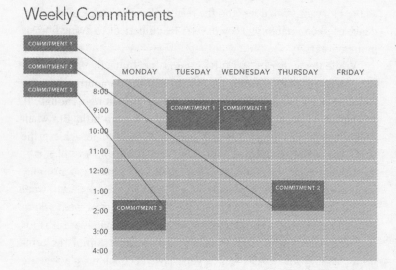

Weekly Commitments

The gray blocks represent your day-to-day whirlwind; the black blocks represent your weekly commitments to move the WIG scoreboard. If you actively schedule them into your week, the whirlwind is less likely to draw your focus away from the WIG.

What would happen if you pulled one of those black blocks out of your week? Would it remain empty?

Think about the last time you were relieved to learn that a meeting had been cancelled, freeing an hour in your schedule. How long was it before three other meetings and five urgent requests were all competing for that one open spot? In terms of the diagram, how long would it be before the whirlwind devoured that open time, turning it gray?

When we ask this question in our sessions, every leader knows the answer: "Immediately!" The gray doesn't want the black in your week. In other words, the whirlwind will consume every moment of time and every ounce of energy it can. Parkinson's Law states: "Work expands so as to fill the time available for its completion," and nowhere is this principle of expansion and consumption of time and energy more true than with your whirlwind. Execution on your WIG is all about driving the black into the gray, no matter what it takes.

Now, think of the diagram as representing the combined energy of a week from your entire team, not just from you. In this new context, the black represents the energy of every member of your team as they keep their commitments every week. This is the kind of focused energy that produces results. If you keep the cadence of accountability, week after week, your team unleashes this focused energy against the lead measures that have a direct effect on the WIG.

This weekly discipline also has a real effect on morale. Think about the last time you had an all-gray week, a week of long hours consumed by the endless crises of the whirlwind. The worst part of it was the sickening feeling in the pit of your stomach that, despite killing yourself all week, you didn't really accomplish anything.

If your all-gray weeks become a regular experience, you feel the life draining out of you as a leader. Even worse, you will see the same feeling reflected in the engagement and the performance of your team.

WIG sessions are the antidote to all-gray weeks. When the discipline of holding WIG sessions is sustained—when you and your team force the black into the gray every week—not only will you make consistent progress toward your goals, you'll also begin to feel that you, rather than the whirlwind, are in charge.

WIG SESSIONS AND ENGAGEMENT

Mark McChesney, the older brother of one of our authors, wanted only one thing growing up: to design cars. Mark worked very hard to achieve his dream and was eventually hired as a designer for one of the big three automakers in the United States. Almost all of the designers on Mark's team had the same dream, a dream that they are now living by spending every day doing the one thing they wanted to do more than anything in the world: designing cars.

You would think that their level of engagement would be off the charts. However, here is the fascinating part of this story: This design department has the lowest engagement scores of any team within that giant organization. That's right, people who are doing the one thing they always wanted to do have the lowest scores. How can people who have made a career doing what they love have low engagement?

In his book *The Three Signs of a Miserable Job,* Patrick Lencioni describes brilliantly three reasons individuals disengage from work.

1. **Anonymity**: They feel their leaders don't know or care what they are doing.
2. **Irrelevance**: They don't understand how their job makes a difference.
3. **Immeasurement**: They cannot measure or assess for themselves the contribution they are making.[21]

All three of Lencioni's signs are present in the automotive design department. First, the designer's original work is changed so much by the time it actually becomes a product that the originator is often forgotten (anonymity). Second, the product is released years after designers work on it, so they may not be able to see their contribution in the final product (irrelevance). And third, evaluations of performance are extremely subjective (immeasurement).

Lencioni's three signs not only explain what's happening in the design department, as well as in many other jobs, but also describe life in the whirlwind perfectly—what we have called an "all-gray week." The good news is that Discipline 4, if done right, is the cure for all three.

On a team that keeps the cadence of WIG sessions, the individual members are not anonymous. On the contrary, they are in the spotlight at least once a week. They are also not irrelevant, because they can see exactly how their commitments are moving the lead measures that drive a wildly important goal. And they are definitely not suffering from immeasurement: They have a clear and public scoreboard that is updated weekly to reflect their performance.

The full impact of the WIG session won't be felt right away. It often takes three to four weeks before a team establishes an effective rhythm in which they learn to stay focused on the WIG and avoid talking about the whirlwind. But soon the meeting begins to feel more productive; and after a few more weeks, something important starts to happen. The lead measures actually begin to move the lag measure and the team starts to feel that they are *winning*.

A DIFFERENT KIND OF ACCOUNTABILITY

Our on-line system used for running WIG sessions, my4dx.com (explained beginning on page 194) has captured millions of commitments from teams all over the world. More than 75 percent of those commitments have been kept, despite the whirlwind. This real-world data shows that WIG sessions create real accountability and follow-through.

However, it's the particular *kind* of accountability created in a WIG session that we want you to understand.

Often the very word *accountability* has a strong negative connotation. If your boss says, "Come see me in an hour; we need to have an accountability session," you can be fairly certain it's not a good thing.

However, the accountability created in a WIG session is very different. It's not organizational, it's *personal*. Instead of accountability to a broad outcome you can't influence, it's accountability to a weekly commitment that you yourself made and that is within your power to keep. And, one-by-one, you report your results not only to the boss, but to each other. The question you ultimately answer in a WIG session is, "Did we do what we committed *to each other* we would do?"

When the answer is "yes," when members of a team see their peers consistently following through on the commitments they make, they grow in respect for each other. They learn that the people they work with can be trusted to follow through. When this happens, performance improves dramatically.

Take the experience of Nomaco, a leading company in engineered polymer-foam extrusions. In short, they make amazing things out of colored foam, from high-tech insulation to swimming-pool toys.

As one of three Nomaco manufacturing plants, Tarboro in North Carolina was a good plant. They were beating budget on all fronts—costs, profitability, and safety—but they did not yet feel that it was a great plant, because although they were improving, they were not producing breakthrough performance.

The plant's organizational structure was traditional, and despite an open and friendly environment, people still depended on the plant manager to supervise, monitor, make all the decisions, and, essentially, ensure everyone in the plant was doing what they were supposed to be doing.

4DX brought the breakthrough they were looking for. In the eighteen months after adopting 4DX, Tarboro Plant:

- Cut more than $1 million in costs off the production line
- Came in more than 30 percent below budget for the fiscal year
- Experienced no lost-time accidents and only one recordable accident
- Beat projected budget for the following fiscal year in the first quarter

Of 4DX, the plant manager concluded, "It is simply a strong tool to ensure success in any type of initiative an organization chooses to bring on board. Whether it is Six Sigma, lean manufacturing, or self-directed work teams . . . 4DX will get you the results you are desiring to achieve."

The key to this shift was in the WIG sessions.

At Tarboro, every team held WIG sessions weekly. All employees reported on how they were moving the needle, changing the score, and achieving the WIG. Each week, they came up with new ideas to keep the scoreboard green. The WIG sessions kept them focused on achieving the wildly important goals, but more than that, the sessions enabled them to think together, make decisions together, help one another, and celebrate their wins.

As a result, the Tarboro plant created a culture of highly engaged employees who held themselves, *and each other,* accountable for results.

Julian Young, president of Nomaco during the 4DX implementation, summarized the impact of WIG sessions in this way: "The WIG sessions have a lot more energy than your traditional, old-fashioned manufacturing meetings. They have improved productivity substantially at each of our locations and have made accountability incredibly simple."

Over the years, we've observed thousands of WIG sessions like those at the Tarboro plant, and this experience has made one thing clear: The accountability to their peers that is created in the WIG session is an even greater motivator of performance for most individuals than accountability to their boss. In the end, people will work hard to avoid disappointing their boss, but they will do almost anything to avoid disappointing their teammates.

However, to reach this level, you still need to understand one additional point. We've said that the first three disciplines set up the game but until you apply Discipline 4, your team isn't *in* the game. But now we want to say it even more clearly: The level of importance you place on the WIG session will directly determine the results your team produces. Based on your consistency, your focus, and your own modeling of making commitments and following through, you will establish the WIG session as either a high-stakes game or a low-stakes game in the minds of your team.

Think of this point applied to a game played in the preseason versus the playoffs. In preseason, you'd like to win, but lose in the playoffs and your team goes home. Which type of game drives the highest level of play? Simply put, if the game doesn't really matter, why should your team care? This is why real accountability inspires the team to engage at the highest level of play.

CREATING AN INNOVATIVE CULTURE

Some people don't like the fact that WIG sessions are so structured. Actually, when done right, WIG sessions are also highly creative. Structure and creativity together produce engagement, as eminent brain scientist Dr. Edward Hallowell has discovered. The most motivating situations, he says, are those that are "highly structured *and* full of novelty and stimulation."[22]

The cadence of accountability can release the creativity of the team.

When you think of a team that has a culture of discipline and execution, you don't expect to hear that they are also creative and innovative. However, we've regularly seen all of these characteristics in teams that apply 4DX well.

The WIG session encourages experimentation with fresh ideas. It engages everyone in problem-solving and promotes shared learning. It's a forum for innovative insights as to how to move the lead measures, and because so much is at stake, it brings out the best thinking from every team member.

Towne Park is a great example. The largest provider of valet parking services for high-end hotels and hospitals, Towne Park has always been extremely well run. When Gaylord Entertainment (one of Towne Park's largest customers) had great success as an early adopter of the 4DX, the leaders at Towne Park became interested as well.

Towne Park was already measuring virtually every aspect of its business: Did attendants open the door for you and your guests when you arrived? Did they use the proper hotel greeting? Did they offer you a bottle of water? Their execs could tell you all this, as they were literally measuring everything they thought mattered to their customers.

Still, they decided to apply 4DX to the wildly important goal of the company, increasing customer satisfaction, to see if they could improve it even more. While developing lead measures in Discipline 2, they realized that one thing they weren't measuring might actually be their point of highest leverage in pleasing the customer: How long it takes the customer to get his or her car back.

So, they chose reducing retrieval time as the most predictive lead measure for further improving customer satisfaction. Although they had always known this was an important aspect of the business, they had never measured it because it isn't an easy measure to get, even for a company that believes in measurement. They knew that collecting retrieval-time data would require them to clock when the customer called for the car and when the valet arrived with the car. The elapsed time between the two points, the *retrieval time,* would then need to be consistently captured for all teams in all locations.

You can imagine how difficult it would be to gather this data in the whirlwind of incoming and outgoing cars, so difficult that some leaders argued that it couldn't be done. However, because they were committed to their WIG of unparalleled customer satisfaction, and because they believed retrieval time was the most predictive and influenceable measure for achieving it, they committed to tracking it. Like all great leadership teams, once the decision was made, they found a way.

Initially, they wondered if retrieval time was really influenceable because of all the external factors that impact it, such as the location of the parking area and the distance to the car. Despite these worries, they were able to reduce retrieval time dramatically.

How? The teams figured it out because they were highly engaged in the game. Once the lead measure went up on the scoreboard, the valets began finding new ways to win. For example, they started advising arriving guests to call before checking out so that their car would be waiting for them." Whenever the guest called in advance, the valet knew the retrieval time would be zero.

The valets also began to ask what day the guest planned on checking out. If it was later in the week, they would park the car in the back of the lot. As the day of departure drew closer, they would move the car forward so that retrieval time would be reduced.

These and a host of other innovations not only reduced the lead measure of retrieval time, but immediately raised the lag measure of customer satisfaction. Towne Parke was winning, but without the team's engagement in the game, these ideas might never have surfaced, let alone been implemented.

However, a Towne Park team in Miami, Florida, faced an obstacle that seemed insurmountable: A four-foot-high concrete wall ran down the middle of the parking garage, forcing the valets to drive around it to retrieve every car.

After several months of trying to compensate for the wall, a *literal* breakthrough came during their WIG session. James McNeil, one of the assistant account managers, committed to his team that the wall was coming out. He obtained clearance from the hotel's engineer who confirmed that the wall was not load-bearing, borrowed a concrete saw, and recruited several other supervisors to help. Starting early the following Saturday morning, they cut and hauled out several tons of concrete; by the end of the day, the wall was gone.

If you're a leader, you should be fascinated by this story. If a Towne Park executive had ordered the team to do something as far outside their normal responsibilities as removing a concrete wall, what do you think the team's reaction would have been? At best, resistance, and at worst, mutiny, even from a good team.

But because the lead measure had become a high-stakes game, one the players didn't want to lose, the effect was the opposite. Taking out the wall was their idea; and their desire to win was so strong, you couldn't have kept them from doing it. Necessity really is the mother of invention. Once they made retrieval time a high-stakes game, the creativity and invention followed.

What's critical to understand is that this level of engagement seldom if ever comes from a command-and-control approach—that is, one that relies exclusively on the formal authority of the leader. Authority alone at best yields only compliance from a team.

By contrast, 4DX produces results not from the exercise of authority but from the fundamental desire of each individual team member to feel significant, to do work that matters, and ultimately, to win.

That kind of engagement yields true commitment, the kind of commitment that led a Towne Park team to tear down a wall. And it's only that kind of commitment that produces extraordinary results.

In section 2, we'll give you precise guidance on how to achieve that kind of commitment through the cadence of accountability.

THE POWER OF 4DX

Now that we've examined each of the 4 Disciplines of Execution, we hope you sense their power to transform your culture and your business results. When we introduce leaders to 4DX, they often believe they are already doing most of what we teach. After all, goals, measures, scoreboards, and meetings are familiar topics. But, once 4DX is implemented, these same leaders report in their teams a dramatic paradigm shift that produces predictable results, often for the first time

If you contrast 4DX with the familiar practices of annual planning, you can see how different this paradigm is from the typical mindset about goals.

The annual goal-setting process usually begins with the creation of a master plan for the year, focused on a large number of objectives. Then each objective is broken down into the many projects, milestones, tasks, and subtasks that must be accomplished over the

LINK: http://www.4dxbook.com/qr/BestMoment

Scan the image above to see a short video of what leaders face when driving strategy.

coming months for the plan to succeed. The deeper the planning process goes, the more complex the plan becomes.

Despite this growing complexity, the leaders may feel symptoms of what we call the "planning high." It's that hopeful feeling they get as they say "This could really work!"

Finally, they create a set of colorful PowerPoint slides to explain the plan, and then deliver a convincing formal presentation. Sound familiar so far? If so, there's only one step left after the plan is presented: watching it slowly fall into obscurity as the changing needs of the business, none of which were accounted for, make the plan less and less relevant.

Now, in contrast, think back to the experience of Younger Brothers Construction and their WIG to reduce accidents. No matter how detailed or strategically brilliant their annual plan might have been, it could never have foreseen that in week thirty-two, a leader would need to meet with crews nine, eleven, and thirteen to focus on safety glasses. In other words, the very information needed to drive the highest level of results that week would not be in the plan, and it never is.

However, in Discipline 4, the team plans weekly against their lead measures, in essence, creating a just-in-time plan based on commitments that they could not have imagined at the beginning of the month, let alone the beginning of the year.

The constant weekly energy applied against the lead measures creates a unique form of accountability that connects the team directly to the goal, again and again.

If Younger Brothers had attacked their WIG without the lead measure of safety compliance, they would still have been able to make weekly commitments but against a less specific target. Can you imagine each team member making a commitment to reduce accidents this week? It would seem so broad as to be overwhelming to them, like trying to boil the ocean.

Even worse, imagine the perspective of the leaders. Can you hear them saying in frustration, "These are all adults who've been working construction for years. If they don't care about their own safety, what am I supposed to do about it?"

Once people give up on a goal that looks unachievable—no matter how strategic it might be—there is only one place to go: back to the whirlwind. After all, it's what they know and it feels safe. When this happens, your team is now officially playing not to lose instead of playing to win and there is a big difference. Simply put, 4DX gets an organization playing to win!

Think of 4DX like the operating system on your computer. You need a powerful operating system to execute whatever programs you choose to install. If the operating system isn't equal to the task, it doesn't matter how beautifully designed the program, it won't work consistently on your computer.

Likewise, without an operating system for executing your goals, no matter how beautifully designed your strategy, it won't work consistently. Even if you achieve results, you won't be able to sustain them, or surpass them, year after year. 4DX ensures the precise and consistent execution of any goal you choose to install in your team or organization and creates a foundation for greater success in the future.

One of the key reasons that 4DX works so powerfully is that it's based on timeless principles; and it's proven to work with virtually any organization in any environment. We didn't invent the principles of 4DX; we simply uncovered and codified them. Others have used the same principles to effectively change human behavior in the service of a goal.

In 1961, Jean Nidetch of Queens, New York, was losing patience with dieting. She was uncomfortably overweight and found it difficult to stay on a diet. She failed to achieve her goal every time she tried. So when she decided to try a diet she obtained from the NYC Board of Health, she decided to try a new approach: She invited a few friends who were also fighting their weight to meet each week and check on each other. They set reasonable, bite-sized goals to lose a pound or two per week. They carefully monitored their intake of calories and gauged the amount of exercise they were getting.

Over a period of about two years, they achieved their weight-loss goals, and they did it together.

Jean's weight-loss club continued to add members and, in 1963, incorporated as the Weight Watchers organization. Since then, Weight Watchers has grown into an international network of clubs, with a product line of diet drinks, sugar substitutes, and publications. "My little private club has become an industry," said Jean Nidetch.

No other program has matched their record for helping large numbers of people maintain a healthy weight.

The success of Weight Watchers is due to the same principles that underlie the 4 Disciplines:

- Discipline 1: Careful focus on a clear lag measure: losing a certain amount of weight within a certain time frame— *from X to Y by when.*
- Discipline 2: Acting on the high-leverage lead measures of calorie intake and output through exercise, measures that the participants can control. These lead measures are expressed in terms of points that are easily tracked.
- Discipline 3: Regular scorekeeping and monitoring of the lead measures and the lag measure. A compelling scoreboard engages people and keeps them on track toward the goal.
- Discipline 4: The cadence of accountability: the weekly meeting with others who have the same goal. They share stories, check the scoreboard (the scale), celebrate successes, and talk about lapses and what to do about them. Many participants say that the weekly weigh-in is the most motivating thing about the program.[23]

The principles underlying 4DX are universal and timeless, a conclusion we have confirmed again and again in working with some of the best companies in the world.

Section 2

Installing 4DX with Your Team

As you've learned in section 1, 4DX is an operating system for achieving the goals you must achieve.

In section 2, you'll learn what to expect when you install 4DX with your team and the specific steps for doing so. You'll benefit from the experience of thousands of work teams who've committed themselves to the same exhilarating challenge.

Please keep in mind that 4DX is not a set of guidelines, but a set of disciplines. Installing 4DX will require your finest efforts, but the payoff will be a team that performs consistently and with excellence.

This section is designed to guide you in installing 4DX. Think of it as a field guide with all the information to ensure your success. If you're a senior executive who will lead the efforts of others in implementing 4DX, you'll find it a valuable overview of the journey. If you're a leader who will be implementing 4DX with your own team, you'll find a detailed road map of that journey. You'll appreciate its value once you begin.

In either case, you'll likely refer to this section many times during implementation and again over the years as your experience with 4DX grows.

What to Expect

The famous Greek myth of Sisyphus tells of a man whom the gods punish by requiring him to push a boulder up a mountain. Each time he reaches the peak, the stone rolls back down and he has to push it back up the mountain all over again, for eternity!

It's a little like the feeling of leaving work at the end of an exhausting day without being able to point to a single significant accomplishment, and knowing that tomorrow you'll begin pushing that boulder all over again.

Jim Dixon, the general manager of Store 334 in a large grocery chain, felt very much like Sisyphus every day. Store 334 had the worst financial performance of 250 stores in the division. People didn't want to shop there, and they didn't want to work there either.

Every day when Jim came to work, he would do what he called the "head slap" over the same old problems. Shopping carts and trash all over the parking lot. Broken bottles in the aisles. Big gaps in products on the shelves. Nothing in that store happened until Jim told somebody to do it, or he did it himself. Midnight often found him stocking shelves or mopping up spilled milk. Not only had he hired people to do these things, he had hired people to *hire* people to do these things.

Like Sisyphus, Jim felt he was pushing the same boulder up the hill every day just to watch it roll down again. He never had time or energy to actually move the store forward in a significant way.

Jim had been considered a high-potential leader when he was put in charge at Store 334. Now, he seemed to be a low-potential micromanager. When we met him, he'd been working sixteen days straight and hadn't taken a vacation in over a year. Sales were way down while employee turnover was up. The vice president of human resources confided to us, "Jim's either going to quit, or we're going to have to let him go."

With all he had to do, you can imagine how delighted Jim would be to go to a 4 Disciplines workshop on top of everything else. And in December, too, which is the busiest time of the year for the grocery business.

For Jim and his department heads, the wildly important goal was no mystery. If they didn't meet the year-over-year revenue figure, the store itself was in danger of closing. Nothing else really mattered. However, the tricky problem was determining their lead measure: What could they do differently that they weren't doing already? What would have the most impact on driving up store revenues?

Jim and his team were pretty sure that if store conditions improved, revenue would improve. A clean, attractive, fully stocked store should draw more customers. So each department individually came up with the two or three most important things to measure for that department, and they decided to score themselves daily on a one-to-ten scale.

- For the meat department, fresh cuts in a crystal-clear display.
- Shelves in the produce department fully stocked by five in the morning.
- For the bakery, hot, fresh bread on the racks every two hours.

At the end of this process, Jim and his team had a plan! They would start executing immediately, and the assistant manager and the department heads would update the scoreboard daily. The bet was that as store conditions improved, so would year-over-year revenue. It felt like it might work.

That morning they posted the scoreboards, and that night the employees tore them down. The next day they put the scoreboards back up again, but the whirlwind of day-to-day pressures sucked the department heads right back to where they had been before. After two weeks, the five departments were averaging thirteen out of fifty on a scale they'd created themselves! Jim was frustrated, and the wildly important goal was in trouble.

Later in this section, you'll see why—and learn the rest of this story.

STAGES OF CHANGE

Because changing human behavior is such a big job, many leaders face challenges like these when installing 4DX. In fact, we've found that most teams go through five stages of behavior change. In this chapter, we hope to help you understand and manage your way through these stages.

Stage 1: Getting Clear

Let's follow Marilyn, the leader of the surgical nursing unit at a large inner-city hospital, as she installs the 4DX with her team. She and her team face a whirlwind like no other, as lives literally depend on how well they execute dozens of surgeries every day.

Marilyn's team had recently seen a sharp rise in *perioperative incidents*—things that go wrong in surgery. Despite the raging whirlwind of an operating room, they all

> **STAGE 1:** Getting Clear
>
> The leader and the team commit to a new level of performance. They are oriented to 4DX and develop crystal-clear WIGs, lag and lead measures, and a compelling scoreboard. They commit to regular WIG sessions. Although you can naturally expect varying levels of commitment, team members will be more motivated if they are closely involved in the 4DX work session.

shared a passion for reducing these incidents that endangered their patients.

In a 4DX work session, they translated this focus into a wildly important goal: Increase surgeries without perioperative incidents from 89 percent to 98 percent by December 31.

The team then carefully reviewed the factors that caused the most incidents, as well as those that created the greatest risk to patients, and isolated two lead measures that would give them the greatest leverage: Achieve 100 percent compliance on all pre-surgery audits at least thirty minutes before surgery, and double count surgical items following 100 percent of surgeries.

Now that Marilyn and her team had a wildly important goal (Discipline 1) and two Lead Measures (Discipline 2), they designed a simple scoreboard (Discipline 3) for tracking their performance and scheduled a weekly WIG session to hold themselves accountable for continuous progress (Discipline 4).

As they closed the team meeting, Marilyn looked forward to the launch the next week. She had never felt clearer about a goal and a plan. The rest, she thought, would be easy.

Of course, she was underestimating the task. The reason this happens is the inherent difficulty of changing human behavior in the midst of a raging whirlwind. Success starts by getting to crystal clarity on the WIG and the 4DX process. Remember your key actions in implementing 4DX:

- Be a model of focus on the wildly important goal(s).
- Identify high-leverage lead measures.
- Create a players' scoreboard.
- Schedule WIG sessions at least weekly and *hold* them.

Stage 2: Launch

Marilyn launched the 4DX process beginning with the first surgery of the week: Monday morning at seven. By noon, the team was already struggling. The lead measure required the nurses to do equipment audits twenty minutes earlier than normal, but the schedule change and a new checklist confused everyone.

With a full surgical schedule and a nurse home sick, Marilyn's hands were full and her team scrambling. That first morning taught her about the problems of executing in the midst of the whirlwind.

Marilyn also noticed some were more willing to change than others. Her top performers were succeeding, and although it wasn't easy, they relished the challenge. However, two of her most senior nurses still wondered why the change in the audit routine was needed and complained about the added stress. Furthermore, Marilyn saw that the newer nurses, who were not yet confident in their roles, were actually slowing down the audit.

> **STAGE 2:** Launch
>
> Now the team is at the starting line. Whether you hold a formal kickoff meeting, or gather your team in a brief huddle, you launch the team into action on the WIG. But just as a rocket requires tremendous, highly focused energy to escape the earth's gravity, the team needs intense involvement from the leader at this point of launch.

That week, Marilyn realized that what was simple to plan was very difficult to launch. She faced not only a whirlwind, but a team with mixed motivations.

The launch phase of 4DX is not guaranteed to go smoothly. You will have your models (those who get on board), your potentials (those who struggle at first), and your resisters (those who don't want to get on board). Here are some keys to a successful launch:

- Recognize that a launch phase requires focus and energy—especially from the leader.
- Remain focused and implement the 4DX process diligently. You can trust the process.
- Identify your models, potentials, and resisters (more on these groups below).

Stage 3: Adoption

Marilyn worked hard to maintain focus on the WIG. Her team adjusted schedules and refined methods of scorekeeping. She trained and coached her potentials. She counseled the resisters about the need for change.

Each week they worked at the lead measures and they slowly improved. When they met in their weekly WIG sessions, they first reviewed their scoreboard and then individually made commitments of their own to move the needle on the scores.

Before long, Marilyn sensed the team finding its rhythm, and the incident rate declined. As the team saw that the lead measure was

> **STAGE 3:** Adoption
>
> Team members adopt the 4DX process and new behaviors drive the achievement of the WIG. You can expect resistance to fade and enthusiasm to increase as 4DX begins to work for them. They become accountable to each other for the new level of performance despite the demands of the whirlwind.

working, their excitement grew. For the first time in many months, they began to feel that they were winning.

Recognize that adoption of the new 4DX process will take time. Adherence to the process is essential to your success on the WIG: be respectful but diligent about sticking with the process. Otherwise, the whirlwind will quickly take over. Remember these keys to successful adoption of 4DX:

- Focus first on adherence to the process, then on results.
- Make commitments and hold each other accountable in weekly WIG sessions.
- Track results each week on a visible scoreboard.
- Make adjustments as needed.
- Invest in the potentials through additional training and mentoring.
- Answer straightforwardly any issues with resisters and clear the path for them if needed.

Stage 4: Optimization

Over the next eight weeks, Marilyn was pleased with her team's progress and with the steady, though small, decline in surgical incidents. But the team would have to pick up the pace to reach the WIG by the end of the year, and she wasn't sure what more they could do.

In the WIG session later that day, her nurses surprised her by proposing changes to the lead measures. First, they wanted to reposition the equipment trays in the operating room so that they could do their audits more quickly and accurately. Second, if they audited the operating rooms for both first and second surgeries simultaneously at the beginning of the shift, they

> **Stage 4:** Optimization
>
> At this stage, the team shifts to a 4DX mindset. You can expect them to become more purposeful and more engaged in their work as they produce results that make a difference. They will start looking for ways to optimize their performance—they now know what "playing to win" feels like.

could stay ahead of schedule the rest of the day. Third, they suggested the patient transport team notify them as soon as the patient was on the way to surgery, giving them time to cross-check the operating room a final time.

Marilyn was pleased and surprised that her team had found these ways to optimize their performance. It struck her that if she had proposed these things herself, the team probably would have resisted the extra work. But because the ideas came from them, they were not only willing but excited to carry them out.

Marilyn had created a game that mattered, and now her team was playing to win.

The nurses took ownership of the process. They kept coming up with new ways to move the lead measures, and the lag measure continued to rise. Their weekly commitments were precise and their follow-through excellent. The WIG sessions were tightly focused on results.

However, what really fascinated Marilyn was a new level of engagement and energy she had never seen before.

If you're consistent about 4DX, you can expect team members to begin optimizing it on their own. Here are keys to making the most of this stage:

- Encourage and recognize abundant creative ideas for moving the lead measures, even if some work better than others.
- Recognize excellent follow-through and celebrate successes.
- Encourage team members to clear the path for each other and celebrate it when it happens.
- Recognize when the potentials start performing like the models.

Stage 5: Habits

Marilyn proudly walked to the podium amidst enthusiastic applause at the hospital's annual meeting. It was hard to believe that only eleven months before she had been facing a crisis—the rising incident rate could have impacted her job and, much more important, the lives of her patients. Now, she and her team were being recognized for having exceeded their goal and for the lowest incident rate in the hospital's history.

Stage 5: Habits

When 4DX becomes habitual, you can expect not only to reach the goal but also to see a permanent rise in the level of your team's performance. The ultimate aim of 4DX is not just to get results, but to create a culture of excellent execution.

Marilyn knew that the change in her team went far beyond the achievement of their goal; they had fundamentally changed the way they performed and, in the process, had developed habits of execution that would ensure future success. The behavior changes that had been so hard to make were now standard performance for her team. In essence, the practices that reduced surgical incidents were now a normal component of her whirlwind, but because of them, her whirlwind had become far more manageable.

112

As a result, she knew the team could sustain a whole new level of focus and commitment; and as they turned to a new WIG, they were on a winning track.

LINK: http://www.4dxbook.com/qr/HealthCare

Scan the image above to see a series of video case studies on 4DX in health care.

4DX is habit forming: Once the new behaviors become ingrained in the day-to-day operation, you can set new goals and still execute with excellence again and again. Here are keys to help the team make 4DX habitual:

- Celebrate the accomplishment of the WIG.
- Move immediately on to new WIGs in order to formalize 4DX as your operating system.
- Emphasize that your new operating standard is sustained superior performance on lead measures.
- Help individual team members become high performers by tracking and moving the middle.

MOVING THE MIDDLE

As we've said, people generally deal with change in one of three ways:

Models. The models are not only the top performers but the most engaged. They embrace 4DX enthusiastically and use it to take their performance to a higher level. They are also the ones you'd most like to clone.

Resisters. The resisters are the opposite. When you introduce 4DX, some will immediately tell you why it won't work and how impossible it will be to implement given the demands of their whirlwind. Others will withdraw from the effort and hope no one notices, but 4DX makes their resistance highly visible to everyone. As one of our clients remarked, "When you implement the 4 Disciplines, there's no place to hide."

Most people fall in the middle between the models and the resisters. They represent your greatest potential leverage for improving performance.

Potentials. The potentials are those with the capacity to be top performers, but who haven't arrived. Some may lack the focus on goals or the specific knowledge they need to improve. Others may need the added pressure of accountability to motivate them.

The performance of any group of people generally looks like this:

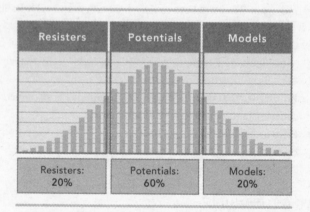

There's a big bulge in the middle.

Natural variability in any system produces this bulge, called a *normal curve*. You will always have a top 20 percent (the pockets of excellence), the bottom 20 percent (the inevitable weak performers) and the middle 60 percent, the majority who could do better if they were motivated to.

These are the potentials, the people who could contribute much more if only they knew how. Of course, the numbers vary, but what if that middle 60 percent performed more like the top 20 percent?

What would it mean to your performance if the graph looked like this instead?

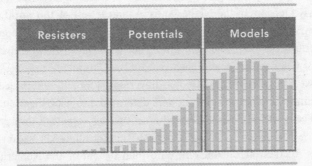

The curve shifts toward better overall performance as the middle performers consistently rise to the level of the top 20 percent. In other words, because more people are doing things better, the curve shifts right and tight all the time. Meanwhile, in an ordinary team, normal performance remains left and loose.

- A hotel satisfied with normal guest-satisfaction scores is left and loose. After all, nearly everyone is satisfied, right?
- A high-school faculty happy with normal graduation rates (which also means normal dropout rates) is left and loose.
- A hospital whose administration is content with keeping infections within accepted norms is left and loose. (And in this case, one may well ask if accepted norms *are* acceptable, since we're talking about preventable suffering and death!)

None of these organizations will make the leap to great performance as long as they are content with the left-and-loose normal curve.

However, even these organizations have pockets of great performance—teams who are consistently right and tight.

One example of great performance is Erasmus Medical Center near Rotterdam in the Netherlands. As in the rest of the world, European hospitals face a disturbing increase in lethal hospital-acquired infections (HAIs), which are estimated to account for two-thirds of the 25,000 hospital deaths each year on the Continent.

At Erasmus Medical Center, infections were still within acceptable limits, but administrators were determined to wipe them out. To achieve their WIG they adopted a set of lead measures they called *Search and Destroy,* which eliminated nearly all HAIs within five years. To their credit, the entire hospital system of the Netherlands followed their lead.[24]

By definition, hospitals are filled with sick people. Germs abound. And most hospitals seem content with infection rates within accepted norms. However, for a high-performance team like the administrators of Erasmus Medical Center, the only acceptable infection rate is *zero*. That meant moving the middle in a big way.

The Erasmus team moved a left-and-loose curve to right and tight within a matter of months. Vulnerable patients stopped getting sick and dying. Most hospitals do not lack the know-how to get the same results, but, as famous University of Kentucky basketball Coach Adolph Rupp said, "Whenever you see a man on top of a mountain, you can be sure he didn't fall there."

If you could move the middle toward the summit of performance, the impact on results would be significant. You do that by consistently motivating new and better behavior, which is the aim of 4DX.

In our experience—whether with hospitals, grocery chains, engineering firms, hotels, software companies, power plants, government contractors, or multiunit retail operations—the outcome is almost always the same: A new culture of high performance along with consistent results.

Getting there isn't easy and doesn't happen overnight. It takes focus and discipline *over time* to implement 4DX and to make it stick. The pattern to expect usually looks like this.

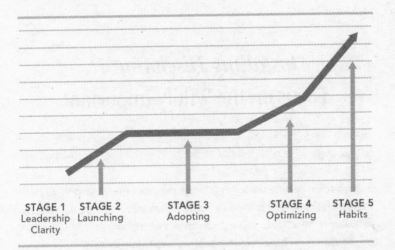

STAGE 1
Leadership
Clarity

STAGE 2
Launching

STAGE 3
Adopting

STAGE 4
Optimizing

STAGE 5
Habits

Initially, results improve quickly, but we've noticed a plateau period as the team works to adopt the new mindset. Once team members become habituated to 4DX, it starts to pay real dividends.

We began this book by pointing out that possibly the single greatest challenge you will face as a leader is driving a strategy that depends on changing human behavior.

4DX is a proven system for meeting that challenge, not just once, but again and again. In the following chapters, we will take you step by step through each discipline so you can apply it with your team.

Installing Discipline 1:
Focus on the Wildly Important

Superb team performance begins with selecting one or two WIGs. Focusing on these vital few goals is the foundational principle of 4DX: Without it, your team will get lost in the whirlwind.

Many teams have multiple goals—sometimes dozens, all of which are priority one. Of course, that means that nothing is priority one.

A client put it best: "When you work on that many goals, you actually work on none of them, because the amount of energy you can put into each one is so small, it's meaningless."

Selecting the right WIG is crucial. Leaders often hesitate to narrow their focus because they worry about the consequences of choosing the wrong WIG or failing to achieve it. Still, when you choose a WIG, you're starting a game that matters; one where the stakes are high and the team can make a real difference. Discipline 1 is necessary if you're going to play to win.

STEP 1: CONSIDER THE POSSIBILITIES

Begin by brainstorming possible WIGs. Although you might feel you already know what the WIGs should be, you might end this process with entirely different WIGs. In our experience, this happens often.

You'll do this brainstorming differently depending on the kind of organization you belong to and the place of your team in the organization:

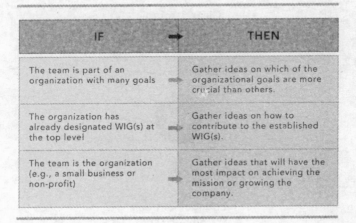

IF	→	THEN
The team is part of an organization with many goals		Gather ideas on which of the organizational goals are more crucial than others.
The organization has already designated WIG(s) at the top level		Gather ideas on how to contribute to the established WIG(s).
The team is the organization (e.g., a small business or non-profit)		Gather ideas that will have the most impact on achieving the mission or growing the company.

Getting Input

You have three options:

- Brainstorm with peer leaders, especially if you are all focusing on the same organizational WIG. If you're concerned that they might not understand your team's operation, their outside perspective will still be valuable, particularly if you depend on them or they depend on you.
- Brainstorm with your team members or with a representative group. Obviously, if they are involved in selecting the WIG, they will take ownership of it more readily.
- Brainstorm alone. You will still be able to validate the WIG with the team when you develop lead measures.

Top Down or Bottom Up?

Should WIGs come from the leader or from the team?

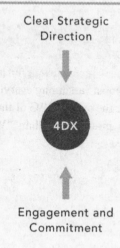

Clear Strategic
Direction

4DX

Engagement and
Commitment

With the 4 Disciplines, leaders provide top-down strategic direction in defining the WIG, while team members provide active input that increases their engagement and commitment to the WIG.

Top Down: A leader who imposes WIGs without input from the team might have problems getting team ownership. If she drives accountability mostly through her authority, she probably won't develop a high-performance team and will pay a price in lost retention, creativity, and innovation.

Bottom Up: WIGs that come exclusively from the team might lack relevance to the overall WIG. Without strong direction, the team could lose valuable time and energy in getting consensus on every move.

Top Down *and* Bottom Up: Ideally, both the leader and the team participate in defining the WIGs. Only the leader can provide clarity about what matters most. The leader is ultimately responsible for the

WIG, but shouldn't engage team members solely through the exercise of authority. To reach the goal and to transform the team, team members must have active input in defining the WIG: "No involvement, no commitment."

Discovery Questions

We've found these three questions useful in discovering the WIG.

- "Which one area of our team's performance would we want to improve most (assuming everything else holds) in order to achieve the overall WIG of the organization?" (This question is more useful than "What's the most important thing we can do?")
- "What are the greatest strengths of the team that can be leveraged to ensure the overall WIG is achieved?" (This question will generate ideas in areas in which your team is already succeeding, but where they can also take their performance to an even higher level.)
- "What are the areas where the team's poor performance most needs to be improved to ensure the overall WIG is achieved?" (This question will generate ideas around performance gaps that, if not improved, actually represent a threat to achieving the overall WIG.)

Don't settle for just a few ideas for the WIG. Gather as many ideas as you can reasonably capture. Our experience shows that the longer and more creative the list of possible WIGs, the higher quality the final choice.

Think what, not how. Don't make the common mistake at this point of shifting the focus from the WIG itself to how to achieve it. The "how" is the new and better behavior that will lead to the WIG. That discussion comes later in Discipline 2.

A five-star hotel chain had this overall WIG: Increase total profit from \$54 million to \$62 million by December 31. Various departments in one hotel brainstormed ideas for their team WIGs:

Housekeeping	Clean guestrooms like they've never been cleaned before. We're already the best—let's get better!
Restaurant	Make alliances with local sports and culture venues.
Valet Parking	Ensure no one waits for their car.
Reception	Move guests through the system more quickly. No more queues at the registration desk.

Let's look at the actual list of ideas from one department, Event Management. Since this group can impact profit both by increasing revenue and reducing expenses, they brainstormed ideas to do both.

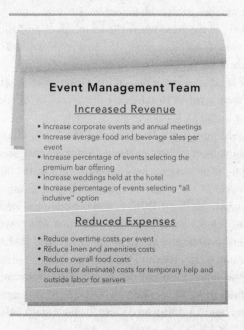

Event Management Team

Increased Revenue

- Increase corporate events and annual meetings
- Increase average food and beverage sales per event
- Increase percentage of events selecting the premium bar offering
- Increase weddings held at the hotel
- Increase percentage of events selecting "all inclusive" option

Reduced Expenses

- Reduce overtime costs per event
- Reduce linen and amenities costs
- Reduce overall food costs
- Reduce (or eliminate) costs for temporary help and outside labor for servers

STEP 2: RANK BY IMPACT

When you're satisfied with your list of candidate team WIGs, you're ready to identify the ideas that promise the greatest potential impact *on the overall organizational WIG.*

Calculating the impact of a team WIG depends on the nature of the overall WIG:

If the overall WIG is	Then rank the WIG in terms of
A financial goal	Prospective revenues, profitability, investment performance, cash flow, and/or cost savings.
A quality goal	Efficiencies gained, cycle times, productivity improvements, and/or customer satisfaction.
A strategic goal	Service to the mission, competitive advantages gained, opportunities captured, and/or threats reduced.

Susan, who runs the event management team, is responsible for meetings, banquets, and special events. In step 1, they identified team WIGs that would contribute to the overall profit WIG.

To narrow this list, they calculated the financial impact of each idea. It wasn't hard to identify the ideas that would generate the most profit for her team, but that was not the right focus.

The real challenge was to rank the ideas in terms of impact *on the overall organizational WIG*; in other words, to isolate those that would generate the most profit for the *entire hotel*. When they did that ranking, corporate events and weddings rose to the top because they generated revenue beyond the event itself, through rooms booked by out-of-town guests, restaurant meals, even spa services.

Avoid the trap of selecting WIGs that improve the team's performance but might have little to do with achieving the overall WIG.

In the end, Susan and her team chose two candidate WIGs that would clearly have the greatest impact on the overall WIG:

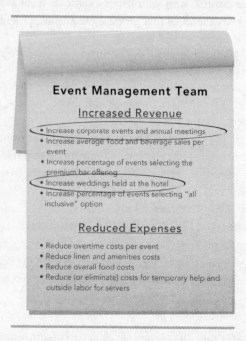

Event Management Team

Increased Revenue

- Increase corporate events and annual meetings
- Increase average food and beverage sales per event
- Increase percentage of events selecting the premium bar offering
- Increase weddings held at the hotel
- Increase percentage of events selecting "all inclusive" option

Reduced Expenses

- Reduce overtime costs per event
- Reduce linen and amenities costs
- Reduce overall food costs
- Reduce (or eliminate) costs for temporary help and outside labor for servers

A major drug company used this same narrowing process to identify their WIG: Shorten time to market for new products from approximately seven-and-a-half years to five years. For this company, one year's sales of a blockbuster product averages more than $1 billion, so the old saying, "time is money," is no joke to them.

Clive, who runs the regulatory affairs division, oversees the process of getting drugs approved by the medicine control authorities of various nations. Every new drug has to go through a complex application process that's different for each country.

In step 1, the team came up with these candidate WIGs:

1. Write application documents that meet the criteria for every country, instead of a different application for each country.

2. Hire some former regulators as consultants.
3. Eliminate mistakes in the application documents.
4. Lobby governments to broaden their criteria for fast-tracking a new drug so that it can get to market faster.

Some team members argued forcefully for candidate WIG 2 because they felt the department lacked expertise. Others believed government agencies were to blame and wanted to spend their efforts on candidate WIG 4. WIG 1 was also important because meeting so many different criteria was so frustrating.

But when they examined their ideas in light of the overall WIG to *shorten time to market,* they discovered something they hadn't noticed before: The authorities kept sending applications back to get mistakes corrected and unclear things explained. These delays were actually doubling the amount of time it took to get approval.

From that point, candidate WIG 3 was the obvious choice for the team's entire focus.

In a similar example, a large Scandinavian shipping company announced three goals for the year: To improve quality and productivity and reduce costs.

Stein was responsible for loading and unloading containers at a company facility in Norway. He recognized that the corporate goals were hazy, but he was eager for his team to contribute measurably to all three emphases.

Many reasonable candidate WIGs came out of a 4DX work session, such as:

- Increase maintenance of the onshore cranes to reduce downtime.
- Get everyone certified in Six Sigma to improve the loading process.
- Rebuild the depot at the rail head to smooth the flow of containers to the ships.

Each candidate WIG impacted one of the three company goals, but not all of them at once.

Now Stein had read on the Web about a Malaysian port that had recently broken the world record for the number of container moves per hour. The team there had off-loaded a giant ship in seven hours—half the average time.

He told the team all about it. Their competitive spirit was fired up and their energy led to the choice of a final WIG: Double our number of container moves per hour. It would require maximum productivity and maximum quality, but the cut in hours would automatically mean a cut in costs.

STEP 3: TEST TOP IDEAS

Once you've identified a couple of high-impact WIG candidates, test them against four specific criteria for a wildly important goal:

- Is the Team WIG aligned to the overall WIG?
- Is it measurable?
- Who owns the results—our team or some other team?
- Who owns the game—the team or the leader?

Is it aligned? Is there a seamless line of sight between the candidate WIG and the overall WIG? To create meaningful team WIGs, you should have a clear line of sight between your team (in the center) and the WIGs of the overall organization (if they can be identified).

Although this test may seem obvious, many teams become so excited about an idea that they forget achievement of the overall WIG is the top priority. If the idea fails this test, eliminate it and choose the next most high-impact idea from the list.

Is it measurable? As one of our clients put it, "If you're not keeping score, you're just practicing." A game without a clearly measurable score will never be a game that matters.

A WIG requires that a credible measurement be in place *from the day you begin executing.* If significant effort is required before you begin measuring, as with the performance of a system that hasn't been developed yet, it should be crossed off for now. Once the system is running, reconsider it, but time invested in a game without a score is time lost

Who owns the result? Does the team have at least 80 percent ownership of the result? This test is about eliminating significant dependence on other teams. The conceptual measure of 80 percent can help you determine how much your team will have to depend on other teams to achieve the WIG.

If it's less than 80 percent, neither team will take responsibility and accountability will be lost.

Of course, if two teams own the same WIG, joint ownership can be a powerful driver of performance, so long as both teams, and both leaders, understand that they win or lose together.

Who owns the game—leader or team? Is it a leader's game or a team game? This final test is more subtle than the others, but equally important. The question is whether results are driven by the performance of the leader or the performance of the team.

If the WIG depends too much on functions that only the leader performs, the team will quickly lose interest in the game. The team WIG should depend primarily on what the team does, not just the leader.

Failure to pass any of these tests should lead you to reevaluate the idea you're considering. Don't ask the team to play a game that's flawed; under the pressure of accountability, those flaws will quickly become apparent.

STEP 4: DEFINE THE WIG

Once you've selected and tested your ideas for high-impact team WIGs, make them as clear and measurable as possible. Define the WIGs according to the following rules:

- Begin with a verb.
- Define the lag measure in terms of *X to Y by When*.
- Keep it simple.
- Focus on what, not how.

Begin with a Verb

Simple verbs focus the mind immediately on action. Almost all multisyllable verbs have simple equivalents.

Long, overwrought introductions are also unnecessary. Just state the WIG:

THIS	NOT THIS
Cut costs... Grow revenue... Raise customer satisfaction score... Add one plant... Launch product...	In order to drive increased value to our shareholders, enhance the careers of our employees, and remain true to our fundamental values, we will be implementing a Wildly Important Goal this year to...

Define the Lag Measure

Lag measures tell you if you've achieved the goal. They mark a precise finish line for the team. Write lag measures in the format *from X to Y by when,* as these examples show.

Current Result (From X)	Desired Result (To Y)	Deadline (By When)
11% error rate	4% error rate	July 31
8 inventory turns per year	10 inventory turns per year	fiscal year end
12% return on investment per year	30% return on investment per year	within 3 years

The resulting WIGs look like this:

- Decrease routing error rate from 11 percent to 4 percent by July 31.
- Raise annual inventory turn rate from eight to ten by fiscal year end.
- Increase our average ROI from 12 percent to 30 percent within three years.

Keep It Simple

Earlier, we shared the startling fact that 85 percent of working adults cannot tell you their organization's most important goals. Among the many reasons for this: Most organizational goals are vague, complex, and pretentious.

THIS	NOT THIS
Raise our customer-loyalty score from 40 to 70 by December 31st.	"We are committed to enhancing and enriching our relationships with our customers."
Increase customer utilization of our investment counseling service by 25% this fiscal year.	"Our principal aim for the coming fiscal year is to facilitate investment, infrastructure, and access growth through effective coordination."
Launch three $10 million bio products within five years.	"We hope to foster industry innovation by addressing needs for bio-based resources through biotechnology."

Focus on What, Not How

Many teams define a clear goal but then complicate it by adding a lengthy description of how the goal will be achieved.

THIS	NOT THIS
Increase guest retention from 63% to 75% over the next two years.	Increase guest retention from 63% to 75% over the next two years through providing exceptional customer experiences.

You will identify *how* you plan to achieve the goal when you develop lead measures in Discipline 2. The WIG should focus exclusively on *what* the team plans to achieve.

Make Sure the WIG Is Achievable

We often encounter leaders who believe in setting goals that are far beyond anything their team can achieve, while privately acknowledging that they'll be satisfied if they get 75 percent of the goal. This type of gamesmanship can significantly undermine your ability to drive engagement and results.

We want to be very careful here. We're not advocating goals that are easy to reach. Set a goal that challenges the team to rise to their highest level of performance but not beyond it. In other words, create a WIG that is both *worthy* and *winnable*.

The Deliverable

The deliverable for Discipline 1 is a team WIG and lag measure.

At the hotel, Susan's team ultimately selected "increase corporate events" as the WIG, because they believed it would generate more revenue and, consequently, more profit for the hotel.

Susan then considered carefully the lag measure. Defining the gap between X and Y is a critical decision. The gap had to be challenging but realistic. She needed to create not only a game that mattered, but a *winnable* game.

The final WIG for Susan's team was significant, clear, and challenging:

Increase revenue from corporate events from $22 million to $31 million by December 31.

Having experienced Discipline 1, you now know that the simplicity of this WIG is deceptive. However, the team now has a clear focus on what matters most, a focus that can be sustained beyond the day-to-day requirements of your team's operation. Like a compass, the WIG provides clear, consistent direction toward a result that's *wildly important.*

What If Your WIG Is a Project?

Sometimes, your wildly important goal will be the successful completion of a major project. If this is the case, the principles of Discipline 1 still apply, but you'll need to pay particular attention to setting your lag measure finish line.

So far, we've used examples of lag measures that are based on numerical values, such as profit, customer satisfaction, or number of accidents. But with a project, your first inclination may be to set a lag measure of 100 percent completion. While this may seem obvious, it's usually far less precise than a numerical value. And because of other factors, such as scope expansion, 100 percent completion may turn out to be impossible to actually measure.

With projects, it's far better to establish a lag measure that relates to the *business outcome* the project is designed to meet. As legendary Harvard marketing professor Theodore Levitt put it, "People don't want to buy a quarter-inch *drill.* They want a quarter-inch *hole.*"[25]

So, instead of defining your lag measure solely as "Complete and implement the new CRM system by Dec 31," you might establish a more precise lag measure by adding measures such as the following:

- Meeting 100 percent of the specified marketing functions
- Providing full integration with Microsoft Outlook
- Including full functionality for smartphones and tablet PCs

Because they are more focused and more precisely defined than completion, these types of measures will provide a clear finish line and an accurate measure of success. (For a description of project lead measures, see page 149.)

TRY IT
Use the WIG builder tool to experiment with your ideas for a wildly important goal for the team.

WIG Builder Tool

1. Brainstorm ideas for the WIG.
2. Brainstorm lag measures for each idea (from X to Y by when).
3. Rank in order of importance to the organization or to the overall WIG.
4. Test your ideas against the checklist on the facing page.
5. Write your final WIG(s).

Ideas for the WIG	Current Result (From X)	Desired Result (To Y)	Deadline (By When)	Rank

Final WIG(s)

_____

_____

_____

_____

Final WIG(s)

Did You Get It Right?

Check off each item to ensure your Team WIGs and lag measures meet the standard:

☐ Have you gathered rich input both top down and bottom up?

☐ Will the Team WIG have a clear, predictable impact on the overall organizational WIG or strategy, not just on team performance?

☐ Is the Team WIG the most impactful thing the team can do to drive achievement of the overall WIG?

☐ Does the team clearly have the power to achieve the WIG without heavy dependence on other teams?

☐ Does the WIG require the focus of the entire team, not just of the leader or a subgroup?

☐ Is the lag measure written in the format "from X to Y by when"?

☐ Can the WIG be simplified any further? Does it start with a simple verb and end with a clear lag measure?

Installing Discipline 2:
Act on the Lead Measures

Great teams invest their best efforts in those few activities that have the most impact on the WIGs: the lead measures. This insight is so crucial and so distinctive, yet so little understood that we call it the secret of excellence in execution. Unlike lag measures, which tell you if you *have* achieved your goal, lead measures tell you if you are *likely* to achieve your goal. You will use lead measures to track those activities that have the highest leverage on the WIG.

Lead measures must be both *predictive* of achieving the WIG and *influenceable* by the team, as these examples show:

Team	Lag Measure	Lead Measure
Hospital Quality Improvement Team	Decrease mortality rate in the hospital from 4% to 2% this year.	Evaluate susceptible patients twice a day against pneumonia prevention protocols.
Shipping Company Dispatching Team	Reduce trucking costs by 12% this quarter.	Ensure 90% of all trips are with fully loaded trucks
Restaurant	Increase average check amount by 10% by year end.	Suggest the specialty cocktail of the day to 90% of all tables.

Each of these lead measures is both predictive and influenceable. The team can manageably act on the lead measure, which in turn will move the lag measure.

Acting on lead measures is essential to superb performance, but it is also the single most difficult aspect of installing 4DX in your team.

There are three reasons for this:

- **Lead measures can be counterintuitive.** Most leaders focus on lag measures, the bottom line results that ultimately matter. This focus is only natural. But you cannot *act* on a lag measure because it's in the past.
- **Lead measures are hard to keep track of.** They are measures of new and different behaviors, and tracking behaviors is much harder than tracking results. Often, there is no readily available system for tracking lead measures, so you might have to invent such a system.
- **Lead measures often look too simple.** They demand a precise focus on a certain behavior that might look insignificant (although it isn't), particularly to those outside the team.

For example, a retail store chose this lead measure for driving sales: Limit out of stocks on top items to twenty or fewer per week. Can this very common measure really make an important difference? And shouldn't they be doing that already? But if this simple lever is applied inconsistently, customers who can't find what they want will not return.

Often, lead measures simply close the gap between knowing what to do and doing it. Just as a simple lever can move a big rock, a good lead measure provides powerful leverage.

TWO TYPES OF LEAD MEASURES

Before you and your team begin to develop lead measures, we want you to understand more about the types and characteristics of these powerful drivers of execution. To begin, there are two types of lead measures: small outcomes and leveraged behaviors.

Small outcomes are lead measures that focus the team on achieving a weekly result, but give each member of the team latitude to choose their own method for achieving it. "Limit out of stocks to twenty or fewer per week" is a small-outcome lead measure where a variety of actions could be applied. Whatever actions they choose, with a small-outcome lead measure the team is ultimately accountable for producing the result.

Leveraged behaviors are lead measures that track the specific behaviors you want the team to perform throughout the week. They enable the entire team to adopt new behaviors at the same level of consistency and quality, and provide a clear measurement of how well they are performed. With a leveraged behavior lead measure, the team is accountable for performing the behavior, rather than for producing the result.

Both types of lead measures are *equally valid* applications of Discipline 2 and are powerful drivers of results.

WILDLY IMPORTANT GOAL

Reduce average monthly accidents from 12 to 7 by December 31st 2011

SMALL OUTCOME	LEVERAGED BEHAVIOR
LEAD MEASURE	LEAD MEASURE
Achieve average safety compliance score of 97% each week	Ensure that 95% of all associates wear safety boots every day

This example is drawn from our implementation at Younger Brothers Construction, where the wildly important goal was a lower accident rate. They chose the small outcome of Compliance to Safety, which involved driving multiple new behaviors. If they had believed that their team would be unsuccessful focusing on this many behaviors, they could have chosen to begin with a single leveraged behavior of, say, wearing safety boots (one of the six safety standards) and over time incorporated the additional behaviors as new habits for the team.

WILDLY IMPORTANT GOAL

Increase average weekly sales
from $1m to $1.5 m by
December 31ˢᵗ 2011

SMALL OUTCOME	LEVERAGED BEHAVIOR
LEAD MEASURE Limit out-of-stocks on top items to 20 or less per week	**LEAD MEASURE** Complete 2 additional shelf reviews each day, filling all holes on top items

---

This example is drawn from our work with a large grocery chain, where one of the most powerful drivers of increased sales was ensuring that the highest selling products were always available to customers. They chose to focus on a leveraged behavior, "Complete 2 additional shelf reviews," in which every member of the team could participate.

What we want you to see from these examples is that both types of lead measures give your team real leverage for achieving the goal. It's not a question of which is a better lead measure. It's a question of which is a better lead measure *for your team.*

Here are the steps for arriving at high-leverage lead measures.

Step 1: Consider the Possibilities

Begin by brainstorming possible lead measures. Resist the temptation to choose quickly—our experience has taught us that the more ideas generated, the higher the quality of the lead measures.

We've found these questions useful in discovering the lead measures:

- "What could we do that we've never done before that might make all the difference to the WIG?"
- "What strengths of this team can we use as leverage on the WIG? Where are our 'pockets of excellence'? What do our best performers do differently?"
- "What weaknesses might keep us from achieving the WIG? What could we do more consistently?"

For example, a grocery store has this WIG: "Increase year-over-year sales by 5 percent." Here are some candidate lead measures:

Identify New and Better Actions

- Greet people at the door between 5 and 7 p.m. (rush hour) and offer to help them find what they're looking for.
- Take grocery orders by text and email and have them ready for customers to pick up.

Leverage Pockets of Excellence

- Build creative new product displays in every department every month.
- Adapt the customer-service checklist the bakery uses to all departments in the store.

Fix Inconsistencies

- Conduct shelf reviews for out-of-stock items every two hours.
- Minimize queues to two customers at any time

Stay solely focused on ideas that will drive the WIG. Don't drift into a general discussion of good things to do rather than things that will impact the WIG, or you will end up with a long list of irrelevancies.

A famous example of a productive lead measure is the 15 percent rule at 3M Company. For decades, this great company has held out the strategic WIG of creating a flow of great new products that never stops. To drive this goal, they adopted the lead measure of requiring their research teams to devote 15 percent of their time on projects of their own choice. The author Jim Collins comments:

"No one is told what products to work on, just how much to work. And that loosening of controls has led to a stream of profitable innovations, from the famous Post-it Notes to less well-known examples as reflective license plates and machines that replace the functions of the human heart during surgery. 3M's sales and earnings have increased more than forty-fold since instituting the 15 percent rule." [26]

The ideal lead measure, like 3M's 15 percent rule, is extremely fruitful in driving the WIG and is within the control of the team.

Step 2: Rank by Impact

When you're satisfied with your list of candidate lead measures, you're ready to identify the ideas that promise the greatest potential impact on the Team WIG.

In service of the hotel's WIG to increase profitability, the event management team has set this WIG: Increase Revenue from Corporate Events from $22 million to $31 million by December 31.

In a 4DX work session, Susan led her team in brainstorming lead measures for this WIG:

Now, Susan and her team narrowed the focus to three ideas that would have the greatest impact on achieving their Team WIG:

1. **Increase the number of site visits.** Susan's team knew from experience that whenever they could influence a customer to visit the hotel, their success at winning the contract for the event was significantly higher.

Event Management Team

WIG: Increase revenue from corporate events from $22 million to $31 million by December 31st.

Lead Measure Ideas

- Increase the number of site visits we conduct
- Develop contacts at new local corporations
- Explore additional opportunities for events with existing clients
- Attend trade shows for corporate events
- Develop and implement a new marketing program
- Improve our banquet food options
- Upsell our premium bar package
- Upsell our expanded audio visual package
- Generate more high quality proposals
- Join meeting planner associations and attend meetings
- Contact former clients lost to other hotels and win them back

2. **Upsell the premium bar package.** Since margins were highest on products in the premium bar package, every event that upgraded to this option increased not only revenue but profitability.

3. **Generate more high-quality proposals.** The proposal was the last step in the sales process, so the more often prospects advanced to this stage, the more likely they would buy. The idea was to make sure each proposal went through a checklist of winning quality standards.

WATCH OUT

After producing the list of candidate lead measures, we often hear team members say, "We need to do all of these things." No doubt they are all good things to do, but the more you try to do, the less energy you have to give to any one thing.

Additionally, narrowing the focus to a few lead measures permits stronger leverage. As we often say, "A lever must move a lot to move the rock a little." In other words, the team must press hard on the lead measure to move the lag measure. Too many lead measures, and you dissipate that pressure.

Step 3: Test Top Ideas

Once you've identified a couple of high-leverage lead measures, test them against these six criteria:

- Is it predictive?
- Is it influenceable?
- Is it an ongoing process or a "once and done"?
- Is it a leader's game or a team game?
- Can it be measured?
- Is it worth measuring?

IS THE MEASURE PREDICTIVE OF ACHIEVING THE WIG?

This is the first and most important test for a candidate lead measure. If the idea fails this test, even if it's a good idea, eliminate it and choose the next most impactful idea from the brainstorming list.

CAN THE TEAM INFLUENCE THE MEASURE?

By influence, we mean to ask if the team has at least 80 percent control over the measure. As in Discipline 1, this test eliminates significant dependencies on other teams.

These are candidate lead measures that Susan's event management team might have proposed as an alternative to uncontrollable lag measures:

THE 4 DISCIPLINES OF EXECUTION

Uninfluenceable Lag Measures	Influenceable Lead Measures
Raise food-and-drink profitability by 20%	Upsell premium bar package and improve banquet options
Win back former clients	Contact former clients lost to other hotels and generate persuasive proposals to re-sign
Book more conventions	Participate actively in the convention planning association monthly meetings

Remember, the ideal lead measure is an action that moves the lag measure and that the team can readily take *without a significant dependence on another team*.

IS IT AN ONGOING PROCESS OR "ONCE AND DONE"?

The ideal lead measure is a behavior change that becomes habitual and brings continuous improvements to the lag measure. Although an action taken once might bring temporary improvement, it is not a behavior change and has little effect on the culture of the team.

Here are some examples that might have been used by Susan's team and that illustrate the important differences this test reveals:

Ongoing process (Do This)	Once and done (Not This)
Ensure that every client is aware of our audio-visual capabilities and receives a customized set-up	Upgrade our entire audio-visual system
Maintain 100% compliance to the banquet table setting checklist	Holding a training session on the standards for setting up banquet tables
Attend all Chamber of Commerce meetings and contact all companies opening new locations in our city	Join the Chamber of Commerce

Although the once-and-done ideas can make a temporary difference—possibly a big one—only the behavioral habits the team develops can drive permanent improvements.

IS IT A LEADER'S GAME OR A TEAM GAME?

The behavior of the team must drive the lead measure. If only the leader (or one individual) can move the lead measure, the team will quickly lose interest in the game.

For example, a quality initiative requires the leader to audit the process frequently, and an outcome is continuously improving audit results.

If the proposed lead measure is more frequent audits, it fails this test because only the leader can do audits. But if the proposal is to respond in a timely manner to all audit findings, it becomes a team game. The actions to drive an audit score involve everyone on the team.

In the same way, candidate measures such as filling open positions, reducing overtime hours, or improving scheduling are usually examples of a leader's game in most organizations. Remember, lead measures connect the team to the WIG, but only if it's the team's game to play.

CAN IT BE MEASURED?

As we've said, lead-measure data is hard to get, and most teams don't have systems for tracking lead measures. But success on lag measures absolutely requires successfully tracking the lead measures.

If the WIG is truly wildly important, you must find ways to measure the new behaviors.

IS THE LEAD MEASURE WORTH MEASURING?

If it takes more effort than its impact is worth, or it has serious unintended consequences, it fails the test of a lead measure.

For example, one large fast-food retailer hired inspectors to visit each franchise regularly to measure compliance with the company's standards. The inspectors were widely considered to be spies. Team members felt disrespected. To the direct cost of hiring this army of inspectors, company leaders could add the cost of mounting distrust and sinking morale.

Ultimately, the lead measures developed by Susan's event management team passed all the tests. In the testing process, they discovered that nearly every site visit they conducted resulted in a successful proposal. So they decided to focus on conducting more site visits and following up with proposals.

Step 4: Define the Lead Measures

Answer these questions as you put the lead measures in final form:

ARE WE TRACKING TEAM OR INDIVIDUAL PERFORMANCE?

This choice will affect your scorekeeping, the design of your scoreboard, and, ultimately, how the team is held accountable. Tracking results for individual performers creates the highest level of accountability but also the most difficult game to win because it demands the same performance from everyone. Alternatively, tracking team results allows for differences in individual performance while still enabling the team to achieve the outcome.

ARE WE TRACKING THE LEAD MEASURE DAILY OR WEEKLY?

To reach the highest level of engagement, team members need to be able to see the lead measure scores moving at least weekly; otherwise, they will lose interest fast. Daily tracking creates the highest level of accountability because it demands the same performance from every associate every day, where weekly tracking allows for varying performance each day as long as the overall result for the week is achieved.

Here is an example of the *same lead measure* with individual and daily scoring, as well as daily and weekly tracking.

Individual Score	Team Score	
Engage 20 customers per Associate per day with a warm greeting and offer assistance	Engage 100 customers per day as a team with a warm greeting and offer assistance	Measured Daily
Engage 100 customers per Associate per week with a warm greeting and offer assistance	Engage 700 customers per week as a team with a warm greeting and offer assistance	Measured Weekly

These considerations should play a part in your decision making:

Individual Score	Team Score	
• Every team member must achieve the lead measure • Personal accountability is very high as tracking is done by person • Scorekeeping is very detailed	• The team can win even when individual members underperform • Results from high performers can mask those from low performers	Measured Daily
• Individuals can win for the week even if some daily goals are missed • The team wins only when every member performs • Scorekeeping is detailed	• The team can win for the week even when daily goals are missed • Results from high performers can mask those from low performers • The team wins or loses together	Measured Weekly

WHAT IS THE QUANTITATIVE STANDARD?

In other words, "How much / how often / how consistently are we supposed to perform?"

At Younger Brothers, the lead measure was 97 percent compliance with six safety standards. How did they arrive at 97 percent? How would you?

You decide based on the urgency and importance of the WIG. Remember that the lever has to move a lot to move the rock a little. If safety compliance is only 67 percent, going for 97 percent will move the rock a lot—and if lives and limbs are at stake, that rock *needs* to move dramatically. Choose numbers that challenge the team without making it an unwinnable game.

For example, in the Netherlands, every patient admitted to a hospital is swabbed for infection, a key lead measure for wiping out HAIs. Obviously, swabbing every patient consumes time and resources, but it can be managed. Other countries with a higher tolerance for HAIs, or perhaps less of a problem, might screen some but certainly not all patients: For them, zero HAIs is not a WIG.

Sometimes you discover the numbers through trial and error. A building-materials client sent two email blasts out every week before a sale, but got little response from the blasts. When they experimented with sending out three emails, they were flooded with business. There was something magical about three emails instead of two. Who knew?

If you'll be measuring an activity your team already does, it's essential that the level of performance go up significantly beyond where it is today. Otherwise, you'll be playing out a familiar definition of insanity: *Doing the same things you've always done, but expecting different results.*

WHAT IS THE QUALITATIVE STANDARD?

In other words, "How well are we supposed to perform?"

Not all lead measures have to answer this question. Still, the most impactful lead measures set the standard not only for how often or how many, but also how well the team must perform.

At Younger Brothers, the six safety standards are the qualitative component of the lead measure. For a team in a lean manufacturing facility, it might be compliance with value stream maps.

DOES IT START WITH A VERB?

Simple verbs focus the mind immediately on action.

WIG	Lead Measure
Make $2 million in new revenue by quarter end	*Complete* 500 more outbound calls per week
Raise our win rate on bids from 75% to 85% this fiscal year	*Ensure* all proposals achieve 98% compliance with our quality writing standards
Improve customer loyalty score from 40 to 70 within two years	*Achieve* 99% server availability each week
Increase inventory turns from 8 to 10 this year	*Send* 3 emails to contacts for every special offer

IS IT SIMPLE?

State your lead measure in as few words as possible. Eliminate opening explanations, such as "In order to achieve our WIG and to exceed the expectations of our customers we will . . ." What comes *after* the words "we will" is the lead measure, and it's all you need to say. A clear WIG statement captures most of what you would say in a prefacing statement anyway.

SPECIAL NOTE ABOUT PROCESS-ORIENTED LEAD MEASURES

Another way to identify powerful lead measures is to look at your work in the form of process steps, particularly if you already know that your WIG comes out of a process (examples would be a sales revenue WIG from a sales process, a quality WIG from a manufacturing process, or a project completion WIG from a project management process).

The example here is a basic eleven-step sales process.

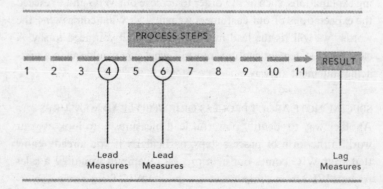

Processes always present the same challenges: Is the process getting us results? Are we even following the process? Do we have the right process?

Somewhere in every process there are leverage points, critical steps in the process where performance falters. If these leverage points become lead measures, the team can apply concentrated energy against them.

In this chart, the team has decided that a significantly better job on needs analysis (step 4) and business cases (step 7) would have the greatest impact on their results. They have made their bet.

The team now defines lead measures for these leverage points. They'll ask, "How do we measure whether a good needs analysis has taken place?" "How do we know we have a good business case?" This kind of lead measure is vastly more effective than proposing to improve an entire process all at once. In that case, the leader would spread their energy pushing change across the whole process, and the team would never break the old habits.

4DX gives a leader the ability to lock down the most critical points of a process and then move on to the next most critical points.

CAN PROJECT MILESTONES BE GOOD LEAD MEASURES?

If your WIG is a single project, your project milestones may be effective lead measures, but you'll need to evaluate them carefully. If the milestones are both *predictive* of project success (for a description of project lag measures, see page 131) and *influenceable* by the team, they can be good candidates. However, they must also be *significant* enough for weekly commitments to be made against them. The smaller or more granular the milestones are, the less opportunity for weekly commitments. A milestone that requires less than six weeks to complete is generally not significant enough to serve as a good lead measure.

Alternatively, if your WIG consists of multiple projects, your lead measures are more likely to be procedures that you are using to ensure success in all projects, such as the completion of formal scoping, functional requirements definition, project communication, or testing procedures. In this case, you should choose the *most predictive* and *influenceable* components of your project process as lead measures.

THE DELIVERABLE

The deliverable for Discipline 2 is a small set of lead measures that will move the lag measure on the WIG.

The final lead measures for Susan's team were clear—and challenging:

- Complete two quality site visits per associate per week.
- Upsell our premium bar package to 90 percent of all events.

Discipline 2 provides Susan with a clear, concise, and measurable strategy for improving her team's performance *and* delivering great results for the hotel.

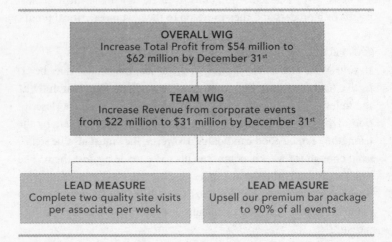

OVERALL WIG
Increase Total Profit from $54 million to $62 million by December 31st

TEAM WIG
Increase Revenue from corporate events from $22 million to $31 million by December 31st

LEAD MEASURE
Complete two quality site visits per associate per week

LEAD MEASURE
Upsell our premium bar package to 90% of all events

Discipline 2 is exciting for many teams, and with good reason. They have not only a clear WIG with a defined finish line, but also some carefully constructed lead measures for achieving the WIG; for many, it is the most *executable* plan they've ever made. They're confident they've done everything necessary to make it happen and that from here it's all easy.

They could not be more wrong.

Despite the beautiful game they've just designed, it will disappear into the whirlwind within days of the launch unless they go on to Discipline 3.

TRY IT

Use the Lead Measure Builder tool on the next page to experiment with creating lead measures for your WIG.

Lead Measure Builder Tool

1. Insert the Wildly Important Goal and lag measure in the top box.

2. Brainstorm ideas for lead measures.

3. Brainstorm methods for measuring those ideas.

4. Rank in order of impact on the WIG.

5. Test your ideas against the checklist on the facing page.

6. Write your final lead measures.

Ideas for lead measures	How to measure?	Rank

Final Lead Measures

Did You Get It Right?

Check off each item to ensure your team's lead measures will move the lag measure of the WIG:

☐ Have you gathered rich input on the lead measures from the team and others?

☐ Are the lead measures predictive—that is, the most impactful things the team can do to drive achievement of the Team WIG?

☐ Are the lead measures influenceable—that is, does the team clearly have the power to move the lead measure?

☐ Are the lead measures truly measurable? Can you track performance on the lead measures from day one?

☐ Are the lead measures worth pursuing? Or will the data cost more to gather than it's worth? Will these measures lead to unintended consequences?

☐ Does each lead measure start with a simple verb?

☐ Is every measure quantified—including quality measures?

Installing Discipline 3:
Keep a Compelling Scoreboard

Discipline 3 is the discipline of engagement. Even though you've defined a clear and effective game in Disciplines 1 and 2, the team won't play at their best unless they are emotionally engaged—and that happens when they can tell if they are winning or losing.

The key to engagement is a big, visible, continually updated scoreboard that is compelling to the players. Why do we put so much emphasis on the scoreboard?

In a recent FranklinCovey survey of retail stores, we found that 73 percent of the top performers agree with this statement: "Our success measures are visible, accessible, and continually updated." Only 33 percent of the bottom performers agreed with the statement. Top performers are thus more than twice as likely to see and interact with some form of compelling scoreboard so they can see if they are winning or not. Why is this so?

Recall three principles.

PEOPLE PLAY DIFFERENTLY WHEN *THEY* ARE KEEPING SCORE

People give less than their best and finest effort if no one is keeping score—it's just human nature. And note the emphasis: People play differently when *they* are keeping score. There's a remarkable difference between a game where the leader scores the team and a game where the players score each other. It means that the team takes ownership of the results. It's their game to play.

A COACH'S SCOREBOARD IS NOT A PLAYERS' SCOREBOARD

A coach's scoreboard is complex and full of data. A players' scoreboard is simple. It shows a handful of measures that indicate to the players if they are winning or losing the game. They serve different purposes. As leader you can guide, but you can't build a players' scoreboard without the involvement of the players.

THE PURPOSE OF A PLAYERS' SCOREBOARD IS TO MOTIVATE THE PLAYERS TO WIN

If the scoreboard doesn't motivate energetic action, it is not compelling enough to the players. All team members should be able to see it and watch it change moment by moment, day by day, or week by week. They should be discussing it all the time. They should never really take their minds off it.

In this chapter, you'll learn how to involve the team in creating a compelling scoreboard. You'll also see how different scoreboard designs drive different behaviors.

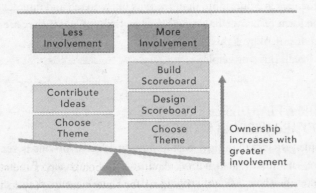

We've found that the more the team is involved in designing the scoreboard, illustrated in this graphic by giving the team more distinct responsibilities, the more the scale is tipped to instill their ownership.

Step 1: Choose a Theme

Choose a theme for your scoreboard that displays clearly and instantly the measures you are tracking. You have several options.

TREND LINES.

By far the most useful scoreboards for displaying lag measures, trend lines easily communicate *from X to Y by when.* The goat shows you where you should be now if you're planning to get Y by a certain time and, therefore, whether you're winning.

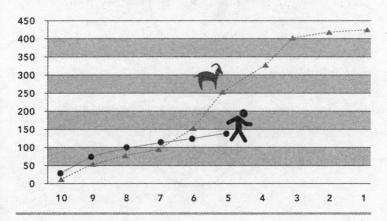

BEAT THE GOAT

WIG: Book 428 Exhibitors for
Outdoor Convention by Oct. 30

SPEEDOMETER.

Like an automobile speedometer, this scoreboard shows the status of the measures instantly. It's ideal for time measures (cycle time, process speed, time to market, retrieval times, etc.). Consider other common gauges such as thermometers, pressure meters, rulers, or scales.

BAR CHART.
This scoreboard is useful for comparing the performance of teams or groups within teams.

LEAD MEASURES

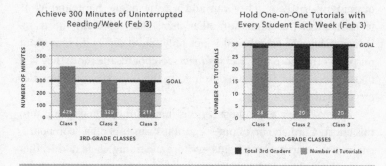

ANDON.

An andon chart consists of colored signals or lights that show a process is on track (green), in danger of going off track (yellow), or off track (red). This kind of scoreboard is useful for showing the status of lead measures.

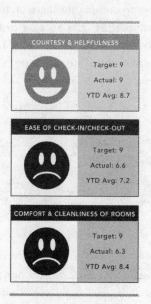

PERSONALIZED.

When team members can personalize the scoreboard, it's often more meaningful to them. They can add a team name, photographs of team members, cartoons, or other items that represent the team. Personalizing the scoreboard is not only fun, it serves an important purpose—the more they feel it's *their* scoreboard, the more they will take ownership of the results. Achieving the WIG becomes a matter of personal pride.

We've seen even the most serious-minded individuals jump into this effort. Cardiac nurses put surgical instruments on a scoreboard, engineers set up flashing lights, motorcycle-riding chefs add leather chaps. When the scoreboard becomes personal, they become engaged.

Step 2: Design the Scoreboard

Once you've determined the theme or type of scoreboard you want, the team should design the scoreboard with these questions in mind:

IS IT SIMPLE?

Resist the temptation to complicate the scoreboard by adding too many variables or supporting data such as historical trends, year-over-year comparisons, or future projections. Don't use the scoreboard as a communication board to post reports, status updates, and

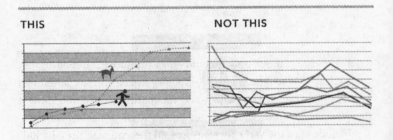

THIS   NOT THIS

Team members can immediately see if they're winning from the scoreboard on the left, but they would have to study carefully the scoreboard on the right to understand it—there are too many variables to interpret.

other general information that distracts the team from the results they need to see. In the midst of the whirlwind, simplicity is the key to keeping the team engaged.

CAN THE TEAM SEE IT EASILY?

Post the scoreboard where the team will see it often. The more visible the scoreboard, the more the team will stay connected to the game. If you want to motivate the team even more, post it where *other* teams can see it as well. If your team is dispersed geographically, the scoreboard should be visible remotely (more on electronic scoreboards in the chapter Automating 4DX).

DOES IT CONTAIN BOTH LEAD AND LAG MEASURES?

Include both actual results and target results. The scoreboard must answer not only Where are we now? but also Where should we be?

THIS		NOT THIS	
Planned Units End of May	105	Actual Units End of May	97
Actual Units	97		
Net Gain/ (Loss)	(08)		

If the team can see only the units they produce each month, they can't tell if they're winning or losing. They need to see the number of units planned—it also helps to do the math for them and show if they're up or down on the goal (net gain or loss).

Include both the WIG lag measure and the lead measures. Include legends and other minimal labels to explain the measures: Don't just assume that everyone knows what they are. (Remember, 85 percent of team members we surveyed could not name their most important goals!)

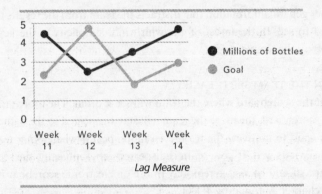

Lag Measure

Week	Unit 1	Unit 2	Unit 3	Unit 4	Unit 5	Unit 6	Unit 7	Unit 8	Unit 9
11		✓							✓
12	✓	✓		✓	✓		✓	✓	✓
13	✓	✓	✓	✓		✓	✓	✓	✓
14	✓	✓		✓	✓	✓	✓	✓	✓

Lead Measure

This team's WIG was to produce a certain number of bottles of water each week. The lead measure was to do maintenance on the bottling units on a strict schedule—as long as the bottling units were up and running, they could meet the goal.

When they noted a correlation between a drop in maintenance and a drop in production, they became more consistent about the lead measure and shot past the goal.

CAN WE TELL AT A GLANCE IF WE'RE WINNING?
Design the scoreboard so that in five seconds or less the team can determine whether they are winning or losing. This is the true test of a players' scoreboard.

Step 3: Build the Scoreboard

Let the team build the scoreboard. The greater their involvement, the better—they will take more ownership of it if they build it themselves.

Of course, the size and nature of your team will make a difference. If they have very little discretionary time, the leader needs to take more of a role in producing the actual scoreboard. Still, most teams embrace the opportunity to create their own scoreboard and often volunteer their own time for it.

Finally, it doesn't matter much what medium you use for the scoreboard. You can put up an electronic sign, a poster, a whiteboard, or even a chalkboard, as long as it meets the design standards discussed here.

Step 4: Keep It Updated

The design of the scoreboard should make it easy to update at least weekly. If the scoreboard is hard to update, you'll be tempted to put it off when the whirlwind strikes—and your wildly important goal will disappear in the noise and confusion.

The leader should make very clear:

- Who is responsible for the scoreboard.
- When it will be posted.
- How often it will be updated.

AN EXAMPLE

Let's follow Susan's event management team as they design and build a scoreboard.

Applying Discipline 1, they set a Team WIG to increase revenue from corporate events from $22 million to $31 million by December 31. They then applied Discipline 2 to identify two high-impact lead measures:

- Complete two quality site visits per associate per week.
- Upsell our premium bar package to 90 percent of all events.

With the game clearly defined, Susan and her team were now ready to build a scoreboard. They began by defining clearly on the scoreboard the WIG and lag measure:

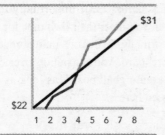

WIG

Increase revenue from corporate events from $22 to $31 million by December 31st

Next they added lead measure 1 with a detailed graph for tracking individual performance.

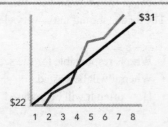

WIG

Increase revenue from corporate events from $22 to $31 million by December 31st

Lead Measure

Complete two quality site visits per associate per week

ASSOCIATE	1	2	3	4	5	6	7	AVG
KIM	1	1	2	2	4	X	X	2
BOB	2	2	3	2	X	X	3	2.4
KAREN	1	3	2	X	X	2	2	2
JEFF	0	0	X	X	1	1	1	.6
EMILY	3	X	X	4	3	2	4	2.8
RICHARD	X	X	2	2	2	4	4	2.8
BETH	X	1	2	5	2	4	X	2.8
TOTAL	7	7	11	15	12	13	14	2.3

Finally, they added lead measure 2 and a bar graph to track upsell attempts.

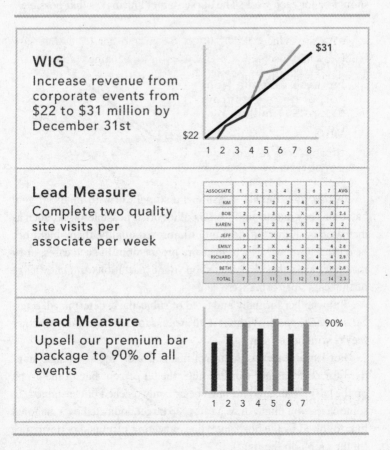

With the WIG on top and the lead measures clearly charted, Susan's scoreboard easily meets the design standards.

It's simple, not overloaded with data. It has only three major components, and each component is crystal clear and quantifiable.

It's visible, with large, dark fonts and easily grasped visuals.

It's complete. The entire game is shown. The Team WIG, its lag measure, and the lead measures are clearly defined. The team's actual performance versus the target is clear. The scoreboard is motivating because the team can see their actual results in relation to where they should be for each week: The darker target line makes that possible.

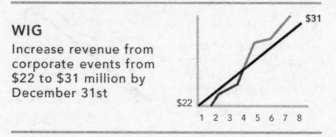

WIG
Increase revenue from corporate events from $22 to $31 million by December 31st

In this case, the lag measure is a straightforward financial goal based on the organization's WIGs. With other possible WIGs, such as increased customer satisfaction or improved quality, there might not be a predetermined way to measure progression. In such cases, draw the target line subjectively based on your expectations and knowledge of the team's performance.

But whether formally budgeted or subjectively determined, *a target line must appear.* Without it, the team can't tell day by day whether they're winning or not.

For lead measures, the target line is usually set as a single standard for performance (for example, the 90 percent bar in the graph on the left). That standard must be not only reached but sustained. In some cases, you might draw a ramp-up target, indicated by a diagonal line, followed by the horizontal line indicating sustained performance (in the graph on the right).

Lead Measure
Upsell our premium bar package to 90% of all events

Lead Measure
Upsell our premium bar package to 90% of all events

The lead measure to complete two quality site visits per associate per week required that the team's performance be reported individually. Each team member recorded on the scoreboard his or her own results each week.

ASSOCIATE	1	2	3	4	5	6	7	AVG
KIM	1	1	2	2	4	X	X	2
BOB	2	2	3	2	X	X	3	2.4
KAREN	1	3	2	X	X	2	2	2
JEFF	0	0	X	X	1	1	1	.6
EMILY	3	X	X	4	3	2	4	2.8
RICHARD	X	X	2	2	2	4	4	2.8
BETH	X	1	2	5	2	4	X	2.8
TOTAL	7	7	11	15	12	13	14	2.3

① Associates track their own performance.

② Associates update the scoreboard.

③ Leader audits performance vs. scoreboard and coaches where needed.

To ensure the credibility of the scoreboard, the leader periodically audits the performance of the team to validate that the scores being recorded match the level of performance observed. The rule here is trust, but verify.

WE CAN TELL IF WE'RE WINNING OR LOSING AT A GLANCE.

Because every graph displays both actual results and the target results, team members can instantly tell whether they are winning or losing on each lead measure as well as the WIG. The colors green and red, when used, can make it even easier to tell how they're doing.

WIG
Increase revenue from corporate events from $22 to $31 million by December 31st

Lead Measure
Upsell our premium bar package to 90% of all events

Note that with lead measure 2, the team wins only when every member performs. The team truly wins when everybody shows green (the lighter color in this chart), indicating completion of two or more site visits that week.

ASSOCIATE	1	2	3	4	5	6	7	AVG
KIM	1	1	2	2	4	X	X	2
BOB	2	2	3	2	X	X	3	2.4
KAREN	1	3	2	X	X	2	2	2
JEFF	0	0	X	X	1	1	1	.6
EMILY	3	X	X	4	3	2	4	2.8
RICHARD	X	X	2	2	2	4	4	2.8
BETH	X	1	2	5	2	4	X	2.8
TOTAL	7	7	11	15	12	13	14	2.3

THE DELIVERABLE

The deliverable for Discipline 3 is a scoreboard that keeps the team engaged.

There's a huge difference in performance between a team that knows about WIGs and measures *as a concept* and a team that actually knows the score. As Jim Stuart said, "Without clear, visible measures, the same goal will mean a hundred different things to a hundred different people." If the measures aren't captured on a highly visible scoreboard and regularly updated, the WIG will disappear into the distraction of the whirlwind. Simply put, people disengage when they don't know the score.

It's the sense of winning that drives engagement, and nothing drives results more than a team that is fully engaged—you'll see that every time you update the scoreboard.

By practicing Disciplines 1, 2, and 3, you've designed a team game that is clear and winnable, but that game is still on the drawing board. In Discipline 4, you put that game into action as everyone becomes accountable—*to each other*—for high performance.

TRY IT

Use the Scoreboard Builder Tool to experiment with scoreboards for your WIG.

Scoreboard Builder Tool

Use this template to create a compelling scoreboard. Test your ideas against the checklist on the facing page.

Team WIG	Lag Measure
Lead Measure 1	**Graph**
Lead Measure 2	**Graph**

Did You Get It Right?

Check off each item to ensure that the team scoreboard is compelling and will drive high performance:

☐ Has the team been closely involved in creating the scoreboard?

☐ Does the scoreboard track the Team WIG, lag measures, and lead measures?

☐ Is there a full explanation of the WIG and measures along with the graphs?

☐ Does every graph display both actual results and the target results *(Where are we now? Where should we be?)*?

☐ Can we tell at a glance on every measure if we're winning or losing?

☐ Is the scoreboard posted in a highly visible location where the team can see it easily and often?

☐ Is the scoreboard easy to update?

☐ Is the scoreboard personalized—a unique expression of the team?

Installing Discipline 4:
Create a Cadence of Accountability

Discipline 4 is the discipline of accountability. Even though you've designed a game that's clear and effective, without consistent accountability the team will never give their best efforts to the game. You might begin well, your team may have the best of intentions to execute, but before long the whirlwind will pull you back into a consuming cycle of reacting to the urgent.

Author John Case described this perfectly in an article in *Inc.* magazine:

> Managers put up whiteboards, chalkboards, and corkboards. They crank out data on defects per thousand, average time spent on hold, and dozens of other performance measures. You can't walk into a plant, warehouse, or office without seeing a metric or two charted on the wall.
>
> For a while, the numbers on the charts improve. People pay attention to the boards and figure out how to improve their performance.
>
> But, then, something funny happens. A week goes by when no one updates the scoreboard. Or maybe a whole month. Somebody finally remembers to enter the new numbers and notices there hasn't been much improvement. So nobody's eager to update the board the next time. Before

long, the boards fall into disuse. Eventually, they're taken down.

With hindsight, that outcome isn't so surprising. What gets measured does get done—but only for a while. Then questions arise: "Why are they always measuring us?" "Who really cares if we make those numbers, anyway?" "Are we still doing that?" A scoreboard can come to feel like a dreaded reminder of "something we should be doing but aren't."[27]

Discipline 4 breaks this cycle by constantly reconnecting team members to the game. More crucially, it reconnects them in a *personal* way. Because they are frequently and regularly accountable to each other, they become invested in the results and play to win.

When leaders hear about Discipline 4, they are understandably skeptical: "*Another* meeting—every week?" "Can you really accomplish that much in such a short meeting?"

After only a few weeks, these same leaders often tell us, as our biggest client did, "I thought another meeting was the last thing we needed. Now, it's the one meeting we won't cancel because it's the most important thing we do."

Discipline 4 asks teams to meet frequently and regularly in WIG sessions in which each member of the team makes *personal* commitments to drive the lead measures.

Because a WIG session might sound like just another quick meeting, you might see nothing much new about it. You're about to see that the cadence of accountability requires real skill and a degree of *precision* if you want your team to perform at the highest level.

WHAT IS A WIG SESSION?
A WIG session is unlike any other meeting you will ever attend.

It has a singular purpose: to refocus the team on the WIG despite the daily whirlwind. It takes place regularly, at least weekly, and sometimes more often. It has a fixed agenda, as illustrated in the model below:

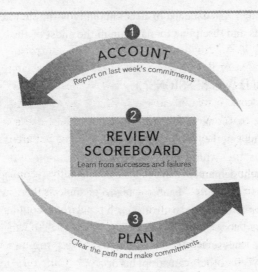

A WIG Session is a short, intense team meeting devoted to these three—and only these three—activities. The purpose of the WIG Session is to account for prior commitments and make commitments to move the WIG scoreboard.

1. **Account: Report on last week's commitments.** Each team member reports on the commitments to move the lead measures that he or she made the prior week.
2. **Review the scoreboard: Learn from successes and failures.** The team assesses whether their commitments are moving the lead measure and whether the lead measure is moving the lag measure. They discuss what they've learned about what works and what doesn't and how to adapt.
3. **Plan: Clear the path and make new commitments.** Based on this assessment, each member of the team makes commitments for the coming week that will raise the lead measures to the required level of performance. Because team members create the commitments themselves, and because they are publicly accountable for them to each other, they go away determined to follow through—it becomes *personally important.*

Although this cadence of accountability is simple in concept, it takes focus and discipline to maintain in the midst of the whirlwind.

WHY HOLD WIG SESSIONS?

- The sessions keep the team's focus on the WIG despite the constant whirlwind of other urgent demands.
- The sessions enable team members to learn from each other about how to move the lead measures. If one person succeeds, others can adopt his or approach. On the other hand, if a course of action isn't working, the team finds out early.
- The sessions give team members the help they need to keep their commitments. If someone runs into a barrier, the team decides how to clear the path.

WIG HUDDLES

Some teams, such as the emergency room team in an inner city hospital, with little to no discretionary time will need to hold an alternative meeting called a WIG Huddle.

WIG Huddles take place once each week for five to seven minutes with the entire team in a circle around the scoreboard where they do three things:

1. **Review the Scoreboard** – reinforcing their accountability for results.
2. **Report on Last Week's Team Commitment** – making a single team commitment to raise their performance.
3. **Make Commitments for the Coming Week**

- The sessions enable the team to adapt on the fly to the changing needs of the business. The session ends with a just-in-time plan that addresses challenges impossible to foresee through annual planning.
- The sessions provide an opportunity to celebrate progress, reenlist the energies of the team, and reengage everyone.

We started thinking hard about WIG sessions after learning from successful business leader Stephen Cooper. When Cooper took over a little company called ETEC in Silicon Valley, it was generating $1 million in red ink every month. Cooper set the WIG to increase revenues tenfold within seven years. To achieve that WIG, he asked each team to identify a few enabling goals with metrics and to reduce their plan to a single sheet of paper.

This exercise provided clarity for each team, but the real key to Cooper's ultimate success was his weekly reviews. He instituted three rules to keep those reviews fast and focused. "People should limit their status reports to four minutes. For each goal, people should cover objectives, status, issues, and recommendations. Finally, the reviews should encourage joint problem solving rather than just reporting."

One of Cooper's team leaders said of these weekly sessions, "[They] stop problems from becoming crises. . . . People have time to react in a comfortable manner instead of a chaotic manner. Each manager takes a few minutes to present and review progress charts, surface problems, and try to solve them. These routines help you to keep your eye on the ball. People move forward with a minimum of direction. It gives everyone their marching orders."[28]

Inspired by Cooper, we experimented for years with different formats for the WIG session. Today, it's a sleek and highly developed concept used by hundreds of organizations to advance their most important priorities.

WHAT HAPPENS IN A WIG SESSION?

To illustrate how a WIG session should work, let's look in on Susan's Event Management Team.

Remember that they have defined a team WIG—to increase revenue from corporate events from $22 million to $31 million by December 31—and two high-impact lead measures:

- Complete two quality site visits per associate per week.
- Upsell our premium bar package to 90 percent of all events.

And they have built a compelling scoreboard.

As Susan and her team begin their WIG session on Monday morning, they have just completed their third month of execution and their scoreboard is up to date.

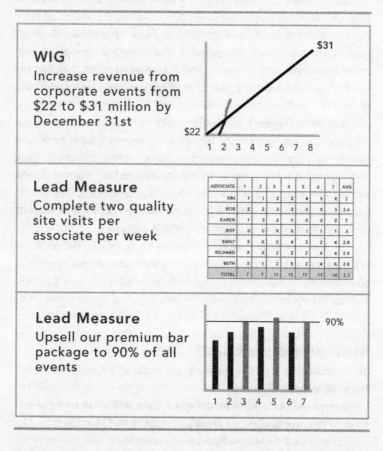

WIG
Increase revenue from corporate events from $22 to $31 million by December 31st

Lead Measure
Complete two quality site visits per associate per week

Lead Measure
Upsell our premium bar package to 90% of all events

Susan: *"Good morning everyone. It's eight-fifteen. Let's get started by reviewing the scoreboard."*

[Review the scoreboard.]

"We have good news today. We've just completed our third month of execution and we are above target for our team WIG of increasing

revenue from corporate events! Our lag measure score for last month is $14M against a target of $10.4M. Congratulations everyone.

"As you can see, last week we raised our site visits on lead measure 1 to a total of 14, our highest result in the past seven weeks. Congratulations to our top performers, Emily and Richard, who each completed four site visits.

"In addition, we hit our highest percentage of upselling so far on lead measure 2 with 95 percent of all events having been offered our premium bar package, but we've missed our percentage goal four out of the last seven weeks. While I know we're pleased with last week's percentage, we have work to do to demonstrate that we can sustain it."

[Report on last week's commitments.]

"Now, for my commitments, last week I committed to work with Kim and Karen for twenty minutes each on improving their upselling scripts for our bar package, as well as practicing their delivery. I completed this.

"I also committed to attend the Chamber of Commerce meeting and to capture at least three new corporate contacts that are not currently holding events at our hotel. I was very pleased to come back with contacts for five organizations, which I'll pass over to several of you this afternoon.

"For next week, I'll complete the final review of our new marketing materials for our premium bar package. Also, I'll interview three candidates for the open position on our team and make an offer to the one that best meets our requirements."

Kim: *"Last week I committed to have face-to-face meetings with two companies that have just opened new offices downtown and I did it. Good news—one of them is scheduled for a site visit next week!*

"On the scoreboard, I completed two site visits, but had an upsell conversation with only one of them, for a score of 50 percent, which I will improve next week.

"For next week, I will have a conversation, by phone or in person, with two of my clients who held their annual meeting with us last year, but haven't committed yet for this year. I want to schedule site visits for

them to see our new banquet room and, hopefully, convince them to sign up for this year."

Bob: *"My commitment last week was to create a special upsell experience for our premium bar package with the three clients that were scheduled for site visits, since they all represent large event opportunities. I did this by getting the chef to create a wine-tasting display, along with light hors d'oeuvres for each client. It went over really well and all three of them upgraded to the premium bar package for their events!*

"On the scoreboard, I had three site visits and had upsell conversations with all of them for a score of 100 percent.

"For next week, I only have one site visit scheduled so far, so I will contact at least five new prospective clients by the end of the day Monday and have at least one of them commit to making a site visit before the end of the week."

Karen: *"My commitment last week was to send a memories packet to ten of my clients who held events with us last year. In each packet, I inserted two or three photos from their event, plus the banquet menu they used, along with a handwritten note from me saying how much I hoped to see them again this year. I completed this and am really pleased to report that four of them called to thank me for the photos and two have agreed to site visits to see the new banquet room.*

"On the scoreboard, I had two site visits and discussed our premium bar package with both of them for a score of 100 percent.

"For next week, I'm going to create memories packets for five more clients from last year and send them out."

Susan's WIG session continues in this way until each member of the team finishes reporting. Note that they are accounting not only to Susan, but to each other for their follow through and for their results.

MAKE HIGH-IMPACT COMMITMENTS
FOR THE COMING WEEK

The effectiveness of the WIG session depends on the consistency of the cadence, but the *results* on the scoreboard depend on the *impact* of the commitments. You'll need to guide the team in making commitments that have the highest possible impact.

Start with this question: "What are the one or two most important things I can do this week to impact the team's performance on the scoreboard?"

Let's break down this question so you understand its significance to the WIG.

- **"One or two":** In Discipline 4, following through on a few high-impact commitments is far more important than making a lot of commitments. You want the team to do a few things with excellence, not a lot of things with mediocrity. The more the commitments, the less likely follow-through becomes. In this context, it's better to make two high-impact commitments and fulfill them exactly than to make five commitments and keep them badly.

- **"Most important":** Don't waste time on peripheral activities. Invest your finest attention and effort in those commitments that will make the biggest difference.

- **"I":** All commitments made in a WIG session are *personal responsibilities.* You're not committing other people to do things, you're committing to things *you* will do. Although you'll be working with others, commit to be accountable only for that part of the effort you can be personally responsible for.

- **"This week":** Discipline 4 requires at least a weekly cadence of accountability. Make only those commitments that can be completed *within the coming week* so that accountability can be maintained. If you commit to something four weeks in the future, then for three of those weeks you're not really accountable. If it's a multiweek initiative, commit only to what you can do this coming week. Weekly commitments create a sense of urgency that helps you stay focused when your whirlwind is raging.

- **"Performance on the scoreboard":** This is most critical: every commitment must be directed at moving the lead and lag measures on your scoreboard. Without this focus, you'll be tempted to make commitments to the whirlwind. While they might be urgent, these commitments will contribute nothing to the WIG.

If everyone answers this question precisely in every WIG session, the team will establish a regular rhythm of execution that will drive results.

Susan's WIG session produced commitments that will make that kind of difference:

- "Work with Kim and Karen for twenty minutes each on improving their upselling scripts for our bar package, as well as practicing their delivery."
- "Attend the Chamber of Commerce meeting and capture at least three new corporate contacts that are not currently holding events at our hotel."
- "Complete the final review of our new marketing materials for our premium bar package."
- "Interview three candidates for the open position on our team and make an offer to the one that best meets our requirements."
- "Complete face-to-face meetings with two companies that have just opened new offices downtown."
- "Create a special upsell experience for our premium bar package with the three clients that were scheduled for site visits."

- "Send a memories packet to ten of my clients who held events with us last year, along with a handwritten note."

Team members are more likely to take ownership of commitments they come up with themselves. Still, the leader should make sure the commitments meet the following standards:

- **Specific.** The more specific the commitment, the higher the accountability for it. You can't hold people accountable for vague commitments. Commit to exactly what you will do, when you will do it, and what you expect the outcome will be.
- **Aligned to moving the scoreboard.** Make sure the commitments move the scoreboard; otherwise, you're just committing more energy to the whirlwind. For instance, the week before your annual budget is due you might be tempted to make a commitment to complete the budget because it's both urgent and important. However, if the budget has little to do with the lead measures, it won't affect the WIG no matter how urgent it seems.
- **Timely.** High impact commitments must be completed within the coming week, but they should also impact the team's performance *in the near term*. If the real impact of your commitment is too far in the future, it won't help to build the weekly rhythm of winning.

This table illustrates the differences between low-and high-impact commitments:

LOW-IMPACT COMMITMENT	HIGH-IMPACT COMMITMENT
I will focus on training this week	I will work with Kim and Karen for 20 minutes each on improving their upselling scripts for our bar package, as well as practicing their delivery.
I will attend the Chamber of Commerce meeting	I will attend the Chamber of Commerce meeting and capture at least three new corporate contacts not currently holding events at our hotel.
I will do some interviews	I will interview three candidates for the open position on our team and make an offer to the one that best meets our requirements.
I will reach out to new clients this week	I will complete face-to-face meetings with two companies that have just opened new offices downtown.
I will call on old clients	I will send a "memories" packet to ten of my clients who held events with us last year, along with a handwritten note.

Note the great strength of commitments specifically aligned to moving the lead measures.

WATCH OUT

Avoid these common pitfalls that undermine the cadence of accountability.

Competing whirlwind responsibilities. This is the most common challenge you and your team will face when you begin applying Discipline 4. Don't mistake whirlwind urgencies for WIG commitments. An effective question for testing a commitment is "How will fulfilling this commitment impact the scoreboard?" If you struggle to answer the question directly, the commitment you're considering is likely focused on your whirlwind.

Holding WIG sessions with no specific outcomes. The cadence of accountability will collapse without disciplined adherence to the WIG session agenda. Every WIG session needs to account specifically for prior commitments and result in clear commitments for the future.

Repeating the same commitment more than two consecutive weeks. Even a high-impact commitment, if repeated week after week, becomes routine. You should always be looking for new and better ways to move the lead measures.

Accepting unfulfilled commitments. The team must fulfill their commitments regardless of their day-to-day whirlwind. When a team member fails to keep a commitment, regardless of all the work you've done to install 4DX, you face *the moment that matters most.*

If you can instill the discipline of accountability in your team, they will beat the whirlwind every week. However, if you're casual about accountability for commitments as well as for results, the whirlwind will overwhelm the wildly important goal.

Let's see how Susan handles this important moment in the WIG session:

Susan: *"Jeff, you're next."*

Jeff: *"Thanks, Susan. Well, I had committed to contact several of my clients from last year about a site visit, but as you all know, I also had a major event taking place in the hotel last week. Since this was my largest group of the year, I wanted to be sure that it was successful, so I gave them a lot of personal attention. And when the projector in the main ballroom crashed, I had to scramble to get another one. I spent a lot of time making sure the client wasn't upset and that things were back on track. Before I realized it, the week was gone and there just wasn't time."*

In essence, Jeff is saying that he couldn't keep his commitment because of his whirlwind; what's more damaging, Jeff believes that he *shouldn't* be held accountable for his commitment if his whirlwind is significant enough. This is where execution breaks down.

Most commitments we make are conditional. For example, when a team member says, "I'll have that report to you by nine Tuesday morning," what he really means is "Unless something urgent comes up." But something urgent *always* comes up—it's in the nature of the ever-present whirlwind.

If you let the whirlwind overwhelm your commitments, you'll never invest the energy needed to progress. The execution discipline starts and ends with keeping your WIG session commitments.

That's why Susan's job as the leader, particularly in the first few WIG sessions, is to set a new standard: Commitments are *unconditional.* As a client of ours says, "Whenever we make a commitment on our team, we know we have to find a way to make it happen, no matter what."

How should Susan respond?

Step 1: Demonstrate respect.

Susan: *"Jeff, I want you to know that the event last week was a huge success, and without you, it could have been a disaster. Everyone on this team understands how hard you worked and how important this client is to us. Thank you for everything you did."*

In this crucial first step, Susan shows Jeff that she respects him as a team member, but she also shows the team that she *respects the whirlwind.* If she skips this step, she'll send two incorrect messages: that Jeff is not valued and that the whirlwind is not important.

Step 2: Reinforce accountability.

Susan: *"Jeff, I also want you to know how important your contribution is to this team. Without you, we can't reach our goal. This means that when we make a commitment, we have to find a way to fulfill it no matter what happens during the week."*

This is a challenging moment for both Jeff and Susan; but because Susan has made it clear that she respects Jeff and the demands of the whirlwind, Jeff should be able to see the importance of doing his best *for the team.*

Step 3: Encourage Performance.

Susan: *"Jeff, I know you want to help us follow through. Can we count on you to catch up next week, by fulfilling last week's commitment as well as the one you were planning on making for next week?"*

Susan gives Jeff the opportunity to report with real pride that all commitments have been fulfilled.

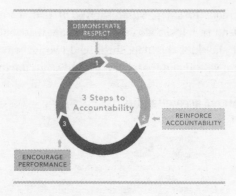

Bringing this important interaction to a successful close is very important. It's important to Jeff because he can now keep his commitment to the team. It's important to the leader because the team sees she's committed to the 4DX discipline. And it's important for the team to know that a new standard for performance is expected.

Without unconditional commitments, you can't drive the black into the gray. The gray whirlwind will simply fill in the black commitments. That's the story of execution breakdown.

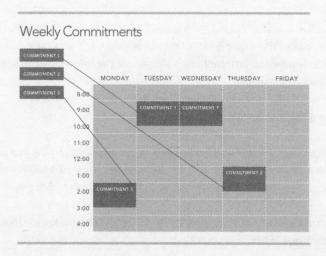

186

Hyrum Smith, one of the founders of FranklinCovey, has said, "If your entire paycheck was based on this one commitment, two things would happen automatically. You would be more careful in making the commitment, and you would be absolutely certain to follow through." This is the purpose of the WIG session: to make commitments intelligently and with the determination to keep them regardless of the whirlwind.

KEYS TO SUCCESSFUL WIG SESSIONS

- **Hold WIG sessions as scheduled.** Keep WIG sessions to the same day at the same time in the same place every week (including electronically), regardless of the whirlwind. If you're gone, delegate leadership of the session to another team member.
- **Keep the sessions brief.** Maintain a brisk and energetic pace. A rule of thumb: sessions shouldn't run more than twenty to thirty minutes. Take too long and the session risks turning into a whirlwind meeting.
- **Set the standard as the leader.** Begin every WIG session by reviewing the overall results on the scoreboard and then *reporting on your own commitments.* By reporting first, you show you're not asking anything of the team that you're unwilling to do yourself.
- **Post the scoreboard.** Update the scoreboard before the session and make sure it's present. You can't hold a WIG session without the scoreboard. It reconnects the team to the game and indicates what's working and what isn't. Without it, the WIG session is just another meeting.
- **Celebrate successes.** Reinforce commitment to the WIG by congratulating both the team and individual members on successfully keeping commitments and moving the measures.
- **Share learning.** Through the week people will discover what does and doesn't move the lead measures. They

will also discover that some measures work better than others. Everyone needs this information.

- **Refuse to let the whirlwind enter.** Limit discussion to commitments that can move the scoreboard. Defer dialogues about the whirlwind, the weather, morning traffic, or sports for other settings.
- **Clear the path for each other.** Remove obstacles for each other. Clearing the path does not mean passing a problem to someone else, but leveraging the strengths of the team. If you agree to clear the path for someone, it becomes one of your commitments for the week and requires the same follow-through as any other commitment.
- **Execute in spite of the whirlwind.** Hold team members unconditionally accountable for their commitments regardless of the whirlwind. If a commitment is missed one week, it must be accounted for the following week.

THE PAYOFF

We began this section of the book with the team at Store 334, who were faltering in their attempt to apply 4DX.

It just wasn't working.

One day, for example, Jim found only day-old bread on the bakery racks and nothing but cookie crumbs in the display case.

"Yolanda!" he called for the bakery manager. She appeared, covered with flour and simmering mad when he pointed at the scoreboard.

"I have too much to do to worry about that scoreboard," she retorted, hands on hips. "I got a big catering order that'll take all day. And I've got to do something about inventory 'cause I'm running out. There's just no time. I'm understaffed."

Sisyphus was alive and well. Despite all the effort choosing the WIG, the lead measures, the scoreboards, nothing had really changed in the store. We pinpointed the reason.

The 4th Discipline was completely missing.

There was no cadence of accountability.

There was no regular, weekly accounting to say, "Here's what I did *last* week, and here's what I'm going to do *this* week, to move that score." So, we pleaded with Jim to meet with the staff and ask each one this simple question: "What is the one thing you can do *this week* that would have the most impact on the scoreboard?"

Jim held his first WIG session the next day. He promised it would take only a few minutes around the store scoreboard. When the department heads gathered, Jim started with the bakery manager.

"Yolanda, what is the one thing, just *one* thing, you could do that would have the biggest impact on the store-conditions scoreboard this week?"

Surprised by Jim's earnest look, Yolanda asked, "You want *me* to choose?"

Jim nodded . . . and waited.

"I guess I could get the back room cleaned out."

"Okay. And how would that move the score on store conditions?"

"Well, it's kind of cluttered. I've got a lot of extra racks out on the floor. If I can get the back room cleaned up, I can get some of that stuff off the floor. It'd look better."

"Great. Just that one thing, Yolanda. That's it." Then he turned to the seafood manager. "Ted, what's the one thing you could do this week that would have the biggest impact on your store-conditions score?"

"I have a big promotion this week," Ted replied. "I'll be focused on the lobster special we are preparing for. That's what I'm doing."

"That's great, Ted, I know that's important and you need to do that, but how is that going to move the scoreboard?"

"Oh, I see what you're getting at." Something clicked for Ted. The special, while important, wouldn't by itself contribute to improving store conditions—the *wildly* important goal. "Yeah, okay. Bobby's been here three weeks and doesn't know how to set up the displays in the morning . . . I'll get him trained, and he can back me up."

"Perfect!" Jim responded.

Ask yourself—who was coming up with these ideas? Jim or his department heads? Do you think that makes much of a difference?

Was Jim micromanaging now? No! The staff members themselves were choosing what to do to move the score. He *had* been micromanaging, not because he wanted to be an overbearing boss but because he didn't know what else to do!

So, Jim's staff met every week around the scoreboard, committing to each other to do just *one* thing to move the score. As the team started working in rhythm, in a cadence of accountability to each other, their attitudes changed and the store changed.

After ten weeks, the average score on store conditions rose from thirteen to thirty-eight on the scale of fifty. Furthermore, their strategic bet paid off. As the scores on store conditions went up, so did the revenue.

Store 334—the worst of 250 stores—went on to out-produce the rest of the zone in year-over-year sales!

A few months later, we were invited to a debrief meeting with the president of Jim's division to hear Jim report on the progress of the store.

He told them, "Things are going so well I didn't even have to go in this morning."

The divisional president asked him, "What has this change meant to you personally?"

Jim replied, "I was going to carry this store on my back until I could get a transfer. Now, you can leave me there as long as you want."

Jim Dixon and his team now knew how it felt to win at a wildly important goal. They didn't need external motivation.

Deep down, everyone wants to win.

SCAN WITH YOUR SMART PHONE

Android - Barcode Scanner
iPhone - Red Laser

LINK: http://www.4dxbook.com/qr/334vid

Scan the image above to see a video about Jim Dixon and Store 334.

Everyone wants to contribute to goals that really matter. It's so disheartening to push and push day in and day out and wonder if you're making a difference. That's why 4DX is so vital. The people at Store 334 learned that. The disciplines make all the difference between just pushing that rock up the hill forever or taking it over the top.

THE DELIVERABLE

The deliverable for Discipline 4 is a regular, frequent WIG session that moves the lead measures.

But far beyond this, the ultimate outcome of Discipline 4 is a cadence of accountability that produces not only reliable results again and again, but also a high-performance team.

Discipline 4 requires real skill and a degree of *precision* in making and keeping important commitments.

Discipline 4 keeps your team *in* the game every week, as the members connect their personal contributions to the most important priorities of the organization. With this comes not only the awareness that they are winning on a key goal, but that they have become a *winning team*.

Which is the ultimate return on the investment you make in 4DX.

TRY IT

Use the WIG Session Agenda Tool on the next page to prepare for a session.

WIG Session Agenda Tool

Distribute this agenda electronically or on paper at the beginning of the WIG Session. After you hold the session, check it against the criteria on the facing page.

WIG SESSION AGENDA			
Where		When	
WIG(s)			
Individual Reports	Team Member	Commitment	Status
Scoreboard Update			

Did You Get It Right?

Check off each item to ensure that the WIG session will drive high performance:

☐ Are you holding WIG sessions as scheduled?

☐ Are you keeping the sessions brief, brisk, and energetic (twenty to thirty minutes)?

☐ Is the leader the model for reporting and making commitments?

☐ Do you review an updated scoreboard?

☐ Do you analyze why you're winning or losing on each measure?

☐ Do you celebrate successes?

☐ Do you hold each other unconditionally accountable for your commitments?

☐ Does each team member make specific commitments for the coming week?

☐ Do you clear the path for each other, finding ways to help team members who encounter obstacles to keeping their commitments?

☐ Do you keep the whirlwind out of the WIG session?

Automating 4DX

Now that we've reviewed the process for installing 4DX in your team, let's explore the powerful support and insight that automating 4DX can bring. In our experience, your chances of successfully implementing 4DX go way up if there are tools and automation to support it. For more information about how to implement the 4DX principles and tools to help you get started, go to team.my4dx.com.

The website also helps you answer these questions: *What percentage of people on my team or within my organization are updating their scoreboards, making weekly commitments against lead measures, and holding WIG sessions?* In this chapter, we will use the capabilities of this software to illustrate how technology can support and enhance your team's ability to produce results—capabilities that you will need, regardless of the technology you use.

LINK: http://www.4dxbook.com/qr/My4DXVid

Scan the image above to see a video that shows you how to use my4dx.com.

CAPTURING THE GAME

Any automated system should fully capture the game you've built in 4DX. In this chapter, we'll describe the five major components of your 4DX game you need from any system.

1. Your team's organizational structure and team members
2. Your WIG and "from X to Y by when" lag measure, as well as your week by week targets for performance
3. Your lead measures and their daily or weekly performance standard
4. Your team's commitments from last week and status on follow through, as well as commitments for next week
5. At-a-glance summary tracking of WIGs, lead measures, WIG sessions and commitments

Although most organizations are data rich, these things are rarely tracked; if so, they are spread across multiple systems so that the data can only be consolidated manually.

In keeping with Discipline 3, your team will develop a physical scoreboard designed to create both public accountability and team engagement. My4dx.com provides an electronic scoreboard for tracking the team's entire performance from the moment you start working on the WIG until you achieve it. More than this, my4dx.com also tracks individual commitments, which the scoreboard doesn't track.

The program ultimately provides you with an execution dashboard, so that you can monitor the entire WIG effort in detail. In my4dx.com, your execution dashboard looks like this:

Let's review the main features of your execution dashboard, using the example of Susan's event management team from the previous chapters.

4DX COMPONENT #1:
The leader and each team member, with specifics about their role, as well as elements of personalization such as photos.

First, notice that the dashboard is specific to Susan and her team. Although many teams in your organization may be using the soft-

196

ware, *each team has its own unique dashboard.* On the upper left you see Susan's name, along with the names of her team members.

4DX COMPONENT #2:
The WIG, a lag measure (X to Y by when), and targets for week-to-week performance.

Moving to the right on the dashboard, you see the WIG for Susan's Team: "Increase revenue from corporate events from $22 million to $31 million by December 31." The only way to tell if you're winning or losing on your Team WIG is to know the score. My4dx.

com displays your lag measure in terms of dollars, percentages, or numbers to create clear accountability.

Each week, the team can record not only their actual performance, but also that performance against their target for the week. This enables the team to instantly answer the questions: *Where are we now? Where should we be now?* From the execution dashboard you can instantly see that Susan and her team are winning at their team WIG, both from the numbers and from the status color green.

4DX COMPONENT #3:
The lead measures, and targets for week-to-week performance.

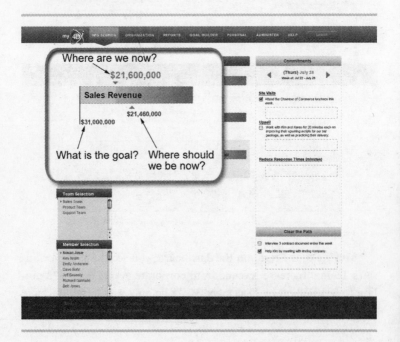

For each lead and lag measure you see only what you need to know. You know where you are now, where you should be, and where you ultimately have to get to. Based on where you are relative to where you should be the indicator is green, yellow, or red. Continuing to the right, you see the two lead measures Susan's team is acting on to drive achievement of their team WIG.

- Complete two quality site visits per associate per week.
- Upsell our premium bar package to 90 percent of all events.

The actual results on the lead measures are entered each week, so the team knows if they are winning or losing on them, and—what's even more important—if the lead measures are *predictive* of moving the lag measures.

From the execution dashboard you can see that Susan and her team are performing well on the lead measure of site visits but are below their target for upsells.

Knowing these things, Susan and her team are now prepared to make commitments that will move the scores on both their lead measures, and ultimately, their team WIG.

> **4DX COMPONENT #4:**
> *Enter commitments and indicate whether those commitments were fulfilled.*

Team members can look back at the commitments they made last week and account to the team for their follow-through. In this example, fulfillment of the commitment is indicated by the check box beside the commitment.

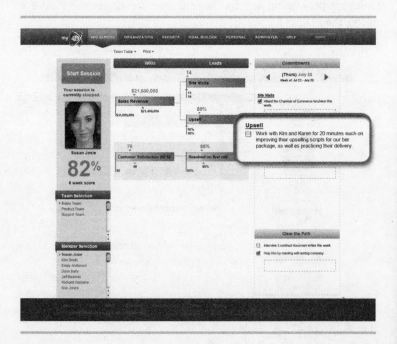

Team members can also make commitments for the coming week to move the scores even further. In the image on the previous page, you can see the expanded view of one weekly commitment for Susan.

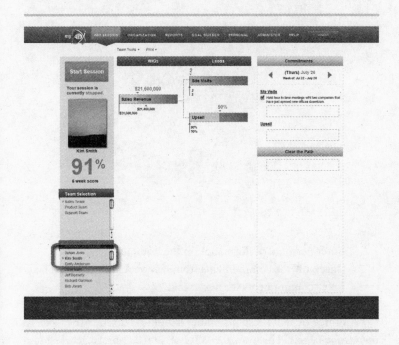

Now, all the components of Susan's game are captured in one location, making the team's overall performance easily and quickly understood.

THE WIG SESSION
Each week, Susan's team meets for their thirty-minute WIG session, using the cadence we've described above.

Prior to the session, each member of her team has three important responsibilities:

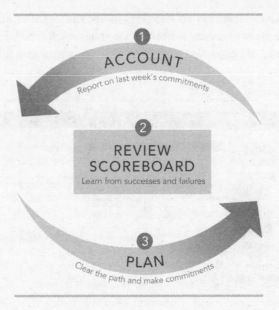

1. Enter personal performance on the lead measures.
2. Check off the commitments from last week that were fulfilled.
3. Enter commitments for next week.

All three of these responsibilities should be taken care of *before the session begins.* This way, the WIG session can move at a fast clip while still providing significant personal accountability as each team member's results are displayed one by one during the meeting.

For example, in the last chapter we read that Kim reported the following results.

Kim: *"Last week I committed to having face-to-face meetings with two companies that have just opened new offices downtown and I completed that. Good news—one of them is scheduled for a site visit next week!*

"On the scoreboard, I completed two site visits, but only had an upsell conversation with one of them for a score of 50 percent, which I will improve next week.

"For next week, I will have a conversation, by phone or in person, with two of my clients who held their annual meeting with us last year, but have not yet committed for this year. I want to schedule site visits for them to see our new banquet room and, hopefully, convince them to re-sign for this year."

While Kim is reporting, Susan advances my4dx.com to display Kim's results.

In this same way, all members of Susan's team can see their individual results displayed as they report on them verbally. At the end of the meeting, Susan once again shows the results for the entire team and offers any final guidance or recognition.

If Susan's team worked in different locations, or if any member were away during the meeting, everyone could easily access my4dx .com through the Internet and view the same display as if they were in the room with the team. This is particularly effective for maintaining accountability with teams that are dispersed geographically; in these situations, the software also serves in place of a physical scoreboard.

AUTOMATING 4DX ACROSS THE ORGANIZATION

We've intentionally limited the discussion of technology supporting 4DX to those capabilities that are most essential to you and your team. For more information, you can visit team.my4dx.com.

> **4DX COMPONENT #5:**
> *At a glance summary tracking on WIGs, Lead Measures, WIG Sessions and Commitments*

However, let us emphasize that the need for automation is even more vital when multiple teams within an organization are launching

4DX. Without these capabilities for at-a-glance assessment of process adoption and results, it will be difficult, if not impossible, to effectively drive results.

To meet this requirement, you will need summary reporting that is graphics based and that instantly shows the execution dashboard for the entire organization. An example of this type of reporting is the Team Status Report from my4dx.com:

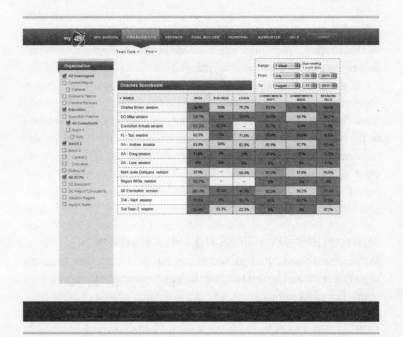

This report, which shows the execution dashboard as one line per team, contains the following information:

Sessions Held: As a percentage, how many team members are attending WIG sessions?

Commitments Made: How many team members are making weekly commitments?

Commitments Kept: How many commitments are executed?
Lead Measures: Where are the lead measures in relation to where they should be?
WIGs: Where are the lag measures in relation to where they should be?

Red, green, and yellow status signals enable you to see in only a few seconds if you're winning or losing for your entire organization.

From an organizational perspective, the leader's job is to "get the red out," starting from the right with WIG sessions and moving to the left toward achieving the WIGs themselves. If this scoreboard is entirely green, all teams in your organization are following the 4DX process fully and achieving the results you set out to get. If participation rates are high but execution percentage rates are low, it means people are making a good effort to identify the activities that drive their scoreboards but are not following through. Leaders can zero in on areas of execution deficiency and provide support.

We believe that two of the greatest drivers of success in 4DX are simplicity and transparency, and with the right technology, you can have both. This means getting a clear line of sight across the organization and showing results for every team in real time. It also means seeing the status of WIGs from the top level to the frontline teams, including everyone's lead and lag measures. Most important, you can see instantly where you're winning and where you're losing.

Section 3

Installing 4DX in
Your Organization

In section 1 of this book, you learned about the 4 Disciplines of Execution as an operating system for achieving the goals you must achieve. Section 2 was about installing 4DX in a work team.

We now want to expand our scope to installing 4DX in an organization made up of more than one team, whether you're a small business or a multinational corporation or something in between.

In section 3, you'll find out what some outstanding leaders have accomplished with 4DX. They will tell you how 4DX has actually transformed not only individual work teams but entire corporations and major agencies of government into high-performance organizations. Their experience shows that 4DX is not just another program, but a transformative operating system for any organization.

Here you'll also learn the specific steps for focusing people on WIGs and rolling out 4DX across the entire organization. The FAQ chapter provides answers to the questions people most frequently ask us.

Like section 2, this section is designed to be a field guide for leaders. Turn to section 3 whenever you need direction and insight into the great challenge of moving a whole organization to execute with excellence.

Best Practices from the Best

Throughout this book, we've presented concepts and methods for implementing the 4 Disciplines, which represent the best of all we've learned when working with thousands of leaders. However, without the opportunity to hear from some of these leaders and to read their own stories in their own words, this book would not be complete.

In this chapter we have chosen four leaders, not only because they are each exceptional in their skills and experiences, but also because they have utilized the 4 Disciplines to achieve extraordinary results, often on a very large scale. These stories show a real-world view of the challenges and the rewards that can be achieved when your team applies these powerful principles, providing a perspective that can be conveyed fully only by those who have implemented them.

ALEC COVINGTON AND NASH FINCH
Alec Covington is President and Chief Executive Officer of Nash Finch, the second-largest publicly traded wholesale food distributor in the United States in terms of revenue, serving the retail grocery industry and the military commissary and exchange systems. Annual sales are approximately $5.0 billion.

The team at Nash Finch implemented the 4 Disciplines of Execution and in only six months produced remarkable results. The following are Alec's insights into 4DX, as well as his description of that experience.

> We've now come through more than six months of implementing the 4 Disciplines and as I look at the results, I can only say it's absolutely fantastic. In fact, it's almost unbelievable how well our team has performed against their WIGs; the process has been followed, the meetings have been conducted as they should have, the regular updates have been there, and finally, the scoreboards are exciting, easy to read, and easy to understand. Today, we have a great story to tell about how our leaders are using the 4 Disciplines to make a difference and leave their fingerprints on our company.
>
> Over my years in this business, I've said many times that, in the absence of a crisis, transformative change is almost impossible. When you walk into a business that's a few days away from bankruptcy, you automatically have everyone's attention. Customers are worried, employees are worried about whether they're going to have a job, vendors are worried about how are they going to get paid, or even *if* they are going to get paid. Because of this uncertainty, customers are willing to change and employees are willing to do things differently. And they are willing to do it today, not tomorrow. So, the crisis gives you full alignment on the sense of urgency and you immediately narrow your focus. Even if you have a hundred problems, you know that you can't possibly solve them in the time that it takes to solve a crisis. That's why a crisis is actually a catalyst for change.
>
> But, when the crisis is over, the next challenge is charting the long-term path. I always dread that period, because it's the one that creates all the frustration, all the stress, and all the disappointments. During that period, the whirlwind always outweighs the strategic plan. It's not a phenomenon that's unique to Nash Finch; it's been true in every company I've been with.

Despite these challenges, we've been able to move our strategic agenda forward, but it's required a different approach in the absence of a crisis. And as we began to implement the 4 Disciplines, it allowed us to have an organized approach that replaced the sense of urgency created by a crisis. The 4 Disciplines allowed us to do what we did when we were having a crisis: focus on only the most important things and drive them forward. And it's worked beautifully.

Now, as we continue to engage in this process and learn more about it, it's become part of our DNA, part of our culture. Today, I can walk into a meeting unrelated to the 4 Disciplines and I will still hear someone in the meeting say, "What's the X to Y by when?" It's a beautiful program that has been deployed well by Nash Finch—one that will chart the path of change within our company for many years to come.

Today we understand our progress, as well as the rest of the way forward. We know what we need to do to achieve our WIGs and land this plane safely. We're also asking, "What will the new WIGs be for next year?" The 4 Disciplines have literally become a part of how we run our business.

We're also celebrating the success that we've had here. We know that we can't leave celebration and fun behind. If we do, we'll be missing one of our building blocks. The 4 Disciplines work perfectly when we combine them with celebration and fun, both for the successes we have and for those individuals and teams that are excelling in that process.

When I travel to facilities and don't see banners celebrating things that have been accomplished, I always ask, "Why?" The answer is always because we're too busy with our whirlwind. But now, we have a new agenda, the 4 Disciplines, along with our WIGs and WIG sessions. In the haste of getting all those things done, we now make sure that we don't fall short on celebration and fun. And you see it in the banners.

I also want to add that I'm a leader who knows that he can't manage everything, so I look for one or two key indicators that can tell me what's really going on in the business. My lead indicator for the 4 Disciplines is the attendance at and consistency of the WIG sessions. That's the only question I ever ask because I believe that if people are engaged, and they're consistent about the meetings and the reports, eventually peer pressure will take over and the rest of the process will take care of itself. It all revolves around participation and engagement.

The second indicator I watch for is how prepared people are in the WIG sessions. And do you know how I gauge that? By how long they last. WIG sessions are designed to be short, concise meetings that move the teams forward. If they're taking too long, something's not working.

You see, most companies have meetings so the leaders can report on how well they did against a goal or an objective that the senior leaders gave them. It's as if the powerful people on high write the tablets in stone, pass them down throughout the company, and then ask you to come in once or twice a year on how well you did. Inspiring, isn't it?

The question we need to be asking is what really have been the results of running things this way. Not much. What the 4 Disciplines allow you to do is to make a major paradigm shift, one in which the senior leaders simply say to the organization that we want to grow and we want to move forward by this much through our WIGs with X to Y by when. Then the leaders and teams that make up the company decide what the team WIGs and lead measures are to achieve them. *They* decide the key elements of how we track progress. The real difference here is that the leaders are then reporting on their own goals, instead of the ones given to them from above.

Today, with the 4 Disciplines, our people talk about the things *they* decided to do, the time frame in which *they* decided to get them done, and the progress *they* made toward their own goals. Corporate America is all about asking people to perform to achieve somebody else's goals; but if it comes down to making or missing *your* goal, that's when the creative juices start flowing. Achieving a corporate budget will never be as important as achieving goals that you set for yourself and keeping commitments that you made for yourself. It's amazing how different the behavior is. This is powerful stuff.

In our company, I don't think we have any bad people; they're all just wonderful. But sometimes they're wonderful people that have been with the company twenty, thirty, or more years, and they just can't get over the fact that we have to make changes. One way of working has to go, and new methods and processes have to come in. For some people, we just can't figure out a way to sell or convince or otherwise make them understand that things have to change. With the 4 Disciplines, you have a process that makes clear what needs to change and it helps hold everyone accountable for accepting and adapting to those changes. It also lets you take the learnings from one way of working and apply them to other parts of the business.

I remember running my first warehouse when I was in my twenties. I didn't understand much about how a warehouse operated because I grew up as a store manager and didn't learn about warehousing until I got involved in the distribution business. I remember walking through the warehouse one day when something caught my eye. Two employees were on break and were playing checkers, and that bothered me. I sat down with the two guys and said, "I'm delighted that you're playing checkers, but why are you playing checkers now?" They said, "We're on our break and this is what we look forward to every day." Do you know what bothered me about that? It was that the work was so boring the only thing these guys could look forward to was playing checkers.

Years later, I was walking through a different facility and I saw a big upright piano. When I asked what an upright piano was doing in the middle of the manufacturing plant, I was told to wait a few minutes and I would see. Soon after, a bell rang and all the employees gathered around the upright piano to sing songs from their Russian homeland. I thought, wouldn't it be something if you could channel that energy and connect it to the business? Instead of singing for fifteen minutes, what if the enthusiasm was about the business?

Today, as I walk through some of our facilities since we've implemented the 4 Disciplines, I see the equivalent of checkers and the upright piano for our employees. They are having fun. They are engaged. It's their checkers; instead of coming to work every day and just pulling cases, they come to work with meaning. More important, they're working on things they can understand. It's not EBITDA, and it's not revenue, and it's not earnings per share. It's how many cases can we select in an hour? It's focusing on things that connect with their world that allows them, in addition to doing their work, to have some element of fun and feeling of accomplishment. This is what makes the 4 Disciplines powerful all the way through the company. When we can do those kinds of things, it's very powerful.

Another thing that I would encourage you to think about, as you're engaged with the 4 Disciplines, is to look for future leaders as you attend WIG sessions. You'll see people that are growing up in your organization, that are becoming leaders. Maybe today they drive forklifts, maybe they receive trucks, or maybe they're inventory control people, but through this process you're going to see them firsthand.

Now, I can't say that without also looking at the other end of the spectrum, because the WIG session doesn't just identify the people that are doing exceptionally well; it also identifies the people who are not showing up for the meetings and who are not making their commitments. These are people that are holding you back, the ones who are keeping you from reaching your goals.

Ultimately, the 4 Disciplines of Execution will enable you to identify, promote, protect, and retain the people who are accomplishing their goals. And it will help you identify those who are not.

The greatest results we've seen are coming from teams that have the most vivid and the most recognizable scoreboards that can be easily understood by the broadest group of people. When we walk into some of these warehouses it's amazing to see how creative people are. Out of a hundred employees, somebody will be an artist. We've proven that over and over again. If you have a problem, take a look at your scoreboard and ask yourself these questions: Is it visible? Does it really connect with the people that need to see the score? Is it simple and easy to understand? Did the people who are going to use it help create it, or was it created for them?

A scoreboard is a very powerful thing. Some of the ones you'll look at might seem like the goofiest things in the world, but they may also be the most powerful, because they mean something to the people that need to see them every day. It doesn't matter that you don't like it. It really doesn't.

The last advice that I would offer is that when you celebrate your accomplishments, don't thank the senior leaders. Please. The senior leaders didn't do anything. I've never seen a single WIG that was accomplished by a senior leader. Let me tell you the way it really works. The senior leaders found the tool. They owned up to the fact that things weren't working and found a process that would help. But it's the leaders and teams down in your organization that embraced it, learned it, used it, and delivered remarkable results. The senior leaders don't need to be thanked. The senior leaders need to thank the leaders and teams down on the front line.

At the end of the day, senior leaders are like golf caddies. If the leaders on the front line tell you they need a nine iron, your job is to give them a damn good nine iron. If they need a new driver, your job is to get them one that will hit the ball farthest. And that's exactly what happens with the 4 Disciplines.

This program has provided a means by which we can pitch the ball and, because of the disciplines and the organization around it, we can actually know that the ball is going to be caught by someone who's accountable on the other side. It's beautiful. It's also provided a means for leaders and teams to get the ball and run with it—to be held accountable for it, but also to be recognized when they do a great job. It's very powerful.

DAVE GRISSEN AND MARRIOTT INTERNATIONAL, INC.

Dave Grissen, President of the Americas for Marriott International, began by implementing the 4 Disciplines in eight pilot hotels. These eight hotels produced results so significant that Dave and his team went on to conduct two progressively larger pilots and ultimately implemented the 4 Disciplines in more than seven hundred Mar-

Scan the image above to see a case study video of Marriott.

riott hotels over the next two years, which is one of the largest and most significant implementations of the 4 Disciplines worldwide.

The following are his insights, as well as his description of that experience.

Let me start by explaining that Marriott, a leading hospitality company, has nearly thirty-seven hundred properties across the globe and approximately one hundred twenty-nine thousand employees in company-operated hotels. The Marriott family established the core values and culture of the organization eighty-five years ago, which are instilled in the employees today. J. Willard Marriott believed that if you take care of your employees, they will take care of your guests, and the guests will come back. The spirit of service reflected in this philosophy is the cornerstone of the company's strong culture, high employee satisfaction, and continued growth. We continue to look for ways to innovate and improve our operations, while enhancing our culture.

Therefore, as soon as I heard about the 4 Disciplines of Execution, I thought it was perfect for our business. It was almost as if someone had watched our operation and designed a process that was customized for exactly what we needed. The best evidence of this is that it's one of those processes that people run toward instead of away from. In fact, we have yet to ask a single hotel to participate; they all come to us and ask to be part of it.

We began our implementation of the 4 Disciplines with eight pilot hotels. By the end of the pilot, every one of them had achieved remarkable results. Perhaps the best example comes from our largest company-operated hotel, the Marriott Marquis in New York City. In the first year of implementing the 4 Disciplines, the team achieved the highest guest satisfaction scores in this great hotel's thirty-year history. Along with this achievement, they also recorded their highest ever results in both revenue and profit. As most leaders know, achieving record results in sales, profit, and the satisfaction of your customers in the same year is quite an achievement.

Based on this success, we then made the decision to implement the 4 Disciplines in over seven hundred hotels in North and South America in pursuit of a *wildly important goal* to become the preeminent lodging company on both continents. We began by establishing a team of experienced leaders within Marriott who would form the core of our infrastructure and who would provide guidance and accountability in partnership with FranklinCovey. Establishing this internal team was an important investment for us, and once that was in place, we were then ready to systematically implement the 4 Disciplines in each of the hotels in our major markets. As you can imagine, this was a large-scale effort, one that required a significant investment from our leaders at every level. But in city after city, the leaders were not only committed, they were passionate about the power of these disciplines and their ability to use them to achieve their wildly important goals.

Over a two-year period, we certified almost four thousand leaders and completed the implementation of the 4 Disciplines in over seven hundred hotels, as well as in our national sales teams and many of our centralized corporate teams, such as human resources and information technology. During this time, about ten thousand employees began using the process and recorded one million commitments toward our wildly important goals. This illustrates the high level of engagement and dedication to the process, as well as the scope of the implementation.

While our plans for further implementation continue, we can now see clearly that the 4 Disciplines of Execution have given us an operating system for focusing large numbers of people on very precise goals and sustaining that focus until they are achieved. This execution platform allows hotels to create their own targeted goals aligned to the company's vision. With this clear vision, employees understand how their day-to-day activities relate to the company's overall business results. And, they feel that they are working toward a common goal. As a result, we have a level of adaptability, focus, engagement, and reporting that is unique in our industry.

As I look back and think about the advice I might offer to other leaders reading this book, I want to offer a few key lessons that I believe are important.

First, design your implementation to fit your culture. While the 4 Disciplines will work in any culture, the method of implementation will vary based on the unique attributes of your organization and your people, and what resonates best with them. In our culture, if I had simply mandated the implementation of the 4 Disciplines at every hotel, it would not have worked. While this might have been the most efficient method, in our culture what was really needed was buy-in. To help us gain this, we had the leaders from the eight original pilot hotels, many of whom have decades of experience with us, gather with leaders from the other hotels at a regional meeting. When the general managers from each of the pilot hotels stood up and acknowledged that the 4 Disciplines had brought their team a better way of focusing and achieving results, it was priceless. And, when they said, "We'll never go back to the way we executed before," it became contagious.

As a leader, you're always tempted to implement the ideas that you believe in most passionately. However, what you must realize is that if you offer the 4 Disciplines as just another good idea, you won't generate the level of commitment needed to be successful. We've all implemented ideas where it seemed that we had buy-in initially, but later realized that the organization simply allowed them to die a quiet death. This doesn't happen because people are against the idea, it happens because they're busy in their whirlwind. Generating buy-in takes longer, but the result is that it really works. You can mandate speed to market of any new program, but the real test is, are they doing it? With the 4 Disciplines, taking additional time to implement it well will result in a more successful rollout and greater results.

Second, realize that it's harder to implement the 4 Disciplines in an organization that's already very successful. When you're failing, it's easy to help your team see their burning platform and, as a result, their need to change. But, when you have an organization that's been really successful for many years, it's harder for them to see why they should try something new. They are also more likely to challenge the validity of new ideas. Leaders who are struggling are ready to accept anything that will help them. Leaders who are succeeding need the time and opportunity to assess an idea on their own and test its worth. The pilot results coupled with our service culture and belief that success is never final helped cultivate this leadership buy-in. Understanding your culture, leaders, and how to implement new ideas is another aspect of why a careful rollout is essential.

Third, the senior leader must focus on holding all leaders accountable. In other words, once they're in, they have to be all in. To do this well, you need the tools, such as reporting systems and regular accountability that the 4 Disciplines and the software (my4dx.com) provide. When the leaders who report to you understand that this is important enough for you to watch every week, they will see that it's real and that it's not going away. The system rolls up to me, and each week I'm reviewing performance. The clearest way you demonstrate that this is how we now execute is by holding them accountable for the results. As soon as you let one leader off the hook, everyone else gets the message and their focus starts to decline. The transparency of the system helps with this since all senior leaders, including me, can view the details at the hotel level. Even leaders who are passionate and committed need the extra pressure of accountability to help them stay focused when their whirlwind is raging.

Fourth, make sure you have the infrastructure to support your implementation. If your implementation is small, having one or two 4 Disciplines coaches may be enough. For the size and speed of the rollout we were planning, I knew that without a sufficient infrastructure we couldn't be successful. Making this level of investment up front is never easy. It requires people of real talent. We chose very experienced people, leaders who had operational experience in our hotels and who had the credibility to influence others and get the job done. Looking back, this was one of the most important decisions we made.

In addition to talented leaders implementing the 4 Disciplines, we also knew that we needed the right tools, systems, and training to support the effort. We branded the program to show our company's commitment to this process and make it part of the culture. We also designed and built reporting tools to track participation and results and used virtual training. Since we were launching across fifteen countries in multiple languages, we needed different training methodologies to implement the program in the desired time frame and ensure speed to market.

Fifth, remember that implementing the 4 Disciplines will raise the engagement of your team. Since I began by emphasizing the importance of understanding your culture, I'll come full circle by emphasizing that the 4 Disciplines can take even a very strong culture, such as the one that we enjoy, to an even higher level. Because each individual on the team sees the impact of their performance on the team's scoreboard every week, they are not only accountable, but are also engaged. They can clearly see that what they do each day really matters. While this has always been true in our company, implementing the 4 Disciplines has helped us to strengthen this level of engagement. As I have stated, each employee has a clear vision of the goals, which are tied directly to our core values. Everyone from our front-line staff to our management teams to our COOs understand how what they are doing impacts the company. And this gives our employees a strong voice; everyone can make a difference. We are innovating at the ground level.

While 4 Disciplines focuses on execution to drive business results, it has the added benefit of giving employees skills to use beyond work and throughout the rest of their career. We've heard countless stories from employees of how they've used the concepts to make improvements in their personal lives. Providing this education and training and investing in our leaders is yet another way our employees are further engaged.

Today, as we continue to roll out the 4 Disciplines, it remains a unique investment in our company and in our people, one that is changing the way in which we operate day to day. Whether we focus our wildly important goals on market share, profit, or guest satisfaction, we know that the 4 Disciplines will enable us to achieve them.

For great business skills or great life skills, the 4 Disciplines is an all-encompassing process about how you hold yourself accountable, how you hold others accountable, and ultimately, how you execute better.

LEANN TALBOT AND COMCAST

LeAnn Talbot is the senior vice president of Comcast's Freedom Region, which includes Comcast's headquarters in Philadelphia and the surrounding areas. Prior to that, she was senior vice president of the Greater Chicago Region (GCR), where she was responsible for marketing, sales, and operations in central and northern Illinois, northwest Indiana, and southwest Michigan. The GCR was one of Comcast's largest operating regions, but also one of the most challenged in terms of performance.

In LeAnn's words, "While the potential was there, the region had not been able to change the trajectory of its performance." Two years later, LeAnn and her team had moved the Greater Chicago Region from last place out of more than a dozen regions to second in the company's internal rankings and rising.

The following are LeAnn's insights, as well as her description of her experience in implementing 4DX throughout the region.

"Do in Chicago what you did in your previous Region—take it to first place." That was the mission I was given by the president of Comcast Cable as I interviewed for the leadership position of the Greater Chicago Region—a region known for two important characteristics: it was one of the largest in size, representing 10 percent of the company, and it was not performing well.

Over the past nine years, the region had remained last in virtually every metric Comcast used to measure performance, despite a succession of leaders. To put it simply, this wasn't a happy place and talented people didn't want to risk the move to the Chicago region because they thought it could negatively impact their careers.

The stage was set. It was clear that we needed to improve our results quickly and show that this important region was on track. And because of the importance of the region, we were also getting a significant level of attention—what we refer to as "the love"—that added additional pressure. Simply put, we needed a disciplined plan to execute with excellence and we needed it now.

We began by ensuring that the right leadership team was in place; one that would create a culture of diverse thought, respect, and accountability. This ultimately meant that 70 percent of the people in leadership roles had to change as we worked to create a visibly engaged team of leaders.

Next, our team needed to believe they could win, so we looked for every opportunity to celebrate a success, no matter how small. At first, they were hard to find. But over the next several months, success bred more success and our team slowly began to believe in themselves. We also had key champions in the company that were engaged with us and they helped to echo our success throughout Comcast, reinforcing the team's new mindset.

With these foundational elements in place, we then knew we needed to find the one focus that would be our primary catalyst for dramatic improvement—a difficult assignment when there were so many areas of our operation needing attention.

We've all heard that "when the student is ready, the teacher appears." And this is exactly what happened for us. One of the leaders on our team happened to attend a luncheon on the 4 Disciplines of Execution. He returned from that luncheon and walked straight into my office saying "We need this." When I listened to the 4 Disciplines audio CD that night on my way home, I had to agree. In fact, I couldn't wait to get started. My team was trapped in its whirlwind, and I was convinced that the 4 Disciplines were the way out.

There was only one problem: as a region, we were not yet achieving our goals. As a new leader, I faced the difficult decision of justifying money spent on a new "program" while we were simultaneously eliminating all but the most critical expenses. More personally, I also worried whether making this investment might mistakenly signal that I didn't believe my team was capable of turning the region around on our own.

In the end, I took the risk. I truly believed that the 4 Disciplines would give us the structure and the focus we needed. Throughout the implementation, I never saw the 4 Disciplines as a training program or even a management program. Instead, the 4 Disciplines were an "operating system" that would enable us to sustain our necessary whirlwind while also moving the needle on our most important objectives. In essence, the 4 Disciplines would give us a way to systematically work the plan we had created and ensure we delivered results, despite the urgent demands of our day-to-day operations.

We began quietly with a pilot in the city of Chicago. As the third largest city in the country, Chicago is a unique environment. Running a cable system there is a significant challenge—one that had resulted in some of our lowest performance metrics. Despite all our efforts, we just couldn't seem to get traction. It was the ideal environment in which to prove the 4 Disciplines, because if they worked in Chicago, we knew they would work throughout the region.

What happened next—to our results, and more importantly, in the engagement of the team—drove the decision to implement the 4 Disciplines throughout the entire region. A key metric in our business, we were able to cut our "Repeat" rate almost in half. (Repeats are when we have to revisit a customer's home to address an issue we've attempted to address at least once prior.) In addition, we doubled the number of customers "saved"—meaning when customers wanted to cancel their services, we were able to convince them to—stay—along with a host of other operating metrics that were all moving in the right direction. Our small investment in the 4 Disciplines helped us reduce costs by more than $2 million in only five months.

Beyond these operating results, the effect on the team was dramatic. I saw tech supervisors—and these are big guys—walking through the halls wearing pink wigs to their "Wildly Important Goal" (WIG) sessions. I saw them in their meetings holding teddy bears, laughing and working together. Front-line technicians were huddled around the scoreboards every week waiting for their results to be posted. And through it all, the needle continued to move substantially on our WIG.

Because we acknowledged the whirlwind with our teams, we gained needed credibility. We were honest in saying that our day jobs would always be there—the whirlwind doesn't go away. But we also promised, and proved, that the 4 Disciplines would allow us to make progress in key areas that would ultimately help to diminish the whirlwind.

We also learned how critical it was to have a 4 Disciplines coach with the teams. To build that resource into the organization is instrumental to the success of the 4 Disciplines and also helped us to grow our own internal experts. Our coaches were HR partners already teamed with the groups, who expanded their responsibilities to fulfill the role of coach, making sure WIG sessions were held each week, that teams found their cadence, scoreboards were created and updated, results were celebrated, and team members were accountable to fulfill their commitments.

We also saw an additional benefit emerge as the teams that had already launched started to "pay it forward" by helping newer teams. Those just launching were invited to attend

WIG sessions and the summit meetings of more seasoned teams. Those who were veterans of the process acted as consultants for other teams. In the end, we chose the 4 Disciplines to help us achieve financial and customer service goals, and the results we produced were extraordinary. But the cultural impact of the 4 Disciplines on our teams was icing on the cake.

Leading the Greater Chicago Region to success didn't happen solely because we launched the 4 Disciplines. We put a solid leadership team in place, quickly assessed our gaps, and developed an action plan that would drive results. But it all came together when we found the operating system—the 4 Disciplines of Execution—that enabled us to navigate the journey to winning.

Today, we're near the top of the rankings and are continuing to improve with respect to our financial and customer-service performance. And we have started to receive recognition as an employer of choice, including being recognized as a "Top 100 Workplace for 2011" by the *Chicago Tribune*. I really wouldn't have thought all of this progress could have happened so quickly when we first began our journey.

I think of the 4 Disciplines like the frame of a house—but I always remember it is a house that could not have been built without talented people, and the drive, hard facts, support from above, strong leaders, and a champion to steer the entire operation.

B. J. WALKER AND THE GEORGIA DEPARTMENT OF HUMAN SERVICES

B. J. Walker has served in the administrations of two governors (Illinois and Georgia) and the mayor of the city of Chicago. In 2004, she was appointed by Governor Sonny Perdue to run the Georgia Department of Human Resources, a massive human-services agency with a combined budget of over $3.2 billion and almost twenty thousand in staff. The agency had oversight of virtually all of the state's human services.

In 2007, she began using the 4 Disciplines of Execution to help move forward reforms across the agency, particularly in areas where errors in frontline practice might result in serious injury and/or death for their clients. Under her watch, a number of key indicators in child welfare, in child support, in welfare-to-work, and in food

SCAN WITH YOUR SMART PHONE

Android - Barcode Scanner
iPhone - Red Laser

LINK: http://www.4dxbook.com/qr/BJWalker

Scan the image above to see a case study video of B. J. Walker.

stamp eligibility continued to make significant and sustained progress.

The following are her insights, as well as her description of that experience.

In 2007, when Governor Sonny Perdue asked me to use FranklinCovey's 4 Disciplines of Execution, I was making slow but steady progress in improving a troubled and crisis-ridden agency. However, we were clearly struggling to achieve consistency in our performance, to fully convince our massive bureaucracy that we were targeting the right priorities, to use metrics as a day-to-day tool in our practice on the frontline, and to weather the storm of what seemed like constant media and political scrutiny. There were many days where I felt challenged and burdened by the need to make so many changes with so little time, and so few people and resources.

Implementing the 4 Disciplines of Execution was a game changer.

First, it convinced me that results are greatest when the game is played as a team, rather than focusing on the talents of a few individual superstars.

Second, it convinced me to stop waiting for reports filled with lag measures to determine whether I was winning or losing—data that always arrived far too late to do anything about it. I played softball for many years, and one of the things I learned is that it's less painful to lose an entire game than it is to endure failure inning by inning. When you operate using only lag measures, it's like posting the score only after each inning is over; you can see that you're losing, but by then it's too late to change your game and the losses just keep coming.

Particularly in a human-services organization, it's easier to just rationalize by saying things like, "I am doing good work. I am helping people. I am extremely busy." But when you do this, you're really just playing the game you know and waiting for the final score. If you lose, it's only a single moment of pain, instead of the day-to-day, week-to-week pressure of your lead measures.

The good news is that when you apply focus to your lead measures, you see them move. And when your lead measures move you start winning on your lag measures! Tragically, most public-sector organizations have never had the experience of seeing a winning score every week, and as a result, seldom think of themselves as winning teams. I made it my responsibility to keep my eye on the score *every week,* making it public. In the end, we sustained this focus and created a team that became used to winning instead of losing.

Third, and perhaps most important, it convinced me that I had to be willing to learn new behaviors. Specifically, I had to learn to lead from a position on the field, as well as from that of a senior executive, to step off the pedestal of mission and into the arena of practice and to move nimbly and intentionally between the leader's view at thirty thousand feet and the team's view on the ground. Implementing the 4 Disciplines makes you learn to lead differently because you want to win.

The 4 Disciplines of Execution will change the way your team moves the needle on their highest priority goals. However, it is up to you to determine what you need to do to embed them into your organization.

We all know how hard it can be to get people to buy into *our* mission and *our* goals, mostly because they are *ours* and not *theirs*. However, when you implement the 4 Disciplines of Execution, you learn to do something different: to use involvement to generate commitment. This begins with cultivating a very specific, and for some, a very different, relationship with your front-line teams, those people who move the transactions that produce results. Whether it's your sales team, customer-service representatives, production operators, or case managers, your first job in implementing the 4 Disciplines is to stimulate an organizational hunger for success on the overall WIG.

On our team this was particularly challenging because there was never much appetite to talk about death, even though serious injury and death were the forces preventing us from successfully executing our mission. It was a war we could not escape. Day after day, we worried about failing, and we also worried about being blamed. So, when we implemented the 4 Disciplines we pulled our WIG right out of the heart of our fear: Reduce by 50 percent the number of incidents that can lead to death and serious injury for people in our care, custody, and oversight.

Once it had been said out loud, everyone on our team could openly acknowledge it as our real mission. Interestingly, it was always the work the team wanted to do, and for many, it was the compelling reason they came back day after day. But creating our wildly important goal allowed us to take *ownership* of what was really our core mission: preventing bad things from happening to vulnerable children and adults. And that ownership created a significant shift in our approach. Instead of waiting to respond after bad things happened, we now proactively planned ways to keep them from happening. Ultimately, we used the 4 Disciplines to make ourselves publicly accountable for reducing death and serious injury and, as a result, began to work as a team to ensure we were successful.

People often ask me what specific aspect of the 4 Disciplines made the biggest difference for my team. My answer is always the same: the weekly WIG sessions. In these powerful meetings, the cadence, the rhythm of asking your people what commitments they are willing to make to move the score forward is the process that erases most of the distance between leaders and the actual day-to-day work in government.

The cadence constantly brings to the surface policy as well as practice issues that are otherwise invisible to (or hidden from) executive leaders. In addition, the WIG sessions allow the knowledge and experience of the front line to be shared throughout the organization, eliminating the gap between what an organization is ultimately accountable for and the actions of the front line that are driving it.

In government, any outcome of significance is almost always a lag measure, whether it's from federal or state entities, governors, or mayors. Usually, it's also a result that has not been achieved in any recent period, if at all. Therefore, the leaders are unlikely to know what behaviors would actually promote success in achieving it or, alternatively, are causing them to fail. They feel accountable, but aren't sure what it will take to move the needle.

WIG sessions close that gap between the leader's vision and the work of the front line by putting everybody in the same room. The flow of data about lead measures and weekly commitments forces leaders to see and hear from the front line regularly and, conversely, it provides the front line with unprecedented access to the eyes and ears of executive leaders when they are in a similar WIG session with them.

I can assure you that the bigger and more bureaucratic the organization, the more significant this effect is. Many private-sector business leaders would be surprised at how easy it is to run a large public-sector organization while never really understanding, let alone being involved in, the day-to-day work. The 4 Disciplines compels even the most senior leader to stay in the room with the frontline and the work.

The second most impactful aspect of the 4 Disciplines was what I referred to as my second job—creating an environment where the right work could be done the right way and for the right reasons. That work is principally seen in Discipline 2: Act on the lead measures. This discipline became the glue that connected the front line to the overall WIG we needed to achieve, as well as to the leaders of their team. It wasn't hard to get the front line to see the importance of their day to day work: They knew how much it mattered. What was difficult was convincing them that the leaders had the same perspective and understanding.

In a human-services agency, where the threat of death and serious injury is always present, it's hard for front-line workers to trust leaders who remain distant. The unspoken question is always, "Who will be thrown under the bus if something goes wrong?" Building trust is a large part of leading the 4 Disciplines successfully.

The best way for leaders to build that trust is by putting them in the middle of the work. Each week, those leaders are accountable for making commitments that help their team, for reporting results of the team's efforts to senior leaders, and for clearing the path of significant obstacles for their team. That's what I call putting leaders in the middle of the work.

For the leaders on my team, these became three absolute requirements:

- **As 4 Disciplines leaders, we must stay the course on our WIGs**. Front-line teams love a sure-footed leader, particularly when the stakes are high, and nothing rattles the confidence of a team like changing the rules in the middle of the game.

- **As 4 Disciplines leaders, we must give the front line what they need**. This means playing the team that is already on the field; we quickly learned that a high-functioning team will take care of its own laggards. While low performers and those who resist change will initially slow down the team's efforts, it won't last long. In 4DX, there is no place to hide, because of the highly visible accountability of results. This also means fixing the bureaucracy when it stands in the way of the front line getting the job done. Often, this means fighting the political battles to change a policy, remove a restriction, confront an issue, or even get more funding. Teams have little use or respect for a leader who cannot clear the path for them.

- **As 4 Disciplines leaders, we must deliver our own messages**. On our team, this meant that the first person to talk about death and serious injury had to be me. If I wanted the teams to do something different, then I had to begin by saying it was safe to change our practices, and even to operate outside the boundaries of existing policy, if it would reduce the number of incidents leading to death or serious injury.

As you know from the opening story in this book, we were ultimately successful in exceeding our wildly important goal: reducing repeat cases of child maltreatment by a stunning 60 percent. From that experience, I want to end with the most important things I learned—things that will help any leader implementing the 4 Disciplines:

- **Embed the language of the 4 Disciplines in your culture.** One of the easiest ways for people to dismiss accountability is to say they are already doing things that are just like the 4 Disciplines. The 4 Disciplines are specific and precise; and unless you implement all of them, you don't see the real benefit. Most important, when the senior leader stops walking and talking the 4 Disciplines, the entire organization immediately stops believing that she is serious.

- **Ensure that your leaders are clearing the path.** You should immediately look for a breakdown in execution if you are not hearing clear-the-path commitments that come all the way from the front line. Always remember: Nonmoving lead measures on the front line mean nonmoving WIGs for the organization.
- **Communicate openly and often to the front line.** Every member of your team needs to see and hear your commitment to the 4 Disciplines and to the achievement of your overall WIG. I sent weekly and often daily emails directly from my inbox to the front line with no layers of leaders in between filtering my message.
- **Make sure people know that it is the work on the front line that matters most.** Your team needs to know that the WIG *must* be achieved. Leadership matters. But, at the same time, they need to know that you know that their work on the front line is what produces bottom-line results. Don't allow the 4 Disciplines to be about you. Make it clear that even if you leave, the 4 Disciplines are about their ability to win.
- **Focus on raising the performance of your B-level leaders to that of your top performers.** The single most powerful way to do this is by consistently and faithfully holding your WIG sessions. Use this discipline to show them how the 4 Disciplines accentuates their leadership, and how the success

of the team comes from them. Midlevel leaders, particularly in large bureaucracies, are often unaccustomed to leading a winning team. It is more often their job to distribute and monitor policies set by others, whether they work or not, and to manage the organization through periods of transition both up and down the chain of command. They need the 4 Disciplines.

- **Be willing to hold the leadership high ground.** In the beginning, some people will criticize the 4 Disciplines as being all about the numbers and not about the people involved. When this happens, you have to hold strong on why the numbers matter. This was particularly true in human services; where the numbers were always about vulnerable people and effectively helping them live better and safer lives, but the principle is true everywhere. As the senior leader, you must be willing to stand behind the laser focus on performance that the 4 Disciplines bring to your work, whether it is about helping children or making widgets.

When I was introduced to the 4 Disciplines of Execution, I was facing the greatest challenge of my career. My twenty thousand employees were completely demoralized, we were under constant media scrutiny because of deaths and accidents involving children, and I was the sixth leader in five years.

Because of these powerful disciplines, and because of the hard work and dedication of all the people who dedicated their lives to this mission, we knew that the children in our care were safer and better protected. We could not have asked for a greater or more significant outcome.

Focusing the Organization on the Wildly Important

(WITH CONTRIBUTING AUTHOR SCOTT THELE)

You can see from these four stories that each leader faced the challenge of focusing the minds and hearts of literally thousands of people on a set of wildly important goals.

When they created focus, their organizations accomplished truly extraordinary things.

In section 1, we introduced four rules to help you narrow the focus of your entire organization:

RULES FOR DISCIPLINE 1

1 No more than **1 to 3 WIGs per person** at the **same time**.

2 The **battles** have to win **the war**.

3 You can **veto, but don't dictate**.

4 A WIG must have a **finish line (from x to y by when)**.

While these rules may seem straightforward, even simple, following them requires tremendous commitment and discipline. Creating focus is never simple for any organization; it only looks simple once it's been accomplished. However, the results are worth the effort. In fact, every successful implementation of 4DX begins when leaders take on the difficult challenge of narrowing the organization's focus.

In this chapter, we will expand on these four rules and show you, step by step, how to translate your organization's complex strategic agenda into a set of focused WIGs with clear finish lines. With actual examples, we'll also show you how to translate those WIGs all the way to the front line. The result: Clarity at every level of the organization and dramatic results at the end of the process.

TRANSLATING ORGANIZATIONAL STRATEGY INTO WIGS: THE CASE OF OPRYLAND

When we first met the leaders of the Opryland Hotel in Nashville, Tennessee, the largest convention hotel in the United States outside Las Vegas, they had dozens of urgent priorities, including:

- Introducing new marketing and advertising programs
- Planning for a 400,000 square-foot expansion of their 2,000-room property
- Launching several initiatives designed to improve their occupancy rate
- Controlling expenses to improve their bottom line
- Engaging in multiple new programs to improve the satisfaction of their guests
- Revamping their convention services
- Identifying ways to help their guests more easily navigate the fifty-six acre property

Like most leaders, they had their hands full. It's likely that you have your own list and no matter how often you try to simplify it, this dizzying list of priorities feels overwhelming. We want you to know that you're not alone.

As the executive team at Opryland began the 4DX process, their crucial first step was focusing the entire hotel on the wildly important. This is never automatic, particularly in larger organizations. It takes work, and that work begins by answering the question, "If every other area of our operation remained at its current level of performance, which one area would we want to improve the most?" Remember to avoid asking the question, "What's our most important priority?" This question will only result in a never-ending debate.

As each member of the executive team expressed their ideas about the one area they wanted to see improve the most, guest satisfaction rose to the top as the most impactful. The primary reason for this is that the experience of the guest literally impacted every other aspect of their business, from revenue to market share. It was also a focus to which every employee of the hotel could make a contribution.

As their focus became clearer, Arthur Keith, the general manager, recommended improved guest satisfaction as the highest-level WIG for the hotel. His role at this point in the process was important and timely. Leaders should be open and should truly listen and explore alternatives, but they may also need to step in at the right moment to help the team reach a decision. The leader must be ready to play both roles, primarily participating in the discussion, but also willing to advocate a position.

Selecting a high-level WIG for an entire organization always feels a little like buying a pair of shoes. You have to walk around in them for a while before deciding if they feel right. Don't force the team to decide on the WIG too quickly. Instead, just select the WIG that seems right, and let the leaders walk around in it as they develop supporting WIGs to ensure its achievement. They can always select a different WIG if it doesn't feel right to apply it across the organization.

A high-level WIG is a serious organizational commitment, so leadership teams are often more than a little hesitant to make a choice. This is why so many organizations rarely achieve real focus. Giving your team the freedom to choose and reconsider their choices frees them to take this step.

Before we go to the next step with Opryland, let's look at where most organizational WIGs come from.

THREE SOURCES OF ORGANIZATIONAL WIGS

We've noticed that almost every leadership team, regardless of industry, size, or geography, chooses a highest-level WIG from one of three areas: financial, operational, or customer satisfaction.

Financial WIGs are measured in dollars, whether top-line revenue, bottom-line profit, or some key measure in between. Surprisingly, less than a third of our clients choose a financial WIG as their first priority, even though financial results are always among the highest priorities.

Operational WIGs focus on production, quality, efficiency, or economies of scale. Most leadership teams focus here initially. These WIGs often focus on key operational measures such as production volume, quality improvements, increased market share, or expansion into new areas.

Customer satisfaction WIGs focus on closing the gap between the current level of performance and the level that represents excellence, whether to customers of a business, patients in a hospital, or guests in a hotel. Unlike financial and operational WIGs, these measures depend on the perception of the customer.

FROM MISSION TO WIG

The highest-level WIG for your organization is not your mission statement. It's also not your vision, nor does it often represent your entire organizational strategy. Your highest-level WIG is a point of laser focus; one to which you will give a disproportionate amount of energy because it requires a change in human behavior.

This diagram helps you see your WIG in context of the overall organization.

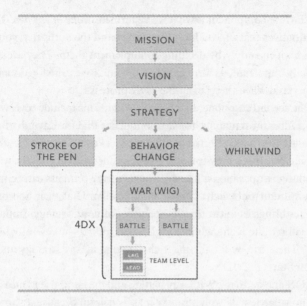

If you're like most organizations, you have a defined mission or purpose statement that clarifies *why* you exist. Once the mission is defined, many leaders articulate *what* success will look like at some point, usually five or more years, in the future. This is your vision. Both your mission and your vision are *aspirational,* meaning they are statements or ideas of what you want the organization to become. You then create a strategy to map out *how* your vision will become a reality. We believe that there are usually three components to an effective strategy.

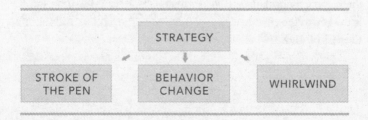

The first component is what we've termed *stroke of the pen.* These are initiatives that, if you have the money and the authority, you can make happen simply by deciding to implement them. They are often critically important, as were many of the initiatives already underway at Opryland when they began the 4DX process.

The second component is the whirlwind. This includes everything your leaders must manage to have confidence that the day job of their teams is being done effectively. While leaders use 4DX to execute key strategic priorities, they must also remain focused on effectively running the core operations. These elements of the business can be monitored through tools such as Norton and Kaplan's Balanced Scorecard.

This brings us to the third component of your strategy: Initiatives that will require a change in people's behavior to successfully implement. These are by far the most challenging in any strategy and the primary target of 4DX.

4DX applies to the WIG, key battles, and the lag and lead measures. This holistic view of your strategy map is helpful because it shows all of your strategic imperatives in their proper place. It also reinforces the critical importance of the whirlwind. Most important, the map warns you against blurring the important boundary around 4DX territory. As you begin to see the effectiveness of 4DX in producing results, you will be tempted to bring more and more initiatives inside this boundary and, if you do, you will lose the narrow focus that is the key to the effectiveness of 4DX.

LINK: http://www.4dxbook.com/qr/StrategyMap

Scan the image above to see a video that gives a more complete description of the Strategy Map.

TRANSLATING BROAD STRATEGY
INTO SPECIFIC FINISH LINES

Once Opryland leaders had chosen guest satisfaction as their highest level WIG, they needed to set the finish line that would define success.

The measurement system for guest satisfaction at Opryland tracked only perfect scores, which they refer to as *top box* scores of five on a one to five scale. This was a very demanding standard, far beyond the normal measures of guest satisfaction. They asked themselves what would be the highest achievable top box score they could get. Their top box score from the previous year was 42 percent (meaning 42 percent of guests gave them a perfect rating), while the highest ever recorded was 45 percent. After much debate, they decided to go for a lag measure of 55 percent.

Having set the high-level WIG, which we sometimes call the *war,* Opryland leaders were ready to move on to the lower level WIGs that would ensure victory; what we've referred to earlier as *battles*.

Once the war is set, defining the battles becomes the leader's key responsibility. The metaphor of wars and battles is helpful for several reasons: First, you should ideally fight only one war at a time; second, all lower-level WIGs (battles) must be aimed at winning the war rather than at any other objective—after all, the only reason to fight a battle is to win the war; and third, you isolate those WIGs that are most essential for success. Leaders must ask, "What is the fewest number of battles necessary to win the war?" The energy level of a team always jumps to a new level when they begin to work on this question, a result we saw clearly at Opryland.

The leadership team at Opryland had never before wrestled with this question. Why? Because they had never forced themselves to narrow their focus to a single war. Like most leadership teams, they were engaged in so many wars that they never even came close to defining battles. And as they tried to identify the battles needed for winning the war for guest satisfaction, they found so many candidates that the effort was almost overwhelming. Every leader listed dozens of possible battles, but then they realized that we weren't asking *how many* candidate battles they could identify: We were asking *how few* were needed to ensure success. This is the question that requires real strategic thinking from the leadership team.

In the end, the leaders at Opryland decided that three critical battles had to be won to raise guest satisfaction to a top box score of 55: arrival experience, problem resolution, and food and beverage quality.

Arrival experience. This battle was essential. Their research had shown that negative opinions of a hotel formed in the first fifteen to twenty minutes were almost impossible to change. The higher the quality of that first experience, the better the overall impression of the hotel.

Problem resolution. The leaders knew that, regardless of their efforts, things would still go wrong. Improving guest satisfaction isn't a question of *if* a problem will occur; it's about what you do *when* it occurs. The response of their teams to guest problems could make or break the guest's entire experience. They wanted their teams to be world class at resolving problems.

Food and beverage quality. Because Opryland is such a large property, guests are less inclined to travel to restaurants outside the hotel. In addition, most of the hotel's restaurants are considered fine dining and are priced accordingly. As a result, guest expectations of the quality of the food are exceptionally high. Meeting those expectations consistently would significantly raise guest satisfaction scores.

The leadership team at Opryland believed that if they could put the energy of the entire hotel behind these three critical battles, they would change the game. Winning those three battles would win the war; and as soon as they realized this, reaching a top box score of 55 percent began to seem possible. This is the real power of a leadership team determining the fewest possible battles; it enables them to see if their war is *winnable.*

Choosing the battles, however, was only half the work. Now they had to set a finish line—*from X to Y by when*—for each battle. They had not only to figure out the top achievable score for each battle, but also to make sure those scores would add up to winning the war.

If the battles won't win the war, you haven't created an effective strategy or a winnable game.

Remember the key principle of leverage: The lever must move a lot for the rock to move a little.

The carefully defined battles that would win Opryland's war for higher guest satisfaction.

The Opryland leadership team spent an entire day defining the war and battles and setting the finish lines for each. When the day was over, Danny Jones, the head of quality and guest satisfaction said, "Now that we're done, it looks so simple, like something we could have written on the back of a napkin over lunch." He was right, but he also knew that the simplicity and the clarity of the plan would be the keys to its effectiveness.

Danny's thoughts were echoed by Arthur Keith, the general manager: "This was the most valuable day we've ever spent together as a leadership team. For the first time, we can articulate in just a few sentences the direction and strategic bets of the entire hotel."

Although the excitement of the leadership team at Opryland was a strong endorsement, the real impact of this work is seen in the teams. At Opryland, seventy-five different operating teams across the hotel were now able to leverage the clarity and direction the leadership team had provided by choosing their own team WIG that would ensure victory in one of the three battles (a process described in on page 136).

For example, the battle for a better arrival experience was largely in the hands of the front-desk team, whose team WIG was to improve the speed of check-in. However, this battle wasn't theirs to win alone. The guest-rooms team had a closely aligned team WIG to increase room availability for guests needing early check-in, which was essential to speeding the check-in process.

The team that really caught our attention was the bell-stand team. For years, this team had struggled to deliver guest bags more quickly. However, faced with antiquated systems and a massive fifty-six acre property to cover, they were still averaging a delivery time of 106 minutes per guest. That's right: Guests had to wait an hour and forty-six minutes for their bags. The bell-stand team knew that, even if the room was available and the check-in fast, their failure to deliver the bags quickly would ultimately hurt the arrival experience score. They chose a team WIG to reduce luggage delivery time from 106 minutes to twenty minutes. After only a few months of intense focus on this team WIG, they exceeded their goal by reducing luggage delivery time to twelve minutes.

The graphic illustrates the 4DX architecture we've just described for winning the battle "arrival experience" within the context of the hotel's war for guest satisfaction.

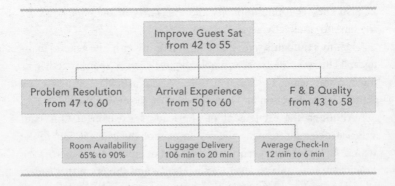

It's important to remember that each of these teams still spent most of their time on the whirlwind: managing the hotel, serving guests, and responding to dozens of unexpected challenges each day. But now, the game had changed. Each team had a wildly important goal they could remain focused on in the midst of their day-to-day responsibilities. And because that Team WIG had a finish line, they were not only accountable for it, they wanted to win.

For each WIG, each team also defined lead measures, created a compelling scoreboard, and met every week to make commitments that would drive those scoreboards, as we described in section 2. Now, when you get seventy-five teams all driving toward the same overall goal, you can do something amazing.

Which they did. After nine months, Opryland not only reached a top-box guest satisfaction score of 55 percent, but went beyond their goal to hit 61 percent. Remember, they had never before scored higher than 45 percent. Now, they achieved almost a 50 percent net improvement in only nine months. Although Gaylord's oldest property, Opryland now led every other Gaylord hotel in guest satisfaction. Although we had been optimistic, even we did not anticipate this level of improvement could be achieved so quickly.

For us, the Opryland story serves as a powerful reminder of the untapped talent and potential that exists in even the best-run organizations when they move from a vague strategic intent to a set of specific finish lines.

LINK: http://www.4dxbook.com/qr/Opryland

Scan the image above to see a case study video of Opryland.

| **FROM:** VAGUE STRATEGIC INTENT | **TO:** SPECIFIC FINISH LINES |

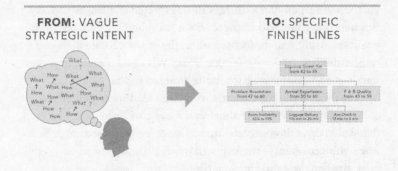

Too many organizational goals are hazy and imprecise, leaving people wondering "what" they are supposed to do and "how" they are supposed to do it. They need clear, unmistakable finish lines so people know exactly what success looks like.

TRANSLATING WIGS THROUGH FUNCTIONALLY SIMILAR ORGANIZATIONS

The seventy-five teams at Opryland were very diverse in their functions, including engineers, housekeepers, front desk clerks, bellhops, and restaurant teams, as well as support services such as finance, accounting, and human resources.

Other organizations, like retail chains, manufacturing facilities, or sales teams, consist of many similar units that perform the *same* functions. The same 4DX principles apply to them; however, in multiunit organizations WIGs translate to the front line quite differently, as we'll see.

Take our experience implementing 4DX with a large retailer with hundreds of outlets. As at Opryland, their overall WIG focused on improving the guest experience. In their case, it was to Increase Likelihood to Recommend (LTR), a customer-loyalty measure devised by business strategist Fred Reichheld. Their research had shown a strong correlation between the profitability of their stores and the likelihood that people would recommend them to their friends. With this WIG in place, the leadership team spent an intensive day defining the *fewest* battles to win the war and finally isolated the three most critical:

- **Improve customer engagement** was of course essential to increasing the willingness of customers to recommend the store. This battle focused primarily on whether their associates were available and eager to help customers find what they needed as soon as they entered the store.
- **Reduce out of stocks** was also critical. If a customer wanted a product that was sold out, not only was the sale lost, the customer was less likely to recommend the store to others.
- **Increase speed of checkout** could make a huge difference. In the speed-driven world of retailing, getting customers checked out and on their way has a disproportionate influence. If the last thing customers remember about the store is a frustrating checkout, it will influence their perception of the whole shopping experience.

You might think the battles they chose were obvious. But, as with Opryland, the leadership team, many of whom had spent decades in this industry, evaluated dozens of candidate battles before settling on these three. They actually drew simplicity out of enormous complexity. It took time, tremendous energy, and a little fighting before they landed on this simple but powerful plan. (When you begin this process, remember that the closer you are to your operation the more complex it is, and often, the harder it is to narrow your focus.)

In the end, does this war-and-battle structure look simple? Yes and that simplicity is one of the keys to a successful implementation. Remember, the greatest challenge is not in developing the plan: It's in changing the behavior of the front-line teams that must execute it while managing the never-ceasing demands of the whirlwind.

Now let's see how this multiunit organization translated the WIG to the front lines. For the sake of simplicity, we'll describe how one region of the company translated the WIGs to districts, and how each district translated it to the stores. Unlike the functionally diverse units at Opryland, these units all performed the same functions; therefore,

The battles selected to increase the likelihood that customers will recommend the store to others.

they all adopted the same WIGs and battles. Still, they had leeway in defining the finish lines.

So, the region chose *from X to Y by when* finish lines that were specific to their region. Then the district leaders, who had helped develop the overall war-and-battle structure, assigned unique *from X to Y by when* finish lines to represent the performance objectives of the district.

The region leader did not dictate the finish lines to the districts; the district leaders took ownership of this responsibility. Regional leaders were free to ask for adjustments if they didn't agree with the numbers. Ultimately, the region leader ensured that districts defined a winning game for the region.

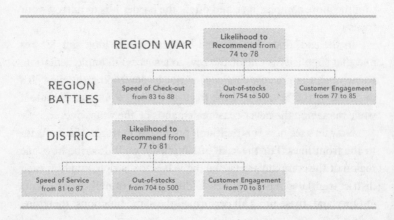

Store WIGs were the same as district WIGs but with unique *from X to Y by when* measures for each store. However, at this level, there was a twist. The stores were given the choice, with oversight from the district leader, to choose the battles that represented the greatest opportunities for the store. If already exemplary in out of stocks or customer engagement, the store could narrow focus to another battle. In this way, two things were accomplished. Store leaders who could choose their own battles were naturally more committed to them; they could also focus on the battle that mattered most.

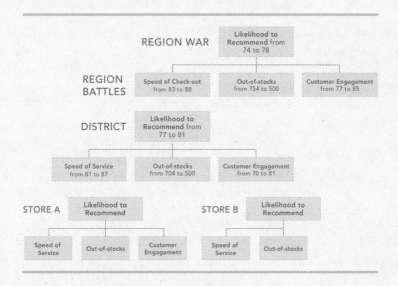

A CLEAR AND EXECUTABLE STRATEGY

In this chapter, we've described an intense but rapid process for achieving a profoundly simple result. At Opryland, with its diverse teams, and at the retail chain with similar teams, high-level WIGs were defined within a day. The result was a clear and simple strategy, but more important, it was a strategy that could be *executed*.

Remember that, for an organization, 4DX is not for your stroke-of-the-pen initiatives. Nor is it for defining all of the measures for monitoring the day-to-day well-being of the operation—the whirlwind. It's for driving behavior changes that have to happen. Because so few leaders and organizations have this kind of discipline, your ability to focus the entire organization on what's *wildly important* might become your greatest competitive advantage.

Rolling Out 4DX Across the Organization

The chapter you are about to read was the most challenging for us to write. Our intention is to describe for you a proven method for installing 4DX, not only with your own team, but also with multiple teams across a larger organization. We've spent years developing this method.

In our first three years of working through 4DX with our clients, we were able to refine the disciplines to the point where we knew they were right, not only in principle but in the practice of producing outstanding results. However, rolling 4DX across an entire organization had us scratching our heads.

From the beginning, our clients embraced the concepts quickly, and in virtually every implementation, we saw pockets of success, which we called *campfires*. A group of aerospace engineers, an individual retail store here and there, a team of software developers, and a manufacturing plant were some of the isolated pockets of excellence we encountered. These pockets almost always had leaders who caught the vision of what 4DX could mean for the team and for them personally. It drove them to produce great results. But replicating this success across a larger organization—turning campfires into wildfires—was evading us.

We knew that our installation process needed the same level of refinement that we had brought to the disciplines themselves, but first, we needed to understand why it wasn't working.

WHAT DOESN'T WORK?

For more than thirty years, FranklinCovey has been one of the most successful training organizations in the world. Given this legacy, it was inevitable that we would first offer the 4 Disciplines as a training solution. It was also wrong.

As Bernard Baruch reportedly said, **"If all you have is a hammer, everything looks like a nail."** Instructor-led training was what we knew how to do, and we did it well. In our earliest offerings, we pulled dozens of leaders out of the whirlwind for a few days to teach them the concepts of 4DX, and they validated the training as highly relevant and engaging. At the end of each session, leaders expressed real passion for what they had been taught. But we, and they, had to learn the hard lesson that embracing a concept is not the same as applying it.

The problem is that the whirlwind is waiting for you the moment the training session is over. By the time you've caught up on the backlog of issues that arose while you were in training, the excitement and momentum you felt for the new concepts are often lost.

It's also difficult to implement new concepts when the people you work with don't have the same understanding that you do, especially if those concepts are counterintuitive. You can find yourself trying to install a discipline that no one's excited about and that runs against the natural tendencies of your team.

Finally, even though the 4 Disciplines are easy to understand, in the end, they are still *disciplines*. It takes real work to make them an established part of organization's operation and culture.

Dr. Atul Gawande expresses this challenge well: "Discipline is hard—harder than trustworthiness and skill and perhaps even self-lessness. We are by nature flawed and inconstant creatures. We can't even keep from snacking between meals. We are not built for discipline. We are built for novelty and excitement, not for careful attention to detail. Discipline is something we have to work at." [29]

Despite these challenges, we often encountered powerful leaders who adopted 4DX and produced extraordinary results. However, they were only a few of the leaders we trained. We realized that enabling an entire organization to produce large-scale results was going to require a system of implementation that ensured a wildfire of organizational success.

WHAT DOES WORK?

As we studied the leaders and teams where we had been successful, we began to develop a very different system of implementing the 4 Disciplines. The following are the key aspects of our approach:

The 4 Disciplines must be implemented as a process, not an event. In this chapter, we will show you six distinct steps for successfully launching the 4 Disciplines across an organization. These six steps apply whether you are implementing the 4DX with your team, or across a larger segment of your organization.

The 4 Disciplines must be implemented with intact teams. Rather than working with isolated leaders from different parts of an organization, we work with all the leaders necessary to achieve the overall wildly important goal. This is critical, because achievement of your overall WIG almost always requires the combined efforts of multiple teams. However, this doesn't mean that you should introduce the 4 Disciplines to an entire organization all at once. In large organizations, we have often found it most effective to work with ten or, at most, twenty teams at a time. If the overall WIG is to increase revenue, for example, we may begin with ten sales managers and their teams, or ten retail stores, or even ten departments within a large production operation. Once the initial teams begin to have success it drives interest in other portions of the organization and makes the continuing implementation easier.

The 4 Disciplines must be implemented by the leader. Our greatest breakthrough came when we realized that the most successful method of implementing the 4 Disciplines was through the

leaders closest to the front line. Instead of relying on one
of our consultants to introduce and launch the disciplines,
we changed our process to instead focus on equipping and
certifying leaders to launch with their teams. From this point,
we will refer to this process as *leader certification*.

There are several reasons that this change made such a significant
difference in our results.

- When you are learning something that you know you
  will ultimately have to teach, you truly learn it. In fact,
  the most powerful way to learn anything is to teach
  it to others, which is a principle we have seen at work
  firsthand in hundreds of implementations.
- When you teach something, you automatically find
  yourself becoming an advocate. When one of our
  consultants taught the process, it allowed the leader to
  stay on the sidelines, but when the leader brought the
  4 Disciplines to the team, he or she had to fully commit.
  In other words, when you are the one advocating the
  Disciplines, you have to be all in or you know they won't
  work.
- If you are the one advocating the 4 Disciplines, you
  are accountable to live them. No credible leader would
  introduce the Disciplines and then knowingly violate
  them by consistently failing to follow through.
- When you introduce the 4 Disciplines, you generate a
  different level of response from the team because of your
  credibility. When the Disciplines come from a consultant,
  an internal trainer, or even a more senior leader within
  the organization, there is a tendency for most teams to
  wait and see if this is real. Usually, the person they watch
  first to determine this is you, their leader. And if *you* are
  the one teaching, advocating, and launching the process,
  they know immediately that it *is* real.

When we describe this method of implementation in our programs, the leaders immediately grasp the benefits, but some are concerned about their own ability to effectively com-

LINK: http://www.4dxbook.com/qr/LCP

Scan the image above to see a short video describing the Leader Certification Process.

municate and launch so many changes. Without question, a successful launch requires careful preparation. But we want you to know that we have seen thousands of leaders, at all levels of skill and experience, create excellent launches.

THE 4DX INSTALLATION PROCESS

The following six-step installation process leads not only to results, but more important, to adoption of an "operating system" for achieving your most important organizational goals over and over again.

Since most of our clients prefer the speed and efficiency of launching multiple teams simultaneously, we will present an overview of how the launch process works with ten teams or more at once. In this multi-team process, which we use to certify leaders in 4DX, leaders work together for a few days to draft team WIGs and lead measures and then to share those results with their teams to get confirmation and buy-in.

Step 1: **Clarify the overall WIG.** If you are leading multiple teams, this is about determining your overall wildly important goal. The specific process for doing this is described on page 235.

Step 2: Design the team WIGs and lead measures. This step usually requires two full days. Leaders learn 4DX concepts at a deep level, reviewing case-study videos and working through real-world examples, all of which are designed to give every leader a firm grasp on the 4 Disciplines and how they are applied.

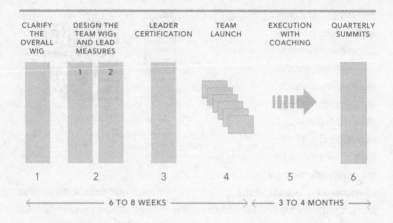

This diagram depicts the six steps of 4DX installation, along with a recommended timeline for the process.

Next, following the process described on page 118, each leader chooses a team WIG that will represent the team's greatest contribution to the overall WIG. Senior leaders play a critical role at this point because they must ultimately decide whether the combined team WIGs will lead to achievement of the overall WIG. In this role, the senior leaders may offer counsel or even veto a team WIG, but they must not dictate what the team WIG should be—only the leader of the team should choose it.

When team WIGs are set, leaders then tackle the most challenging part of the 4DX process: defining lead measures for the WIGs. As we saw on page 136, not many leaders have done this kind of work before. Coming up with predictive and influenceable lead measures is a complex task that often requires multiple attempts.

When all the team WIGs and lead measures are in place, every leader has a clear line of sight from the overall WIG to the contribution of his or her own team. It's a powerful—and often unprecedented—moment of clarity. Please remember that the team WIG and lead measures are not final until they have been validated by the team during a team launch session, which we will cover in step 4. You'll have a hard time getting full commitment from team members who have no opportunity to give input. Remember, "No involvement, no commitment."

Step 3: Leader certification. In this critical step, which usually requires a full day, the leaders learn how to launch 4DX with their teams.

- **Scoreboard design**. Leaders learn not only how to build effective scoreboards but also how to facilitate the team's involvement.
- **WIG session skills.** Leaders learn key skills before holding a first WIG session—in particular, how to hold team members accountable in front of their peers. Some leaders struggle in their first few attempts at effective WIG sessions, so we practice by running mock sessions with other leaders.
- **Launch meeting preparation.** The final and most important stage of leader certification is preparation for the team launch meeting. The success of the launch meeting is essential to the success of the WIG.

Leaders are first prepared to teach their teams a high-level understanding of 4DX. They practice with each other using teaching videos, guidebooks, and presentation slides. In addition, they learn to clearly communicate the overall WIG, along with the draft team WIG and lead measures, and then to facilitate meaningful feedback from the team and make any needed revisions.

When Step 3 is completed, the leaders are now certified to launch 4DX with their teams. This certification also marks the end of the working session with other leaders.

Step 4: Team launch. Leaders schedule and conduct a team launch meeting that usually lasts about two hours. They will present an overview of 4DX for about 45 minutes and then review the overall WIG and the draft team WIG and lead measures. The team then gives feedback and finalizes the team WIG and measures.

In this session, they also design the team scoreboard and assign responsibility for its completion. The meeting concludes with a practice WIG session in preparation for the actual sessions that will begin the following week. This practice session gives the leader the opportunity to discuss the format and ground rules that will be in effect as the team begins its actual pursuit of the team WIG. Particularly for inexperienced or reluctant teams, it's a good practice to attend WIG sessions or summit meetings of more seasoned teams, as LeAnn Talbot of Comcast recommended. 4DX veterans can then answer questions about the process.

Step 5: Execution with coaching. Steps 1 through 4 represent the launch phase of implementing the 4 Disciplines, and although they are critical, they are still the plan for a game that has yet to be played. Step 5 is where the game begins.

Now the leaders and their teams begin the weekly process of driving lead measures to achieve the team WIG, a process that requires discipline and accountability. Week by week, the team evolves and matures, making higher-impact commitments and improving their follow through in WIG sessions. As the lead measures begin to move, the team can see that their focused efforts are actually moving the lag measure; and with each movement, they can see that they are winning.

In our experience, leaders typically need experienced guidance for about three months as they foster new behaviors and encounter unexpected challenges. 4DX coaches help leaders with adherence to the 4DX process, success with lead measures, and preparation for quarterly summits. Our experienced consultants coach leaders while developing strong internal coaches for the organization—a role that is described in more detail in the sections that follow.

Step 6: Quarterly summits. The summit is a meeting at which the leaders report to their senior leaders on progress and results in the presence of their peers. A quarter generally provides enough time to see not only the lead measures moving but also the impact those leads are having on the lag measure. The more senior the leaders who attend the first summit, the greater the sense of urgency to produce results, which is important to making the team WIG and lead measures a high-stakes game.

For many, it will be the first time they meet with senior leaders. It's the first time they get to talk about how their ideas have contributed to the company's goals and to be recognized for their contribution. As Alec Covington of Nash Finch observed, it's a very different experience from receiving orders "on tablets of stone" and being held accountable for goals you don't understand.

When the governor of Georgia, Sonny Perdue, attended the first summit for five agencies of the state government, he watched carefully as leaders explained their team WIGs, lead measures, and results. There was tremendous energy in the room, not only because the governor was present, but more because the leaders who were reporting could see that they were making a difference.

At the end of the meeting, Governor Perdue stood to give a spontaneous closing message. He said, "When I leave office, I don't want any statues made or buildings named after me. I want my legacy to be the employees of this state." As he turned to leave, he gave a clear direction to a member of his staff: "I want every leader in the state to go through this process."

Because quarterly summits combine the power of accountability with the opportunity for recognition, they become a driving force in the leader's implementation of 4DX—a summit is always only a few weeks away.

THE POWERFUL ROLE OF AN INTERNAL COACH

We have found that designating an internal 4DX coach makes a big difference in the success of the installation. We often say that, if accomplishing a wildly important goal is like driving a Formula 1 race car, the 4DX Coach is the head mechanic.

Like a mechanic, the 4DX coach does two things. First, the coach helps with repairs on operational breakdowns in 4DX. The coach guides leaders who encounter difficult resisters, need counsel on the quality of lead measures, or could use help in establishing a cadence of accountability. Also, the coach helps with preventive maintenance, ensuring that the teams adhere to the process and identifying early warning signs of a team that is falling prey to the whirlwind.

We strongly recommend that two individuals share this role to compensate for scheduling conflicts or unanticipated turnover. Internal coaches benefit the organization in the following ways.

- **Responsiveness.** By assigning and developing individuals in this role, the organization creates a significant knowledge resource and immediate front-line support to 4DX leaders. There's no need to bring in resources from outside.
- **Independence.** The more experienced and capable the internal coach, the less need for on-going guidance from outside.
- **Continuity.** As new leaders are hired or promoted, the internal coach can play a crucial role in quickly orienting them to the 4DX process.

Although the internal coach is not a full-time role, selecting the right individuals for the role is crucial. A strong 4DX coach will have a solid knowledge of the business, good communication skills, and the ability to develop and sustain good working relationships. The effectiveness of a coach is largely through influence rather than formal authority.

Over the years, we've seen excellent coaches drawn from many areas: operational management, fast-track leadership programs, quality assurance, and Six Sigma and lean manufacturing belts.

Beyond any other characteristic, a couple of traits are common to the best coaches: interest in and capacity for the role. Coaches with high interest but no capacity beyond their whirlwind responsibilities may be passionate about 4DX, but can't invest the time and energy to ensure the implementation is a success. Those with capacity but no interest can actually slow down the implementation of 4DX and the achievement of results. As one of our clients recently said, "If they're too available, they're probably not too valuable."

In our experience, every highly successful 4DX implementation has been supported by an effective coach. Although achieving your wildly important goal requires the combined efforts of the leaders and their teams, the 4DX coach is essential to a successful implementation and the sustaining of exceptional results.

WATCH OUT

Finally, be on guard against three potential failure points. If you encounter any of these, it might be better to postpone implementation of 4DX until they're resolved.

- **The absence of a goal that really matters**. 4DX is a powerful process for achieving your most important goals, but it's a means to an end, not the end itself. The more important the overall WIG, the more committed the organization and its leaders will be to achieving it and, as a result, the faster they will embrace the Disciplines. Without this focus, the Disciplines will not be as effective.
- **The lack of full commitment from the senior leader.** If the most senior leader is not fully committed to 4DX, the organization will never fully commit. We are not necessarily referring to the CEO but to the most senior leader responsible for the initiative. Implementing the 4 Disciplines, no matter what part of the organization is involved, requires complete commitment. If 4DX is seen as an option for leaders who are interested, your implementation will fail before it begins.
- **Certifying leaders at the wrong level.** It is critical to certify those leaders who are actually responsible for teaching

and driving the 4DX process. You cannot win without them. If you certify leaders at too high a level, the game plan will never reach the front-line team that produces results against the lead measures. In contrast, if you certify leaders at too low a level, they will too often lack the experience to create the best team WIG and lead measures or the authority to hold the team accountable for results.

A useful guideline is to certify the lowest level of full-time leadership above the front line. For example, in a grocery store, the bakery manager would be too low, because those who fulfill this role usually work as individual contributors and would not be considered full time in leadership. The store manager, one level above, would be the right level. In contrast, the plant manager in a manufacturing facility might be too high, making the shift supervisor the right level.

Consider also the amount of discretionary time the leader can put toward 4DX. Leaders who control their own schedules can generally lead a WIG team. It's also essential that team members have enough time to make, schedule, and fulfill weekly commitments.

In this chapter, we've described in general the process we've been through and the issues we've faced hundreds of times in installing 4DX. We've tried to give you the benefit of our trials and our errors.

Implementing the 4 Disciplines with ten or more teams simultaneously, as we do in some part of the world almost every day, involves a number of careful considerations. But in the end, the ability to focus multiple teams on consistently driving lead measures toward a critical goal is deeply powerful. It's key to creating extraordinary outcomes and raising the performance and effectiveness of an entire organization.

4DX Frequently Asked Questions

Here you'll find answers to the questions people most often ask about implementing 4DX. We've grouped the questions under these topics:

- How to generate buy-in and commitment to 4DX
- How to sustain 4DX
- 4DX process tips and traps

We've also answered questions about applying 4DX to certain distinctive types of teams (although the issues discussed should interest any reader).

- Manufacturing teams
- High-tech and scientific teams
- Sales teams
- Government and military teams

Generating Buy-in and Commitment to 4DX
What are the most common mistakes leaders make in implementing 4DX?
The two main mistakes leaders make in this process are a lack of participation and a lack of patience.

First, leaders often unwittingly presume that the success of 4DX

rests with those individuals who have gone through manager certification. While the role of the certified managers is crucial to WIG and
lead measure success, the active involvement of leaders to whom the
certified leaders report is mandatory. Leaders hold WIG sessions with
their direct reports, openly and actively recognizing the contributions
of the certified managers and their team members in this process, reinforcing the principles of the 4DX, and removing barriers to WIG
success and lead measure performance.

Second, all leaders are results driven, so they want results as soon
as possible. However, they often ignore the fact that WIG success depends upon consistent, ongoing performance against the lead measures. If good lead measures have been developed, and if the teams
are performing to these lead measures, the lag measure associated
with the WIG should move, unless external circumstances make WIG
attainment impossible. It takes time. Instead of giving up on the process, the leader needs to patiently reinforce it.

How do you handle the resisters on a team?
First and foremost, understand why they are resisting. Once you have
determined that, you can formulate a solution.

Some resisters have unexpressed concerns about issues outside of
4DX. They just need to be heard.

More often, however, you encounter resisters whose attitudes
you won't change by hearing them out. They may be skeptical about
any change, cynical about new ideas, fiercely independent, or convinced that 4DX is excess bureaucratic overhead rather than a results-
oriented operating system.

If they continue to resist, you need to require their support as
members of a team that is larger than themselves. Usually, they will
begin to see the results the rest of the team members are experienc-
ing and then (sometimes reluctantly and silently) fall in line with the
rest.

What are the most common challenges of running 4DX every week?

How do you deal with them?
Teams often face three challenges: performing consistently on lead measures, keeping the scoreboard current, and attending WIG sessions regularly.

First, team members have to mentally decouple the WIGs from lead measures, meaning that they must focus on consistent and successful performance of the lead measures before they see the lag measure moving. It's like going to the gym every day: You need to exercise patience before you see the changes that result from exercise. If team members are sporadic about their performance against lead measures, they won't see the impact on the lag measures.

Second, team members may feel that keeping a scoreboard current is unnecessary busy-work. Unless the scoreboard is updated, nobody knows the score—they can't see if the lead measures are affecting the lags. Moreover, WIG sessions lose their power without the results of teamwork made visible.

Third, WIG sessions get postponed or canceled and team interest starts draining away. Without regular WIG sessions, people lose focus and no longer feel accountable for their commitments. The WIG session must be sacred. Team members must contribute to the quality of the WIG meeting by making commitments that impact the lead measures and WIG success.

We have seen so many programs *du jour*. How do we overcome our skepticism and get on board with the 4 Disciplines?
Many organizations are repeatedly afflicted with new programs that are in the spotlight one day and forgotten the next. Leaders looking for the next magic bullet thus produce cynicism in the workplace. As Stephen Covey likes to say, "You can't talk your way out of a situation you have behaved yourself into!" So when installing 4DX into a skeptical and disbelieving environment, start small with only one critically important goal that will truly make a difference to the daily lives of people—to the employees and the quality of their work life.

Then, having set just one ambitious and critical goal, be extra diligent in creating scoreboards, updating them consistently, and conducting weekly WIG sessions to prove to the team that they really can achieve a level of success they've never achieved before.

Strive for consistency in the process and a quick win. Once the team absolutely knows they can get significantly better results from 4DX, you can succeed at even more ambitious goals for the future.

Does 4DX need to start at the top of an organization?

No, in fact, it usually doesn't. Most often, 4DX starts somewhere in the middle. There are some obvious advantages if the CEO is involved right from the start, but many great senior leaders or even managers of small teams have successfully launched the process. It can start comfortably almost anywhere and grow.

While it would be great for all members of an organization to align with 4DX to drive results, it isn't necessary. However, a leader who sponsors 4DX needs responsibility for lag measures that are meaningful to upper management. If 4DX is to grow within an organization, senior leaders have to care about the initial results.

What if my boss is always throwing new goals at me?

We get this question a lot, and in a lot of different forms. Here is the bottom line: Most people can't control how many goals get thrown at them, but they *can* control which of those goals they choose to drive with 4DX—those few they consider wildly important.

How do you implement 4DX in a matrixed organization?

The 4DX methodology neither requires nor suggests reorganizing any company, matrixed or otherwise. What is necessary is cooperation and accountability matching.

For instance, a company with a WIG to increase market share might have to rely on a matrixed sales organization operating in multiple geographies: the United States and Canada; Central and South America; Europe, the Middle East, and Africa; and Asia Pacific, and so on. The success of the WIG depends on the cooperative performance of these geographically dispersed, matrixed sales organizations. A 4DX cross-functional team involved in manager certification will ensure that everyone who contributes to the WIG stays focused on the WIG.

Organizational structure is often irrelevant to designating the right team to support a particular WIG; it might take people with many different skill sets from many different parts of the organization.

If I run a support function like HR, finance, or IT, how should I go about selecting a WIG?

We have always found that it is much easier and more effective for the support organizations to choose their WIGs after the line functions (sales, production, and operations) choose theirs. If the line functions are clear on their wildly important goals, a support function can choose WIGs to help enable the achievement of the line WIGs.

For example, if the sales team's WIG is to move successfully to consultative selling, the HR function can set a WIG to ensure that every salesperson gets excellent training in the new model. If the firm's WIG is to move aggressively into social media, shouldn't the IT department with its unique expertise set a WIG to provide the best possible infrastructure for succeeding in social media?

My team works several shifts, so we are never all together. How do I handle the weekly accountability WIG session?

The key word in the question above is *accountability*. The primary purpose of the weekly WIG session is to maintain with all your team's players a cadence of accountability.

There are two parts to accountability. First, team members are accountable to each other to fulfill the personal commitments (only one or two each week) that they make. Second, equally if not more important, each team member needs the personal satisfaction and small win of having done what they said they were going to do and reporting it. This is a subtle form of recognition that each player receives every week when they report on their commitments.

Hence, every effort should be made to give every team member a chance to attend a WIG session or to account for commitments in some way.

With split shifts, a leader might hold several WIG sessions to involve all team members. If a team member works the graveyard shift and the leader rarely sees him or her, a weekly phone follow-up can provide the opportunity for personal accountability and feedback on how the team is doing.

How do we ensure that the message of our WIG is getting all the way through the organization to those on the front lines?
One of the best methods for addressing awareness of the goal is repetition. If the leaders and the 4DX internal coach establish a regular practice of asking individual associates, "What's our WIG?" or "What lead measures are you focusing on?" word will spread quickly, and more and more associates will learn and know the answer.

How do we conduct a weekly WIG session with team members who are seldom in the same place at the same time and who have a big whirlwind to deal with?
Remember that the team members in a WIG session need only from twenty to thirty minutes per week, and those in a WIG Huddle only five to seven minutes each week, so it's not a significant investment of time.

You can hold the WIG session right before or after an existing meeting, or when the greatest number can attend. You can then meet individually with those who cannot.

Remember this key discipline that drives focus and accountability for the WIG: Every member of the team must be in an accountability session around the scoreboard every week.

How do we get a resisting manager to fully adopt 4DX?
The leader is the best resource to help deal with this issue, which should be raised by the coach as a clear-the-path item. Most often, a private discussion with the manager is sufficient to resolve the problem.

Require all managers to report on their adherence to the process. Ask them to report:

- ✓ Team lag measure results for the week
- ✓ Team lead measure results for the week
- ✓ WIG meeting held and attendance percentage
- ✓ Percentage of team commitments fulfilled
- ✓ Personal commitment for last week and results
- ✓ Personal commitment for next week

When reluctant managers are held publicly accountable for these results, and when they hear other managers reporting success, they will almost always respond.

Sustainability of 4DX
What types of recognition work best to keep our teams engaged?
The types of recognition that have the greatest impact include:

- **Public recognition of *individual* performance.** Everyone wants to be recognized for their contribution, especially in front of their peers. Awards like Execution Leader of the Week or Top Performer This Week are greatly appreciated. Just be sure that the criteria for winning are fair and consistently applied.
- **Public recognition of *team* performance.** A team award for the week or month, such as Leaders in Lead Measures for the highest lead-measure performance, can also drive real behavior change.
- **Public recognition of *execution launch*.** A trophy for fastest launch, best scoreboard, or best WIG session can help to lock in the performance behaviors that drive results.
- ***Meaningful* celebration.** As we've said, taking time to meaningfully celebrate team performance is essential to keeping people engaged. The price of pizza or ice cream

is far outweighed by the returns on a small celebration, combined with a meaningful message from the leader.

How do I keep coming up with new and fresh commitments each week? A leader should be at no loss to come up with fresh commitments because the team's execution discipline can always be improved. The discipline of working on the system ultimately distinguishes a leader from an individual contributor. While this may seem challenging at first, it will soon become an exciting part of your role as you come to see the impact you can have.

While individual contributors make commitments to drive the lead measures, the most effective commitments a leader can make will leverage and improve the capabilities of the team. So instead of making direct commitments to the lead measures, the leader makes commitments that enable the entire team to move the lead measures.

As one of our clients says: "Leaders do not get paid for what leaders do. Leaders get paid for what they can get others to do."

If you're struggling for ideas, commit to do something in one of these areas:

- **Training.** There will always be team members who need to be trained or reengaged on the best practices of the team. Choose a team member and train or coach the individual in a specific skill during the coming week. This commitment might also help you to stay at the top of the game.
- **Engaging the team for higher performance.** One of the most powerful practices of high execution leaders is engaging the team in a two-way dialogue about the team's performance and their ideas for making it better. By listening and then implementing the team's ideas, the leader not only improves performance but also increases engagement. In this way, not only does the team do better, but each individual feels valued and respected,

which adds even more emphasis and enthusiasm to their performance.

- **Recognition and modeling.** Identify top performers and recognize them in front of their peers. Everyone wants to model winners. Recognition shows the team the behaviors and levels of performance the leader values. Recruit top performers to coach others.

As a senior leader, what it the most important thing I can do to sustain 4DX?

The most important contribution a senior leader can make is to remain focused on the wildly important goal and resist the allure of your next great idea. Remember, there will always be more good ideas than capacity to implement. Your focus becomes the organization's focus.

Second, ensure that you are modeling the process. Over time, your practices—not just your words—will have the greatest influence on the teams you lead.

Third, follow the suggestions made throughout this book for recognition of outstanding performance by both individuals and teams.

Over the past year, we did everything right. We created WIGs and measures and executed maniacally week after week, but we're not seeing results. What now?

Remember that a WIG is like a strategic bet. When you set a WIG, you're betting on a new product or service, or a new approach to a problem. And then you make an execution bet—you define the critical activities and lead measures and perform those activities relentlessly, in all confidence that the strategic bet will pay off.

But sometimes it doesn't pay off. There is no such thing as a brilliant strategy until it actually works. It's not a brilliant new automobile until it sells like hotcakes in the market. It's not a brilliant new way to improve student achievement until the school shoots past old achievement levels. You are making a bet. Of course, it should be an educated bet, but it is still a bet.

An insurance company made a strategic bet on a new kind of insurance policy targeted at a new market. They devised the approach in great detail, and rallied the sales force to fully engage in the critical actions to realize the goal. They worked maniacally, moving the lead measures on the scoreboards every week exactly according to plan. But, six months into it, the lag measures hadn't moved. Well, during this time a very intense competitor had devised a lower-cost product and delivered it in a leveraged, electronic way. The competitor had made a much better strategic bet.

So, while maintaining your confidence and enthusiasm, set your WIGs with humility and awareness. Place the best strategic bets that you can. But keep one eye on your scoreboards, and the other eye looking over your shoulder.

We've made fast progress on our WIG and it now seems likely that our team will exceed it. Should we raise the goal?
First, congratulations. It's always exciting when a team realizes they will meet or exceed their WIG.

When this happens, the first reaction of a leader is often to raise the goal. While the intention of this decision is good (to drive the team to higher performance), it can disillusion the team. Unless the change is handled carefully, the team will lose their sense of accomplishment and disengage from the new, higher goal. Then reengaging the team is more difficult than initially launching 4DX.

Here are the three most likely scenarios and how to deal with them:

- **The goal was set far too low and the team has already (or will soon) exceed it.** In this case, the right thing to do is to congratulate the team for their performance and then take full responsibility for setting the goal incorrectly. If possible, engage the team in setting a new WIG at a level that will challenge them while still being realistic.
- **The goal was set correctly but the team exceeded the leader's expectations and met it early.** In this case,

congratulate and reward the team for their outstanding performance and declare the original WIG successfully met. Then, set a new WIG for the remaining period of time with a new X to Y. Unless you celebrate their success, team members will conclude that they are running a race where the finish line is always moving out faster than they can run, and they will disengage. So celebrate their success and then involve the team in setting the new stretch goal.

- **Your goal was set correctly, but you benefited from a windfall.** Declare the WIG achieved and move on to a new WIG without delay. Otherwise, your team will falter in adopting 4DX. Remember, your goal is not just to achieve the WIG but to build a high-performance team.

4DX Process Tips and Traps

How do you know when it's time to change a lead measure?

It's dangerous to change a lead measure too quickly. Most teams begin looking for a new lead measure when they reach a plateau on the scoreboard. If the leader responds too soon, all the momentum of the lead measure will be lost, and the team will start over again when giving the original measure more time might have made the difference.

Before abandoning a lead measure, consider these important questions:

- Is the lead measure moving the lag measure? If so, be careful about changing something that's working.
- Is the lag measure moving enough? If not, you might consider raising the standard for performance on the lead measure before changing it. Remember, the lever has to move a lot for the rock to move a little.
- Is the scorekeeping on the lead measure accurate? If not, the team may have a false sense of the value of the lead measure.

- Has the team achieved the lead measure for at least twelve consecutive weeks? This is the minimum time, in our experience, needed for a team to form a habit. If not, they simply don't know yet what consistent performance will bring about.
- Will the performance of the team remain if we remove the lead measure from the scoreboard? If not, it's likely better to stay focused on the lead measure until it becomes a habit, so long as the lead measure is moving the WIG.

Remember that the big-picture aim of 4DX is to establish a new standard of consistency and excellence in some area of the team's operation, then to sustain it long enough to make it a habit.

What if the lead measure is moving but the lag isn't moving?
This is not uncommon, especially as you first begin 4DX. Here are three possible explanations:

- Often, it just takes time. We can't tell you how many times we have seen a delay between the lead and the lag.
- The team might not be consistently moving the lead measure. With all the energy invested in the new lead measure, people tend (consciously or unconsciously) to game the system a little. Be sure that the measurements are accurate and that people are not just showing you what you want to see. (This is one reason we are very leery of tying any kind of compensation to lead measures.)
- The lead measure just isn't predictive. Consider this explanation last because it's often the first conclusion people jump to. If in fact the lead measure is truly not moving the lag, it's time to reexamine your assumptions. We have seen organizations lay to rest beliefs long held but never questioned or tested. Another possibility is

that external conditions have changed so radically that the lead measure no longer applies.

How do you know if you have a good lead measure?

First, we want a measure that is predictive, which is to say that it is not only correlated but causal, not simply necessary but sufficient to move lag measure from X to Y within the time frame.

Look at these two contrasting lead measures for a WIG to increase sales:

A. Sales representative will make x number of visits a week to a client.
B. Sales representative will make x number of visits a week to move the targeted client one or more tiers down the sales cycle as defined by our sales performance model.

Choice A is correlated to the WIG and necessary for its achievement, but compared to Choice B it isn't specific enough to be a sufficient cause of increased sales.

Second, we want the right frequency. Are we acting on the lead measure often enough? Is it the right thing to do, but we just need to do more (or less) of it? Are three client visits a week the right number? Four? The only way to know is by testing the measure.

For years, major drug companies fielded huge sales forces because they believed the more often doctors were visited, the more they would prescribe their products. Doctors soon got weary of the flood of visitors; many banished salespeople from their offices. The frequency of the lead measure was all wrong.

Third, we want a lead measure that will motivate high-quality performance. Are we putting our best and finest effort into the lead measure? If I'm a salesperson, am I not just making sales calls but making excellent sales calls as defined by the team?

Some drug companies finally asked the frustrated doctors how they could help them most. The doctors replied, "Help us learn the science behind your products." As a result, the majors adopted a new sales model. Many pharmaceutical salespeople are now research scientists with a mission to educate rather than to push products. The lead measure of sales success in that industry has changed radically.

If the measure is predictive, done at the right frequency, and done with quality, you have a good lead measure and should see movement in the WIG over time.

How should we align compensation to support 4DX?

There is no one answer to this question.

If your organizational culture and compensation plan rewards performance against clearly articulated objectives at all levels, then compensation aligned to achieving WIGs would be both appropriate and expected. This plan will further reinforce the importance of 4DX as an operating system for achieving results.

If your current compensation plan is not aligned to performance, compensation for achieving WIGs can still be a sound practice. Note, however, that the purpose of a compensation system should not be to get the right *behaviors* from the wrong people, but to reward the right *people* in the first place, and to keep them there—this is the lesson Jim Collins learned in his research for *Good to Great*. Pay for performance on WIGs works fine, as long as you have the right people on the team.

Can 4DX support our performance management system?

It depends on the system.

4DX will support a system that emphasizes performance to specified goals and measures within established time frames. Personal development plans can be aligned to achieving WIGs—if, for example, a WIG requires people to develop certain new skills.

In some cases, our clients have replaced annual performance reviews with WIG sessions, which they feel are more immediate and more useful for gauging the performance of team members. Others have repurposed performance reviews to assess an individual's contribution to WIGs. Still others continue to hold traditional performance reviews in addition to the 4DX accountability system.

I'm having trouble determining whether we are making high-quality commitments each week. Can you tell me what defines a good commitment?

A high-quality commitment has three characteristics:

- **Specific.** Don't settle for a commitment such as "I'm going to focus on upselling." Instead, push for more specifics, such as "I'm going to coach three team members on how to properly upsell our premium wines."
- **Aligned.** Ensure that *every* commitment aligns to the WIG. Don't accept a commitment from the whirlwind. Each week in the WIG session, each team member answers the following question: "What could I do personally this week that would have the greatest impact on achieving our WIG?" This question should generate a weekly stream of new and better answers to match the changing priorities of the team.
- **Timely.** Make sure the commitment can be completed in the coming week. Watch out for multi-week commitments. Be wary of the "I'm making progress" answer.

Is there anything we can do to drive higher performance on a lead measure before we change it?

Yes. First, you are wise to sense that the performance that drives your initial results won't work at the same level indefinitely. The key here is to make careful adjustments that will continue to drive performance.

Consider these ideas for adjusting lead measures.

- **Raise the bar.** If the team has a lead measure for 90 percent performance, challenge them to drive it to 95 percent. Often, a small increase yields a disproportionate result and keeps the team reaching for a higher level.
- **Raise the quality.** If a team is meeting its lead measure performance standard, such as ten upsell conversations per person, then focus on raising the *quality* of those

upsells. Create a best-practice script, have team members role play during the meeting, or recognize those whose quality is outstanding and invite them to coach others.

- **Create a linkage.** If a lead measure has been fully adopted by a team, you can gain additional results by linking it to a closely related additional behavior. In a retail environment, this might mean linking the behavior of greeting every customer within ten seconds and walk them to the product they want. This slight expansion of the lead measure behavior can yield significant results and is far less disruptive than creating and installing a new lead measure.

What should we do when a leader is on vacation? Should we cancel the WIG session/huddle?

No. Consistency and accountability are the most powerful drivers of performance. When the cadence of the WIG sessions is interrupted, the team's momentum is lost. Even in the leader's absence, the performance of the team must continue.

If the leader is absent:

1. **Choose an individual to lead the meeting**—a supervisor or a senior member of the team. Some teams rotate the leadership role from week to week.
2. **Prepare them for success in your absence**—take time to communicate the importance of this responsibility and review the WIG session agenda with them.
3. **Recap and debrief when you return**—ask for a review of the session with the substitute leader as soon as you return. Take time to thank and congratulate them on handling this important responsibility.

Is it a good idea to have more than one coach?

Absolutely. With two coaches or more, they can share the workload of coaching the leaders and get backup or a logical replacement if a coach moves on to different responsibilities.

If you bring on a second coach, be sure to retain the primary, so that you can ensure that the advice and coaching are consistent.

Manufacturing Teams

Can 4DX be used to support methodologies such as lean manufacturing and Six Sigma?

Yes. One of the world's largest carpet manufacturers used a customized form of 4DX to run certain green- and black-belt teams. The 4DX teams cut their project completion time by almost 50 percent.

They found that project delays were due to the lack of involvement by team members trapped in the whirlwind. The Six Sigma work was being pushed back to the black belts and the projects were bogging down. When they ran their Six Sigma projects with visible 4DX scoreboards and held a weekly WIG session "to eat the elephant one bite at a time," not only was completion time cut nearly in half, but the team members had fun winning the game.

4DX can also ensure adoption of the new process changes that result from a Six Sigma project. In this case, 4DX is used to drive a change in behavior, which it was designed to do.

High Tech/Scientific Teams

Can you offer any lessons or watch-outs for leading a team of highly technical people (who are often skeptical) through 4DX?

Most technical individuals are hard wired to assess risk, identify gaps, and innovate to get viable solutions. They are under pressure to deliver on schedule within budget, to exceed customers' moving expectations and changing requirements, and to anticipate future needs—all under the threat of being outsourced. They relish challenges, and they build their careers on analyzing problems and creatively solving them.

If you try to impose 4DX on them as if they don't matter, they will dig their heels in. Unlike most groups, they tend to struggle more and take longer with Discipline 1. The idea of drawing a line in the sand—setting WIGs and measures in place—is often very frustrating for them because they can see all the things that can go wrong. We have found that if we take our time here and let them work though it and keep reminding them of the big picture, they will get there.

The good news is once they get through Discipline 1, they excel at Disciplines 2 and 3. It feels like a puzzle to them, and that's their strength.

How do we apply 4DX to creative or intuitive processes like R&D?
We have seen 4DX applied to many such teams, from R&D groups at pharmaceutical companies to squads of journalists. There is always the initial hesitation: "What we do can't really be managed with something like a lead measure." But we have never found that to be the case. The 4DX process tests their creativity, challenging them to figure out what it is about what they do that is both influenceable and predictive. You can never tell creative people what their lead measures ought to be, but you might be surprised what they come up with.

What kinds of lead measures yield the best results for these kinds of teams?
We have found very powerful lead measures tend to come from the touch points or the handoff within a technical or creative environment. For example:

- Increased interaction and communication earlier in the development process
- Sharing of knowledge with others
- Midstream process checks
- Key stakeholder discussions to assess changing requirements with development underway

Sales Teams
How can 4DX help us execute our new sales process?
4DX is extremely effective in helping people adopt a new sales process because it allows them to focus on specific high-leverage aspects of the process and really get those embedded before moving on to something else. The diagram on page 150 is a good example of this.

Sales is such an intuitive process for most professionals that lay-ing a process over it never feels comfortable. The first time it doesn't work out well, they often abandon the process and go back to what they think works for them. The problem is they are usually trying to eat the whole elephant at once. 4DX not only provides a vehicle for coaching and accountability but also helps a salesperson to get good at the process one bite at a time.

How do you get a sales team to commit to a weekly meeting?

Unless the sales team is held consistently accountable, middle performers will not dial up their game. Salespeople especially need the structure 4DX provides. The process gets sales teams sharing insights into what works, which is essential in a profession in which everyone believes they're already doing all the right things.

Don't most sales teams already have some form of lead measures?

In our experience, while most sales teams measure aspects of their sales pipeline, existing sales measures don't work as viable lead measures because they are not directly influenceable by the team.

Sales managers are often focused on measures that will give them better forecasting (predictability), but these are not usually in the control of the sales force. A predictive but non-influenceable measure does not give a sales team the leverage they need.

Of all people, sales managers are the most intensely focused on lag measures: quarterly volume, weekly bookings, and yearly revenues. Too often, their idea of management is to call team members on the phone and demand the numbers. Therefore, of all people, they are the most in need of effective lead measures. Once equipped with them, sales managers can truly make a difference: They can coach, train, and mentor people on the behaviors that drive results.

Government and Military Teams
Does 4DX add value in a military culture that is already based on a high degree of discipline and execution?

The military has already written the book on the art of execution—in combat, that is. They know how to win battles and stay radically focused despite the fog of war (the whirlwind), but the *garrison military*—that is, out of combat—is swamped by bureaucratic rules, resource constraints, and family demands. They are driven to serve dozens of merely urgent tasks while disregarding truly important goals, such as team readiness or personal development. Our many military clients often say, "It's ironic that a unit in combat can produce miracles, but the same team in peacetime becomes disengaged."

4DX is an effective system for reengaging the military. These are people who want to serve. They are mission oriented. The concept of the wildly important goal energizes them, and accountability is second nature to them.

How do you set WIGs in a government organization with many outside stakeholders pulling it in many different directions?

Government operations don't always seem designed to maximize results. At every turn, there is a tendency to be risk averse. One of our clients recently remarked, "Our government is designed to make change very hard and rewards behavior you might call *good enough for government*." Often, the various checks and balances that are in place make setting WIGs seem almost impossible. Impassioned leaders may have visionary strategic plans and announce them in town halls, but sustained behavior change is incredibly difficult when the employees return to their day jobs and face the whirlwind.

Leaders in public service must spend much more time promoting the WIG with all stakeholders, especially the employees. Involvement in defining the WIGs helps engage their minds and hearts once adopted. Once the employees are engaged and given the opportunity to sharpen and validate the leader's intent, then the WIGs need to be shared with the customers who receive the services. It's much more work and there is risk in being so bold, but it's a formula that produces dramatic results, as we've seen in the story of B. J. Walker and the State of Georgia.

How can implementing 4DX increase employee engagement?

4DX is a system not only for reaching big goals but also for increasing employee engagement and satisfaction.

Usually, employee engagement is gauged through surveys about the workplace, the leadership, and the culture. Let's see how 4DX principles affect these typical measures of employee engagement:

Survey Category	Survey Question	4DX Principle
Measurable Goals	I know what is expected of me at work.	Wildly important goals and lead measures create clear expectations of measurable results.
	I understand how my efforts contribute to our overall success.	Weekly commitments clearly connect individual efforts to organizational goals.
Mentoring and Coaching	The organization encourages my personal and career development.	WIG session accountability provides regular and frequent feedback on performance.
	I receive timely and constructive feedback.	
Communication	Leadership communicates and explains key decisions.	In the selection and communication of WIGs, leaders discuss and clarify what's most important to the organization.
	The organization values my opinion.	Through team involvement in setting WIGs and the weekly cadence of accountability, every team member's voice is repeatedly heard.
	I know what's happening in the organization because leadership keeps me informed.	Conducting WIG sessions and summit meetings communicates and celebrates team performance.

(*continued on next page*)

Survey Category	Survey Question	4DX Principle
Positive Work Environment	I enjoy coming to work.	Belonging to a team with winning mindset and a culture of accountability raises morale and enjoyment of the work.
	I regularly receive recognition or praise for my contributions.	WIG sessions and reports provide many opportunities for high recognition of individual and team performance.
	I am treated fairly at work.	Every individual is able to see that everyone is held accountable in an equal and fair way for fulfilling the commitments they make.
Individual and Team Accountability	Individuals on my team are held accountable for results.	Weekly commitments accounted for in WIG sessions apply to everyone.
	Leadership follows through on their promises.	Leaders go first in a WIG session and candidly report their own follow through on commitments. Leaders are as accountable as anyone else.
Opportunity and Advancement	I have the resources I need to do my best work.	In weekly WIG sessions team members can ask leaders and peers to clear the path of an obstacle or problem, ensuring that each individual is able to succeed.
	Because the team is aligned around a WIG and pursuing lead measures with shared accountability, team cooperation and synergy are maximized.	

Survey Category	Survey Question	4DX Principle
Trust	I trust the leaders of our organization.	Shared accountability, shared commitments, and open communication create a climate of trust.

Bringing It Home

Change is hard.

If you've ever tried to lose weight, improve your marriage, stop smoking or drinking, start a new relationship, develop a hobby, or finish that degree you've been working on for eight years, you know what we mean.

In this chapter, we want to briefly show how these principles of team execution can also be used to help people change their lives and accomplish some important personal or family goal.

It happens all the time. People approach us after a 4DX work session, look around to make sure no one is listening, and whisper: "Do you think 4DX would work in my personal life?"

Our answer? Absolutely. Although we didn't set out to find a better way to accomplish personal goals, we discovered that 4DX is a profound methodology for achieving any goal of any kind, whether at work or at home. Not surprisingly, the principles of focus, leverage, engagement, and accountability, which undergird each of the disciplines, seem to work at any level, be it organizational, team, or personal.

Take the case of Jeffrey Downs, a colleague of ours. After helping numerous organizations apply 4DX, Jeffrey couldn't resist sharing the insights he was learning with his wife, Jami. On her own accord, Jami decided to apply them to a very personal matter.

• • •

When my husband, Jeff, showed me the 4 Disciplines of Execution, I knew I could use those principles in my personal life. I already had a complex life, but now that I was pregnant with our seventh child I knew I had my work cut out for me. In order to keep pace and stay in shape, I had to do something different.

Deciding on my wildly important goal took a lot of thought and energy, even though it now seems so simple. I decided that my WIG would be, "Don't gain more than thirty-six pounds by October 9th."

Naturally, I knew that the two ways to reach my goal were through eating and exercising. Our family had a healthy diet and so I wasn't real concerned about the food. Instead, I focused on the exercise part and I chose one lead measure: "Walk ten thousand steps per day." Sure, there were many other things I could have focused on; however, with the whirlwind of six children and a husband who is on the road three days a week, this was the lead measure that I thought was challenging but doable to get to my WIG.

What transpired over the next nine months was truly remarkable. I no longer focused on my weight. I simply focused on walking by parking far away in the grocery-store parking lot, walking instead of driving to my children's school, or getting up early to walk with friends or my husband. Whenever I had an opportunity to walk, I walked.

Figuring out a simple scoreboard was more challenging than I thought. At first, I started by trying to graph my progress. That didn't work. So, I tried a computer spreadsheet, but it was too hard to consistently find computer time. What finally distilled out of all these attempts was a scoreboard that I hung on my bathroom mirror that had four columns: the day, the number of steps I needed to take that day, the actual steps I had taken that day, and the overall total steps. In a simple glance I could tell where I was, where I needed to be, and whether I was winning or losing.

The key to my scoreboard was not where I was, but rather where I should be. This set the scoreboard apart from any other scoreboard I had ever kept. In the past I just kept track of where I was. Now I was keeping track of where I was compared to where I should be. And that made it a game.

The whole family got in on the game. My children would ask me if I had done my ten thousand steps. My oldest daughter would walk with me when she knew I was tired. My husband was my accountability partner and he and I would go over the scoreboard and I would make commitments on what I was going to do the next week to keep walking.

Something amazing happened during all of this that was completely unexpected. When I learned that I was pregnant with our seventh child, one of my concerns was that my time with my other children would suffer. I thought and prayed a lot about this and didn't know how this concern would be answered. But, by focusing on the simple task of walking, an activity that everyone was aware of and everyone could participate in, my relationships with my children and my husband were actually strengthened. From toddler to teenager everyone could walk with me, and as a result, I grew closer to each.

For example, I did a lot of walking and talking with my oldest daughter. We talked through difficulties she was having with her friends, what college she wanted to attend, and how her boyfriend was treating her. With my other children I learned about their joys and struggles, what they thought about having a large family, and how they felt about a new baby. With my youngest I established a strong bond which I cherish to this day.

When talking with my husband about the 4 Disciplines, he would often refer to the *ancillary benefits* of following them, but I never realized how significant that would be in my life. In the end I did achieve my wildly important goal, gaining fewer than thirty-six pounds. In the process I took 1,751,250 steps. More important, I strengthened family relationships and on October 4, I delivered a healthy baby boy.

• • •

As you read this remarkable story, we hope you were able to spot some of the same insights we noticed.

First, Jami was smart to narrow her focus to only one lead measure. To achieve her WIG of not gaining more than thirty-six pounds she knew she needed to focus on diet and exercise. But because she already ate a healthy diet, watching what she ate wasn't necessary. So why track it? It would only add complexity. Instead, she chose to focus on the single new and different behavior she thought would make the difference, walking ten thousand steps per day. There's a good lesson here. In some cases, the best thing is to focus on the single thing (lead measure) you need to do differently that will make all the difference, instead of the many.

Next, the key ingredient on her scoreboard was the where-I-should-be column. If you don't know where you should be at any given moment, it is hard to tell if you are winning or losing. Always knowing where you are in relation to where you should be is one of the key aspects of a compelling scoreboard. As Jami also learned, finding the right scoreboard, a scoreboard that is motivating and simple and easily updatable, is not easy. In our experience, this is where most people get stuck. They come up with a good WIG, define a lead measure or two, and then never pay the price to put up the scoreboard. Then the whole thing falls apart. Don't let that happen to you.

Finally, there is power in public accountability. Jami's husband was her official accountability partner, but her kids were every bit as involved. Whenever you set a personal goal, your chances for success go way up as soon as you involve others in your goal and have them hold you accountable.

One of our clients tells the touching story of his five-year-old son who just couldn't overcome a bedwetting problem. The family had tried a lot of things, but the problem persisted. "He would wake up in the night and not make it to the bathroom," his dad said.

"After going through 4DX training, I had a light bulb go off. That evening at the dinner table, my son and I started to talk about how we were going to help him make it through the night without wetting his bed. We would make a calendar for every day of the week and go for a month at a time. We put the calendar on the refrigerator so that his mother and his brothers could see the results.

"Every morning after that my son would come down for breakfast and he would report whether he was wet or dry. We had a green crayon and a red crayon. He would draw a green smiley face or a red frowny face depending on how he had fared the previous night. Of course, the first morning he drew a green face the whole family made a big deal of it and gave him high fives and so on. After a full week of greens we made it really special by going for ice cream. Within thirty days, he was sleeping through the night and was dry!

"It seems so simple, but the fact that my son posted a scoreboard and would report to the family every morning—in a cadence of accountability—made it so important to him that he took it very seriously."

Here's a fun scoreboard created by one of our clients who wanted to lose eighty pounds in a six-month period before his son's high-school graduation. His lead measures:

- Walk five miles per day
- No eating after eight in the evening
- Limit intake to 2500 calories per day

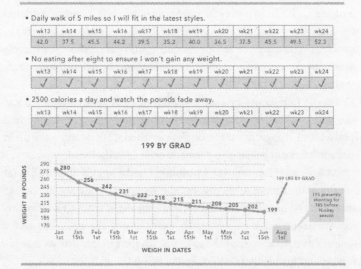

He achieved his goal and then set another WIG to drop fifteen more pounds before his beloved hockey season so he could get out and play with his kids.

Of course, 4DX is about more than just turning around a tough situation. It's also about achieving your highest goals and aspirations.

One of our colleagues sets three WIGs for himself at the beginning of each year—one professional goal, one family goal, and one personal goal. He carefully identifies his lead measures, tracks his scoreboard, and spends thirty minutes each week evaluating progress on his prior commitments and setting new commitments for the coming week. Through this practice he is able to stay balanced and accomplish a great deal.

We know of people who have used 4DX to achieve all kinds of life goals: running a marathon, finishing a degree, learning a new sport, even blending two families. Some of the WIGs we've heard about are profoundly personal.

Another colleague has several young grandchildren. He has a deeply felt personal WIG that they should all know that he loves them and that they can turn to him for anything. Of course, the lag measure is kind of hard to pin down. When asked, he laughs, "I can tell I'm winning if they run up and hug me instead of running away from me."

His lead measure is very clear, however. "I have a strict personal policy of spending time with each one of them every week." On weekends, he might be at the dinosaur museum, the playground, or the soccer field watching them play. Every year he takes them to buy pumpkins for Halloween and to the amusement park and the Renaissance Fair in the summer. He never misses the birthday parties. Sometimes he just shows up in the evening to read a bedtime story or two.

His strategic bet is that careful attention to this lead measure will reap dividends forever. "The lag measure already moves—you should see it move!" he says. "Whenever they see me, they scream and giggle and throw themselves at me. Do you think anything in this world is more wildly important to me than that?"

Another friend of ours, married with children, relates how he worked on a personal WIG of improving the culture of his family over an entire year but felt like he made little progress. He had several lead measures but none of them seemed to be working. In a moment of clarity, he recognized that the single best way he could improve the feeling in his home, the culture, was "to love their mother." In other words, he needed to do a better job of showing his kids how much he adored his wife, their mother, through kindness, gentleness, and small acts of service. So this single measure became his focus, and, as he relates, it immediately made all the difference. "Seeing the love we had for each other as mom and dad seemed to cascade good feelings upon the kids and upon home in general and resolve a multitude of other everyday challenges our family was facing."

So many of the wildly important things in our lives never get the attention we should give them because they aren't urgent. Caring for our health, helping our children, getting more education, strengthening our marriage—these things tend to take second place to the whirlwind of urgencies that require our attention right now.

According to Dr. Ray Levey, founder of the Global Medical Forum, 80 percent of our health-care budget is consumed by five behavioral issues: smoking, drinking, overeating, stress, and not enough exercise. The cause of most disease, he says, is very well known and by and large behavioral. Just changing these five behaviors would eliminate our health-care crisis.

Even after life-threatening heart attacks and strokes, people generally don't change their behavior. "[It's] been studied over and over and over again. And so we're missing some link in there. Even

LINK: http://www.4dxbook.com/qr/GoalSetting

Scan the image above to see a video on 4DX and personal goal setting.

though they know they have a very bad disease and they know they should change their lifestyle, for whatever reason, they can't."[30]

Could it be that the missing link is an operating system for changing human behavior—a system like 4DX?

Do we think 4DX can apply to your personal life? Our answer is a resounding yes! In fact, we think the principles in this book can help you to achieve any great purpose you have in mind.

So, Now What?

Now that you've finished reading *The 4 Disciplines of Execution,* your mind might be spinning. If you're like most people, so much about the 4DX operating system is not in your DNA. To most people, it's counterintuitive to manage things this way. To some people it seems too simple; to others, way too complex.

At the same time, we believe you'll benefit dramatically from experimenting with 4DX. In fact, we believe that once you understand the 4 Disciplines of Execution, you will never lead in the same way again. Years of trial and error have convinced us that the art of execution comes down to the handful of principles and practices in this book.

Actually, we hope your mind *is* spinning—with possibilities!

The question is, now what?

We invite you to try a few simple thought experiments—they won't take long:

Discipline 1: Focus on the Wildly Important

If you haven't already done so, try your hand at drafting a wildly important goal and lag measure for your work team. Ask yourself these questions: "If we achieved that WIG, what would it mean to my team? To my organization? To myself?"

Discipline 2: Act on the Lead Measures

Try drafting lead measures that would drive your WIG to accomplishment. Ask yourself: "How would this new understanding of lead measures change the way we operate?"

Discipline 3: Keep a Compelling Scoreboard

Sketch a scoreboard complete with WIG, lag measure, and lead measures. Ask yourself: "What difference would it make if we focused our best efforts on moving the numbers on that scoreboard? What impact would it have on the team? On our business results?"

Discipline 4: Create a Cadence of Accountability

Visualize your team holding a WIG session around the scoreboard. Ask yourself: "How would regular, frequent WIG sessions change the way we operate? How would our focus and engagement change?"

Finally . . .

Envision for yourself the day you report the achievement of your wildly important goal to your own leaders. What would that day be like for your team? For you?

Now, imagine that day never comes. Imagine you forget everything you've read in this book. Consider spending the future in the midst of a relentless whirlwind where everything is always urgent and the really important priorities are forever postponed.

The great management scientist Peter Drucker observed, "I've seen a great many people who are magnificent at getting the unimportant things done. They have an impressive record of achievement on trivial matters."[31]

But you don't want to be magnificently trivial. You want to make a real difference. You want to make a high-value, high-impact contribution. The 4 Disciplines of Execution can take you there.

If we can help you move forward in any way, we're ready.

But remember, the achievement of your wildly important goal is not the only objective here. 4DX gives you knowledge and skills to do something far more important in the long run—to reignite the passion of your team, to bring focus and discipline to their efforts, and ultimately, to help them see that they are *winners*.

In your career, you will never leave a greater legacy than this. Instilling this sense of winning in the people you work with will not only drive a new level of performance in your organization, but will also equip these people with the skills and confidence they need to become winners in every phase of their lives, as workers, as fathers and mothers, or as leaders in their communities. And that's a legacy that *can't* be measured.

Glossary

4DX: An abbreviation for the 4 Disciplines of Execution.

4 Disciplines of Execution: An orderly pattern of conduct that leads to achievement of an organizational goal with excellence. The 4 Disciplines are based on deep research and field work, as well as fundamental principles of human behavior, and are proprietary to FranklinCovey Co.

Accountability: The ability to report progress or lack of progress using numbers.

"Battle": Within the context of the 4 Disciplines, an enabling or supporting WIG owned by a lower-level team. The principle is to identify the fewest possible "battles" to win the "war."

"Beating the Goat": The point at which a lead measure on a scoreboard is "on target," i.e., where it should be according to plan. The expression comes from a scoreboard created by a 4DX practitioner on which the symbol of a goat is used to represent a lead measure.

Behavioral-Change Strategy: A strategy that requires people— sometimes many people—to do things that are new and different. Because of the difficulty of changing human behavior, such a strategy is usually much more difficult to execute than a stroke-of-the-pen strategy (see entry).

Cadence of Accountability: A recurring cycle of planning and accounting for results. Disciplined execution of WIGs requires a cadence—a rhythm of planning, follow-through, and reporting. This cycle takes the form of a WIG session at least weekly.

Champion: The organizational sponsor of the 4 Disciplines process.

"Clearing the Path": Taking ownership of and resolving a problem or obstacle to achieving the WIG; helping another team member to accomplish an objective. One of the purposes of the team WIG session is to plan how to "clear the path" to execution.

Coach: A person well-versed in the 4 Disciplines who acts as a resource to managers installing the 4 Disciplines in their teams.

Commitment: Within the context of the 4 Disciplines, an individual team member's weekly contribution to achieving a WIG.

Dashboard: A collection of scoreboards by which senior leaders can readily gauge progress on key organizational measures and adherence to the 4 Disciplines. An example is my4dx.com (see entry).

Discipline: A consistent regimen that leads to freedom of action. Without consistent discipline, the team loses the ability to achieve WIGs with precision and excellence, thus losing influence and scope for action.

Discipline 1: Focus on the Wildly Important: The practice of defining crucial goals and narrowing the team's focus to those goals. Work teams who practice Discipline 1 are totally clear on a few WIGs and the lag measures (see entry) for those goals.

Discipline 2: Act on the Lead Measures: The practice of consistently carrying out and tracking results on those high-leverage activities that will lead to achievement of WIGs. Work teams who practice Discipline 2 are clear on the lead measures (see entry) of their goals and track them carefully.

Discipline 3: Keep a Compelling Scoreboard: The practice of visibly tracking key success measures on a goal. Work teams who practice Discipline 3 are continually preoccupied with moving the measures on the scoreboard.

Discipline 4: Create a Cadence of Accountability: The practice of regularly and frequently planning and reporting on activities intended to move the measures on the WIG scoreboard. Work teams who practice Discipline 4 make individual and collective commitments and account for those commitments in weekly WIG sessions.

Execution: The discipline of getting things done as promised—on time, on budget, and with quality. What "executives" are hired to do!

Execution Gap: The gap between setting a strategy or a goal and actually achieving it. This gap is expressed in terms of *from X to Y by when* (see lag measure).

From X to Y by When: The formula for expressing lag measures, tracking movement from a current "X" to a better or more desirable "Y" within a certain time frame. This formula is essential to understanding exactly what it means to "win," to achieve the WIG.

Goal: Any target expressed in terms of lag measures (see entry) that represents improvement in the organization's performance.

Important Goal: A goal with significant consequence and value. Compare to wildly important goal (see entry).

Lag Measure: The measure of goal or WIG achievement. A historical measure of performance, e.g., end-of-year revenue, quality scores, customer satisfaction numbers. Lag measures are typically easy to measure but difficult to influence directly. A lag measure is always expressed in terms of *from X to Y by when*.

Lead Measure: The measure of an action planned and taken as a means to achieving a WIG. Unlike lag measures, lead measures are influenceable by the team and predictive of the goal. Good lead measures are the highest-leverage activities a team can engage in to ensure execution of the WIG; therefore, lead measures are carefully tracked on the team scoreboard. The lead measures constitute the team's "strategic bet" that if they take these measures they will execute the goal with excellence; thus, one purpose of the execution process is to test the lead measures to determine as quickly as possible if the bet is a good one.

Line of Sight: The relationship between goals at each level of an organization, e.g., the link between the daily tasks of a front-line worker and the overall strategy of the organization. Teams in a well-executing organization have clear line of sight at all levels.

Manager Certification: A process in which managers gain the documented ability to lead a team to achieving a WIG by implementing the 4 Disciplines of Execution.

Manager Work Session: A session in which peer managers are oriented to the 4 Disciplines of Execution and draft WIGs and measures for the teams they manage.

Mission: The organization's or team's predefined purpose or reason for being. A WIG is often a goal essential to carrying out the organization's mission or strategy (see entry).

My4DX.com: An online tool for managing (1) adherence to the 4 Disciplines across the organization and (2) achievement of team and organizational WIGs.

Project: A planned undertaking involving defined steps, milestones, and tasks. A project may be undertaken in order to *achieve* a WIG, but the project itself is not a WIG.

Scoreboard: A mechanism for tracking progress on lead and lag measures for a WIG. It should be visible to the entire team and consistently and regularly updated. A scoreboard is "compelling" if it indicates quickly and clearly whether the team is winning or not, thus motivating action.

"Strategic Bet": The hypothesis that certain high-leverage activities will drive the achievement of a goal. This hypothesis must be proven through execution (see lead measure).

Strategy: A plan or method for achieving the mission of the organization or team. A WIG is a goal essential to carrying out the organization's strategy.

Stroke-of-the-Pen Strategy: A strategy that leaders execute just by ordering or authorizing it to be done and that generally does not require a lot of people to do things differently; contrast with behavioral-change strategies that require people to do new and different things.

Summit: A periodic report to senior management on progress on WIGs. It provides the team an opportunity to be recognized and to celebrate their success.

Team: A group of people specifically designated to achieve a WIG. A team may or may not be aligned with a formal organizational chart.

Team Work Session: A work session in which teams finalize their goals and measures and commit to maintaining a cadence of accountability for their goals.

"War": Within the context of the 4 Disciplines, a synonym for the highest-level organizational WIG. Compare to "battle" (see entry). Also called "the overall WIG."

"Whirlwind": A metaphor for the enormous amount of time and energy required to keep the organization at its current level of performance. The "whirlwind" is the main threat to the execution of WIGs; therefore, one of the recurring tasks of the work team is to plan how to clear the path through the whirlwind of demands on everyone's time.

WIG: Abbreviation for wildly important goal (see entry).

WIG Session: A team meeting held at least weekly to account for commitments, review WIG scoreboards, and plan how to improve the scores on the scoreboards. The regular WIG session is essential to maintaining the cadence of accountability, which is key to executing WIGs.

Wildly Important Goal: A goal essential to carrying out the organization's mission or strategy. Failure to achieve this goal will render all other achievements secondary. (Abbreviated WIG.) Compare to important goal (see entry).

Work Session: A meeting in which WIGs, measures, and scoreboards are developed for carrying out key organizational strategies.

Notes

The Real Problem with Execution

1 Patrick Litre, Alan Bird, Gib Carey, Paul Meehan, "Results Delivery: Busting Three Common Myths of Change Management," *Insights,* Bain & Company, Jan. 12, 2011. http://www.bain.com/ publications/articles/results-delivery-busting-3-common-change -management-myths.aspx.

2 See Rafael Aguayo, *Dr. Deming: The American Who Taught the Japanese About Quality* (New York: Simon & Schuster, 1991), 57–63.

3 Tim Harford, "Trial, Error, and the God Complex," TED.com, July 20, 2011, http://www.ted.com/talks/tim_harford.html.

4 See *Who Says We Can't?* FranklinCovey video, 2005.

Discipline 1: Focus on the Wildly Important

5 Quoted in John Naish, "Is Multitasking Bad for Your Brain?" *Mail Online,* Aug. 11, 2009. http://www.dailymail.co.uk/health/article-1205669/ Is-multi-tasking-bad-brain-Experts-reveal-hidden-perils-juggling-jobs.html.

6 Cited in Don Tapscott, *Grown Up Digital* (New York: McGraw-Hill, 2009), 108–9.

7 "Brand of the Decade: Apple," *AdWeek Media,* 2010, http://www .bestofthe2000s.com/brand-of-the-decade.html; "Marketer of the Decade: Apple," *Advertising Age,* October 18, 2010; Adam Lashinsky, "The Decade of Steve," *Fortune,* November 23, 2009, http://money.cnn.com/magazines/ fortune/fortune_archive/2009/11/23/toc.html.

8 Dan Frommer, "Apple COO Tim Cook," *Business Insider,* February 23, 2010, http://www.businessinsider.com/live-apple-coo-tim-cook-at-the -goldman-tech-conference-2010-2.

9 Cited in Steven J. Dick, "Why We Explore," http://www.nasa.gov/exploration/whyweexplore/Why_We_29.html.

10 "Text of President John F. Kennedy's Rice Moon Speech," September 12, 1962. http://er.jsc.nasa.gov/seh/ricetalk.htm.

11 Quoted in "Steve Jobs' Magic Kingdom," *Bloomberg Businessweek,* February 6, 2006. http://www.businessweek.com/magazine/content/06_06/b3970001.htm.

Discipline 2: Act on the Lead Measures

12 Quoted in Aguayo, *Dr. Deming,* 18.

13 Richard Koch, *The 80/20 Principle: The Secret to Achieving More with Less* (New York: Crown Business, 1999), 94.

14 Keith H. Hammonds, "How to Play Beane Ball," *Fast Company,* December 19, 2007, http://www.fastcompany.com/magazine/70/beane.html; Michael Lewis, *Moneyball: The Art of Winning an Unfair Game* (New York: W. W. Norton, 2004), 62–63, 119–137.

15 John Schamel, "How the Pilot's Checklist Came About," January 31, 2011, http://www.atchistory.org/History/checklst.htm.

Discipline 3: Keep a Compelling Scoreboard

16 Teresa M. Amabile, Steven J. Kramer, "The Power of Small Wins," *Harvard Business Review,* May 2011.

Discipline 4: Create a Cadence of Accountability

17 See Jon Krakauer, *Into Thin Air: A Personal Account of the Mt. Everest Disaster* (New York: Anchor Books, 1998), 333–344.

18 See "Everest," FranklinCovey video, 2008.

19 Jack Welch, Suzy Welch, *Winning* (New York: Harper Collins, 2005), 67.

20 From Atul Gawande, *Better: A Surgeon's Notes on Performance* (New York: Metropolitan Books, 2007).

21 Patrick Lencioni, *The Three Signs of a Miserable Job* (San Francisco: Jossey-Bass, 2007), 136–7.

22 Edward M. Hallowell, *Crazy Busy* (New York: Random House Digital, 2007), 183.

23 Suzanne Robins, "Effectiveness of Weight Watchers Diet," Livestrong.com, December 23, 2010. http://www.livestrong.com/article/341703-effectiveness-of-weight-watchers-diet/

What to Expect

24 M.C. Vos, et al., "5 years of experience implementing a methicillin-resistant Staphylococcus aureus search and destroy policy at the largest university medical center in the Netherlands," *Infection Control and Hospital Epidemiology,* October 30, 2009. http://www.ncbi.nlm.nih.gov/pubmed/19712031.

Installing Discipline 1: Focus on the Wildly Important

25 Quoted in Clayton M. Christensen, "What Customers Want from Your Products," *Working Knowledge,* Harvard Business School, January 16, 2006. http://hbswk.hbs.edu/item/5170.html

Installing Discipline 2: Act on the Lead Measures

26 Jim Collins, "Turning Goals into Results: The Power of Catalytic Mechanisms," *Harvard Business Review*, July-August 1999, 73.

Installing Discipline 4: Create a Cadence of Accountability

27 John Case, "Keeping Score," *Inc. Magazine,* June 1 1998. http://www.inc.com/magazine/19980601/945.html

28 Eric Matson, "The Discipline of High-Tech Leaders," *Fast Company*, 1997.

Rolling Out

29 Atul Gawande, *The Checklist Manifesto: How to Get Things Right* (New York: Metropolitan Books, 2009), 183.

Bringing It Home

30 Quoted in Alan Deutschman, "Change or Die," *Fast Company*, May 2005, 53.

So, Now What?

31 Quoted in Rich Karlgaard, "Peter Drucker on Leadership," *Forbes*, November 19, 2004. http://www.forbes.com/2004/11/19/cz_rk_1119drucker.html

Acknowledgments

This book is the product of contributions from literally dozens upon dozens of people from the FranklinCovey organization. Our names are on this book, but we recognize that there are many others who are just as deserving. This truly was a company-wide effort and embodies everything we teach about synergy, where the whole is greater than the sum of its parts. So many contributed in so many different ways. Some were instrumental in the design and development of the 4 Disciplines content. Others refined the methodology through continual application in the field with clients. Still others added an idea or an insight or a new way of viewing an old problem. It seemed that every time we were missing a piece of the execution puzzle, someone showed up who had the answer. The baton was passed again and again as different people led different efforts to commercialize and scale this execution business around the globe. Our heart-felt gratitude goes to everyone who has contributed to this success and particularly to the following individuals:

Jim Stuart, for your extraordinary contribution to Franklin-Covey over a period of many years as a senior consultant and for sharing the principles of execution with the rest of us. Without you, there is no 4 Disciplines. Thank you for your great one-liners and for coining the terms "wildly important," "land one at a time," and "compelling scoreboard," among others. We are forever indebted.

Bob Whitman, our CEO, who recognized years ago that execution was a big idea and then steered us in that direction. Your fingerprints, language, ideas, and influence are all throughout this book. We so appreciate your visionary leadership and support.

The original design and development team (consisting of **Andy Cindrich, Don Tanner, Jim Stuart,** and **Scott Larson**), who conceived and developed the original 4 Disciplines content from scratch. We also wish to thank the subsequent development teams that followed, which included **Todd Davis, Breck England, Catherine Nelson, Blaine Lee,** and **Lynne Snead**.

Mark Josie, for building the initial execution practice, helping to crack the code on implementation, and creating the vision and strategy behind my4dx.com software. We acknowledge your heavy influence on the content and appreciate your pioneering efforts in getting this solution off the ground.

Breck England, our Chief Writing Officer, for contributing greatly to the development of the 4 Disciplines content and for your remarkable talents in helping the authors to write and edit this book. Your contributions raised this book to a whole different level.

Andy Cindrich, a key member of the original design and development team, for your contributions to the content, and for the truly excellent work you have done and continue to do with your clients in execution.

Scott Thele, for your help on the "Focusing the Organization" chapter and your contribution to the Execution Practice.

Doug Puzey, for helping us crack the code on implementation and building our first 4DX Practice.

Jeff Wadsworth, for thought leadership and content creation.

Michael Simpson, for your contribution on applying 4DX to project management and manufacturing.

Michele Condon, for your constant management support, passionate encouragement, and keeping everyone sane.

Catherine Nelson, for leading the charge on early versions of 4DX including the development of Manager Certification.

Todd Davis, for leading the version 2.0 development team and for pointing out that people "play differently when they're keeping score."

Sam Bracken, our general manager over books and media at FranklinCovey, for reestablishing our relationship with Simon & Schuster, negotiating the rights for this book, and for your continual support throughout the lifecycle of the book.

Our publishing team at Simon & Schuster, **Carolyn Reidy, Martha Levin,** and our editor, **Dominick Anfuso,** for your enthusiasm and belief in this work and for your ongoing efforts to market it to everyone under the sun.

Jody Karr, Cassidy Back, and the **Creative Services** team at FranklinCovey, for helping with the numerous graphics in the book.

Don Tanner, a member of the original design team and one of our best consultants, for your early contributions to the content.

Richard Garrison, for your work on 4DX coaching and for enhancing the implementation process, as well as the excellence you bring to your consulting and to our clients.

Rebecca Hession, for your client leadership and extraordinary innovations.

David Covey, for your exceptional support and commitment to our team over many years.

Shawn Moon, for your leadership and your guidance of the Execution Practice.

Scott Larson, for doing a great job as the project leader of the original development team.

Bill Bennett, our former division President, for challenging us at the beginning to "go out and build the world's best solution on the topic of execution. I don't care if you buy it or build it, just do it."

Doug Faber, for your help in expanding the practice and for your many innovative contributions.

Tom Watson, Jeff Downs, Rick Wooden, and **Lance Hilton,** for your leadership in the Execution Practice.

Paul Walker, Marianne Phillips, and **Elise Roma,** for your organizational support over many years.

To **Stephen M.R. Covey,** for helping, in the early days, identify that *Execution* was the issue of our time, and to **Greg Link,** who offered much wise counsel in helping to launch and market the book.

To **Scott Miller** and **Curtis Morley,** for your guidance and support in helping to develop and execute a superb launch plan for this book.

To **Debra Lund,** for your encouragement and friendship, and for the unbelievable way in which you, once again, rounded up so many great endorsements from all over.

Les Kaschner, James Western, Chris Parker, Harvey Young, De'Verl Austin, Coral Rice, Wayne Harrison, Kelly Smith, Craig Wennerholm, Garry Jewkes, Rick Spencer, Bryan Ritchie, and **Pepe Miralles,** for your innovation and dedication to client results.

Index

Page numbers in *italics* refer to illustrations.

311

About the Authors

Chris McChesney

Chris McChesney is the Global Practice Leader of Execution for FranklinCovey and one of the primary developers of the 4 Disciplines of Execution. For more than a decade, he has led FranklinCovey's on-going design and development of these principles, as well as the consulting organization that has achieved extraordinary growth in many countries around the globe and impacted hundreds of organizations. Chris has personally led many of the most noted implementations of the 4 Disciplines, including the State of Georgia, Marriott International, Shaw Industries, Ritz Carlton, Kroger, Coca Cola, Comcast, Frito Lay, Lockheed Martin and Gaylord Entertainment. This practical experience has enabled him to test and refine the principles contained in the 4 Disciplines of Execution from the boardrooms to the front line of these, and many other organizations.

Chris's career with FranklinCovey began by working directly with Dr. Stephen R. Covey and has continued over two decades to include roles as a Consultant, Managing Director, and General Manager within the organization. Chris launched the first 4 Disciplines of Execution Practice in the Southeast Region of FranklinCovey and today has seen it expand around the globe. Throughout this period of significant growth and expansion, Chris has maintained a single focus: to help organizations get results through improved execution.

Known for his high-energy and engaging message, Chris has become a highly sought after speaker, consultant, and advisor on strategy execution, regularly delivering keynote speeches and executive presentations to leaders in audiences ranging from the hundreds to several thousand.

Chris, and his wife, Constance, are the proud parents of five daughters and two sons. His love of family is combined with his passion for boating, water sports, coaching, and trying to keep up with his children.

For more information on Chris, visit www.chris-mcchesney.com.

Sean Covey

Sean Covey is Executive Vice President of Global Solutions and Partnerships for FranklinCovey and oversees FranklinCovey's international operations in 141 countries around the globe. Sean also serves as FranklinCovey's Education Practice Leader which is devoted to transforming education throughout the world through implementing principle-centered leadership.

As the Chief Product Architect for FranklinCovey, Sean organized and directed the original teams that conceived and created *The 4 Disciplines of Execution* and has been an avid practitioner and promoter of the methodology ever since. Sean has also overseen the design and development of most of FranklinCovey's other solutions, including *The 7 Habits of Highly Effective People, Leadership Greatness, Focus, The 5 Choices to Extraordinary Productivity,* and *The Leader in Me.*

Sean is a *New York Times* best-selling author and has written several books, including *The 6 Most Important Decisions You'll Ever*

Make, The 7 Habits of Happy Kids, and *The 7 Habits of Highly Effective Teens,* which has been translated into twenty languages and sold over 4 million copies worldwide. He is a popular and versatile keynoter who regularly speaks to kids and adults and within schools and organizations and has appeared on numerous radio and TV shows.

Sean graduated with honors from BYU with a Bachelor's degree in English and later earned his MBA from Harvard Business School. As the starting quarterback for BYU, he led his team to two bowl games and was twice selected as the ESPN Most Valuable Player of the Game.

Born in Belfast, Ireland, Sean's favorite activities include going to movies, working out, hanging out with his kids, riding his motorcycle, and writing books. Sean and his wife, Rebecca, live with their children in the Rocky Mountains.

For more information on Sean, visit www.seancovey.com.

Jim Huling

Jim Huling is the Managing Consultant for FranklinCovey's 4 Disciplines of Execution. In this role, Jim is responsible for the 4 Disciplines methodology, teaching methods, and the quality of delivery worldwide. Jim also regularly leads large-scale engagements, including the 4DX implementation for Marriott Hotels, Kroger, Ritz-Carlton, and a number of large hospitals. He is a sought-after keynote speaker for events ranging from senior executive sessions to audiences in the thousands.

Jim's career spans over three decades of corporate leadership, from FORTUNE 500 organizations to privately-held companies, including serving as CEO of a company recognized as one of the "25 Best Companies to Work for in America." Prior to joining FranklinCovey, Jim was one of the first leaders to adopt The 4 Disciplines of Execution and used it to drive performance for almost five years. This experience enabled him to significantly enhance the methods by which the 4 Disciplines are taught and implemented around the world.

Jim's teams have won national awards for customer service excellence, business ethics, and an outstanding culture, as well as numerous local and regional awards as a workplace of choice. Jim's personal awards also include being selected for the Turknett Leadership Character Award recognizing CEO's who demonstrate the highest standards of ethics and integrity.

Jim holds a degree in Computer Science from the University of Alabama, a degree in Music from Birmingham-Southern College, and serves on the boards of several local organizations, as well as the Siegel Institute for Leadership, Ethics, and Character.

Jim is most proud of his wonderful marriage of over thirty years to his sweetheart, Donna, being Dad to two phenomenal adults, Scott and Sarah, and "Papa" to his three grandkids. He holds a 3rd Degree Black Belt in tae kwon do and is an avid runner, backpacker, and white-water rafter.

For more information on Jim, visit www.jimhuling.com.

4DX Resources from FranklinCovey

Leader Certification

Leader Certification is a comprehensive program that prepares leaders to apply the 4 Disciplines and then guides them through intensive working sessions, quality reviews, and ongoing coaching to create a successful implementation. This process is described in the chapter "Rolling Out 4DX Across the Organization."

Execution Strategy Sessions

Execution Strategy Sessions are working sessions with senior leaders in which the wildly important goal of the organization is identified, as well as the driving objectives that will ensure its achievement. These sessions usually last one to two days and include developing a full tactical plan for the implementation of the 4 Disciplines. These sessions are described in the chapter "Focusing the Organization on the Wildly Important."

my4dx.com

my4dx.com is a software tool specifically designed to automate 4DX and to support the full adoption of the Disciplines. It provides the ability to capture results, drive accountability, and sustain engagement, as well as offering significant tools for reporting and analysis. These sessions are described in the chapter "Automating 4DX."

4DX Keynote/Overview

The authors are sought-after keynote speakers who regularly deliver keynote speeches and executive overviews to audiences ranging from the hundreds to several thousand. These messages are engaging, high-energy presentations of the 4 Disciplines that are illustrated by stories of successful organizations that have implemented 4DX around the world.

For more information on 4DX resources from FranklinCovey call 1 (800) 882-6839 or visit www.4dxbook.com.